Faith in a Minor Key

Gilbert Friend-Jones

FAITH IN A MINOR KEY

FIRST EDITION

Cover photograph and design: WEG Thomas

ISBN 9781450548908

Printed in the United States of America

For Gabe, Gaia, Johnny, Maia Marion
and all present and future members of my family.

Contents

Acknowledgements

I want to express my appreciation to the following people who contributed so greatly to the publication of this book. They generously donated their valuable time and hard work. Without them, this project would have been impossible to accomplish.

To **Weg Thomas**, photographer, designer, poet and philosopher extraordinaire, for the beautiful cover and the interior design of this book.

To **Penny Schwall** and **Jack Sherman** for their careful reading and respectful reflections on the manuscript.

To **Chris Wakitsch** for her assistance in converting aging documents into electronic texts for editing.

To the staff, officers, members and friends of The First Congregational Church (UCC) of Crystal Lake, IL for their warm-hearted encouragement to bring this project to completion.

To the members and friends of each of the congregations I have been privileged to serve for their unfailing support and inspiration for so much of what is written here.

Foreword

When I was younger, it was easier to distinguish between the pastoral, priestly and prophetic functions of my ministry. Today it seems to me that these all flow from a single motivation: cherishing. To cherish is to be an unabashed activist in caring.

These essays have been collected from newsletters, sermons and other writings over the last 40 years. One will meet many people in the following pages — some well known in their time, and some known only to their families and friends. One will find dreamlike fantasies and political observations, personal vignettes and critical commentaries. Taken together, I hope they reveal something of the cherishing quality of my ministry.

Given the nature of this collection, the reader is forewarned to expect a measure of inconsistency. Some essays are only a few paragraphs long; others run to several pages. Some are completely secular while others address spiritual themes. Some are simple and personal stories while others are theological or philosophical reflections. Some readers will be more interested in my work with Biblical texts, for example, or my reflections on music. Others will pass these over altogether in favor of stories of mimes or a train ride at Christmas. By juxtaposing essays in this way I intend to offer a literary composite of the way ministry actually unfolds — from story to reflection to interpretation to interruption and back to story. The stories provide the living context of my reflections, and the reflections offer an intellectual framework for my stories.

I have organized the material around the great festivals of the Christian liturgical year. This is the way I live my life and the material lends itself to the opening spiral of sacred time. But there is no linear progression here. One piece does not necessarily follow from another, and each essay can be read independently of the others. The reader is encouraged to move freely among these pieces. Read what is most appealing at the moment and put the rest aside for another day.

Finally, if there by anything that is true, honorable, just, pleasing or commendable in all that follows, if there is any excellence or anything worthy of praise, may God be glorified.

Gilbert (Budd) Friend-Jones
Crystal Lake, Illinois USA
All Saints Day, 2010

My Lord God, I have no idea where I am going.

I do not see the road ahead of me.

I cannot know for certain where it will end. Nor do I really know myself,

and the fact that I think that I am following your will

does not mean that I am actually doing so.

But I believe that the desire to please you does in fact please you.

And I hope I have that desire in all that I am doing.

I hope that I will never do anything apart from that desire.

And I know that if I do this you will lead me by the right road

though I may know nothing about it.

Therefore will I trust you always

though I may seem to be lost and in the shadow of death.

I will not fear, for you are ever with me,

and you will never leave me to face my perils alone.

Amen.

Fr. Thomas Merton, OCSO

Advent

The Invitation

I still remember the smells of sweat and sawdust. In my West Virginia hometown the whole community came out when traveling evangelists brought their road shows to town. We worshipped in churches, at the park, or in tents outside of town. We worshiped with singing and shouting, with laughter and tears. No one watched the clock when we got together. No one could imagine a better place to be. What our religion lacked in sophistication we made up for with joyful exuberance.

But as I grew older this was not enough. I had too many questions, and my persistence in asking them made my elders uneasy. These "revivals" were designed not to open my mind or expand my heart but to save my soul from the eternal fires of hell. I believe that my childhood religion was deeply rooted in a genuine faith, but it was too narrowly conceived to sustain the journey of a lifetime.

While I was quite young, and for reasons I still do not understand fully, I walked to a drugstore across town and purchased a recorded symphony. I could not even pronounce the composer's name: Tchaikovsky. The symphony was his *Pathétique*. Closeted in my bedroom, I played it over and over on my sister's Decca phonograph. At first it made little sense to me, but soon I began to hear tunes, themes and particular instruments. The more intently I listened, the more the music revealed itself to me. It had come from another world and it beckoned me beyond the boundaries of my life as I had known it until then.

This invitation to cross some unspecified boundary has become a frequent and welcomed visitor in the intervening years. I heard it again in a loon's call in northern Minnesota, in the plaintive horn of Louis Armstrong, and in the violent rush of spring waters down a New Hampshire mountainside. While walking alone amidst the ruins of Olympia, or preaching in an old Welsh chapel in Swansea, or walking with my children in the Badlands of South Dakota, I felt, like Jacob at Bethel, that "surely God is in this place."

When dancers moved across the stage in a darkened Princeton theater, when an unknown woman played Brahms in a dimly lighted room in St. Galen, or when a single soprano heralded the Easter dawn in a crowded Siberian cathedral, I knew that I was part of a larger reality. Even in the dirty confines of a migrant laborers' camp, or an NAACP-sponsored

2

summer job corps office in Trenton, NJ, or by the bedside of a dying friend, I did not escape God's presence. "Deep calls unto deep. At night, God's song is with me."

Much contemporary religion fails to do justice to the grandeur of God and the ambiguity of the human situation. Too often theology is reduced to clichés and mindless confessions. Religious communities are manipulated as mere political constituencies. A reverence for deeper things — what Aeschylus called "the monarchy of awe" — has disappeared nearly altogether. Yet awe veils a mystery, and from this mystery comes a summons. Humbling ourselves, we hear it. Opening ourselves, we find answers to questions we didn't know resided in our hearts.

Where Yearning Meets with Yearning

As she continued to pray, Eli observed her mouth. Hannah was speaking in her heart. Only her lips moved, but her voice was not heard... (She said) I have been speaking out of my great anxiety and vexation.

(I Samuel 1.12-13,16b)

So many years and miles and cultural mutations lie between Hannah and us. Why should the weeping of a singular Bronze Age woman, dead now these past three thousand years, affect us so? Of what importance to us is the personal tragedy of this semi-nomadic, female inhabitant of the environs of an ancient Middle Eastern shrine called Shiloh? Of what significance to us are her private grief, her marital pain, her familial shame, her inchoate longing for a child? And what do we care about her serendipitous pregnancy?

Yet Hannah's story is so deeply human that it leaps off the page and into our imaginations. We find in her story a common ground. We too have known bitter disappointment. We too have known shame. We too have known the gnawing hunger deep within our souls for something that we cannot have. We too have experienced the barrenness of living with a shattered dream or, worse, living with no dream at all. We too have known "broken places within us that seem never to mend, emptiness within us that seems always to ache, buds within us that seem never to flower."

James Hillman is one of the inspired voices behind the current revival of interest in spirituality and care for the soul. "Would you know yourself?" he asked. You are not what you have. You are not what you do. You are not even what you are. You are, he said, what you yearn for.

What are your deepest longings? What keeps you awake at night? What troubles you most deeply? When you are alone within the Shiloh of your heart, what intense desire rises from your depths? What unspoken pain demands expression? What fulfilling hope reaches for articulation?

Hannah's first prayer is a simple and obvious desire to have a child. Those of us who have experienced fertility problems can identify with our sister from antiquity. This is invariably one of the most painful texts in all of Biblical literature for us to hear. For many of us there is still a primordial urge to bring forth new life from within our own bodies, to give living expression to a love we share, to form a link in the unbroken chain of passing generations. Although most of the world has long since abandoned myths of blood and breeding, yet we judge ourselves incomplete. We feel inadequate when we are unable to birth or deliver a child. Though our reason tells us that there is more to life than biology, and more to family than genetics, still we feel denied participation in one of life's greatest gifts. The loss of the possibility of birthing a child can be spiritually devastating. We understand Hannah's prayer.

If we get nothing else from this text, already we have accomplished much. We have entered into true human community with one whom, because of time and circumstance, we might have considered alien. We have discovered a kindred soul.

But there is more. Hannah's prayer is not a single melody, but a veritable cacophony of demands clamoring to be acknowledged. There is envy of other family members. There are hurt feelings. There is shame, and hope. Fear and bitterness tumble over one another. There is tenderness from her husband, scorn from other women in the hill country, and feebleness in that old judge, Eli.

Prayer begins with this jangling racket. It is a place of longing and doubt, of bargaining and surrender and finally, of blessing. Barry and Ann Ulanov, professors of literature and theology respectively, have written a modern classic called *Primary Speech — A Psychology of Prayer*. "(Prayer is) the noisy clamoring of all the parts of us demanding to be heard. The clamor is the sound of a great river flowing in us... ." Images from our life stagger into our prayer, shape it, crowd it, demand to be heard and taken into account. We become aware of the best and the worst within us. "Our best parts, if left unlived," observed the Ulanovs, "can be as poisonous as our worst parts, if left unhealed."

Have not many of us experienced this phenomenon? Indeed, the very stresses that drive us to this kind of intense prayer make focusing more difficult. Matters both great and trivial overwhelm our conscious attempts to bring our needs to God. It may be that our longings and deprivations are so vivid that our conscious selves can endure them only for a little while. We may fear what they reveal about us. While grief, rage, pain, guilt or fear can be unpleasant, they may have taken root and become familiar companions in our daily journeys. It can be difficult to imagine life without them, and so we distract ourselves from our prayer.

Such evasions are rarely successful. Beneath all the diversions, our soul's dull ache remains. Again and again we find ourselves returning to what we think to be its cause: Dear God, if I might have a child... Dear God, if I might not have cancer... If you would heal my friend... If I might get that job... If I might pass the exam... If she comes back to me... We continue to set the agenda. We continue to prescribe the remedy. We continue to set the course, not knowing or not trusting in the goodness of God's purposes for us.

But our prayers have a life and voice of their own, observed Saint Augustine, quite apart from our own voices. If we continue in our prayer, we will feel God pulling us in other directions, into larger, deeper, stronger currents than the ones that course through our conscious life. Indeed, observed Saint Paul, we do not know how to pray as we ought but the Spirit of God helps us in our weakness and intercedes for us with sighs deep for words. (Romans 8.26)

Prayer takes us ever deeper into the core of our self and through it into the origin of all self. In our most earnest prayers we not only express our deepest yearnings. We encounter Another who has been yearning for us. "God is more intimate than the most intimate of ourselves," said the French theologian, Francois Varillon. "'Intimate' means, as 'immanent' cannot, that God embraces the soul in love."

When we come before the altar of our Shiloh, to the place of our greatest honesty and vulnerability, we discover that our yearning for healing meets with God's yearning for wholeness. In our deepest prayer we begin to perceive that God is tugging at us, trying to pull us into a life of increasing joy.

Prayer expands our spiritual horizons, deepens our imaginations and opens us to utterly new possibilities for living. "Praying to God, to the source of being," wrote Edmund Husserl, "gives us more being, more self." It enlarges the stature of the soul (Bernard Loomer) and adds depth, range and greater capacity for relationships.

Although her anguish was very private, and she approached the altar by herself, Hannah was joined by another: old Eli. He waited with her, listened respectfully, counseled and finally blessed her. Nor need we ever be alone with our pain. God will provide someone. She or he may be a pastor, spiritual director or Stephen Minister. Friends or family members might become our spiritual companions. We can be and often are spiritual caregivers for each other.

Prayer is the place where God's abounding love for us, the contingencies and limitations of our circumstances, and our own deepest aspirations come together. If it is true, as the psychiatrist Hillman wrote, that wisdom is "the union of love and necessity," then prayer is the place where wisdom makes a home. It is the place where grieving can be accomplished, and where we begin to develop a vocabulary of hope.

One of Galway Kinnell's poems, Saint Francis and the Sow, addresses Hannah's situation, if we listen very closely:

> The bud
> stands for all things,
> even for those things that don't flower,
> for everything flowers, from within, of self-blessing;
> though sometimes it is necessary
> to reteach a thing its loveliness,
> to put a hand on its brow
> of the flower
> and retell it in words and in touch
> it is lovely
> until it flowers from within, of self-blessing.

Hannah's prayer took her deeply into her own loveliness. In her "sighs too deep for words" broken places began to mend. Into her empty spaces a new grace began to flow. She began to flower from within, of self-blessing.

She matured from the conventional young woman of the hill country with scripted longings engraved upon her soul into a woman of wisdom, originality and character. The union of love and necessity vastly enlarged her soul. Henceforth she would listen to her inner voice. She would live from her sacred, central self.

When she emerged from the temple at Shiloh, Hannah was a new person. Yet, paradoxically, she was more Hannah than she ever had been before.

She relinquished to God what she most dearly desired. Because of this act of desperation and faithfulness, all of sacred history pivoted. In the tearful prayer of a singular Bronze Age woman, an epoch ended, and an epoch commenced. Yearning met with yearning, and the world began again.

Einstein at the Door

Can any good thing come out of Nazareth?

(John 1: 46)

In 1899, the Einstein family transferred their son, Albert, from a Catholic school to the Luitpold Gymnasium in Munich. Teachers in Luitpold, like those in other schools of the same time and place, exercised a ruthless and sometimes brutal discipline over their students. Conformity was the rule. Einstein was miserable there. Over the next six years this quiet, taciturn young man developed an intense hatred for all educational disciplines; most of the teachers held out only the weakest of hopes that he would ever achieve anything of significance.

One teacher stood apart from the others. He was the odd one out. He went his own way. He encouraged his pupils to think for themselves. He inspired a passionate interest in the continuing influence of classical cultures on contemporary life. His name was Reuss, and Einstein never forgot him.

The teachers' low estimation of his potential was confirmed in Einstein's early years. He grew up to become only a second class Swiss patent officer. But from that unpretentious position we know that he launched an intellectual revolution, and the rest is history.

Many years after he had become famous the world over for his work in physics and his humanitarian witness, Einstein happened again to be in Munich. He decided to call on his former master, Reuss, now living in retirement. The scene that followed is a classical example of missed opportunity.

Einstein knocked on the door. Reuss opened it. Reuss looked at the disheveled man standing before him. The jacket was worn, the trousers baggy, the hair unkempt. Einstein introduced himself, but Reuss was unable to remember the name. Certain that the man before him was a beggar, Reuss fumbled nervously at the door. Einstein quickly terminated the interview and hurriedly walked away. We are left to wonder if Reuss ever learned about the famous visitor he once had turned away.

Reuss is more to be pitied than condemned. His true story raises the most unsettling questions in me. In what ways am I like him? Have I become a prisoner to my fears, my stereotypes, my own sense of being right, my own standards of respectability? Who has come to my door that I have failed to see? What great opportunities have come into my life — perhaps even were sent into my life — and I never knew them, because I was not open to the "packaging" in which they arrived?

Truth comes in ways we do not expect and may not desire. "He had no form or majesty that we should look at him, nothing in his appearance that we should desire him . . . He was despised and we held him of no account." (Isaiah 53:2-3) It takes courage to remain in the presence of the stranger, the one most threatening, and even more to recognize our long lost ties of kinship. Yet in this "other" resides the means of our own redemption.

Tell Me About Your Darkness

The people who walked in darkness have seen a great light; those who lived in a land of deep darkness - on them light has shined.

(Isaiah 9: 2)

Tell me about your darkness, and I will tell you about mine.

If you talk to me about the plight of the homeless woman wrapped in rags and sleeping on a bed of crumbled newspapers and soiled blankets on a dark Chicago street on a cold winter night, I will understand. But do you know darkness, you who shop the malls, and drive the interstates in your late model cars? If you take me into the pale green room at the end of the brightly lighted hall in that little nursing home, if you have me sit with the frail woman who is sitting with the frailer man who has been her companion these many years, I will recognize the darkness in her soul. But, I ask, does the darkness ever threaten you, as you spread the linen napkin across your lap? If you transport me across the world, to Rwanda, Chechnya or Kosovo, to all the villages of desperation where the four horsemen of the apocalypse have slain the children of hope, I would see it and know it, would I not? But is there darkness in your life too, you who buy a hotdog at Wrigley Field, you who are led quietly to your seat before the opera begins, you who push the elevator buttons to ascend to your office in the sky?

If we were to visit together the jail in Woodstock, or the emergency room of any hospital in the land, if we could listen to the endless staccato bursts crackling continuously over police radios, then the darkness itself would become so thick, and so tangible, that it would be nearly impenetrable. It would threaten to choke us with its reality. But as we leaf through old magazines in the quietness of our doctor's waiting room, as we wander from aisle to aisle filling our shopping baskets with good things, as we swipe our plastic cards and type in our access codes, we can ignore that for a while. We keep ourselves busy. Engaged. Wired. Connected. But sometimes, in spite of it all, we are fearful. The darkness is within as well as without. It forms the background for the foreground of our purposeful activity. It haunts our dreams and our waking moments.

This darkness of which I speak is a shape shifter, ever present yet ever elusive. Hard to see and harder to name. It takes many forms in the course of a lifetime: loneliness, disappointment, boredom, resentment, despair. Jean-Paul Sartre once called it "nausea." It is the omnipresent "deep darkness" through which, alas, we all must go. We are the people who walk in darkness and the heart of darkness dwells in us all. Whether we live in Ceylon or Chicago, Cape Town or Crystal Lake, the land of deep darkness is our land.

But the people who walked in darkness have seen a great light; we who live in a land of deep darkness — on us the light has shined. Therefore I invite you to tell me about your darkness, and I will tell you about mine. Tell me about the light you see, and I will tell you also about what gives me hope.

Within every darkness there is light. This light is the call of Life; darkness will not — cannot — overcome it. Although we walk in darkness we are children of the light. We come from light, we return to light, and we are invited to live in the light all the days of our earthly journey.

This is the "First Light" of all creation. Moses beheld it at Sinai. The disciples fell down before it on Mount Tabor. Sakyamuni was overcome by it while sitting beneath the bodhi tree. Mohammed glimpsed this light on Mount Hira (also called Jabal Nur) three miles north of Mecca. Benedict was given a direct vision of it toward the end of his life at Monte Cassino. Julian of Norwich saw "showings" of it in her cell in Norwich, England. When Martin Luther King, Jr. encountered it at his kitchen table in Montgomery, Alabama, modern history took a different turn.

For me the light shined most fully from a manger in a stable in the village of Bethlehem 2000 years ago. It came in flesh and blood to reveal to us our ancient destinies. Though we walk through a valley of deep darkness we do not fear: not in the nursing home, at the dinner table, or in the lawyer's office. Beyond the thunder at our picnic, beyond the threatening clouds that darken our horizons, we know the sun shines brightly. The light has shined on us.

Ask the Horse

O Jerusalem! Jerusalem! You who slay the prophets and stone those sent to you! How often I would have gathered your children as a mother hen gathers her chicks under her wing, but you would not.

(Matthew 23:27)

Dainin Katagiri is a local Zen Roshi. He recently said that contemporary civilization is like a rider who storms through a village on a runaway horse. People shout, "Where are you going?" He yells back, "Ask the horse! Ask the horse!"

Wherever we look we see violence and destruction. The past and the future have become mirrors of our present turmoil. Looking backward, we see gunslingers and brawlers. Looking forward we see Battlestars and Terminators. The next generation is becoming acclimated to interstellar violence. We are preparing them to fight on a cosmic scale.

Once we were confident of our purposes and destiny. We trusted the advances won by education, the inventions spawned by technology and the idealism generated by liberal faith.

This confidence has been shaken. The vast gains of knowledge, our technological strides, the rich accumulations of centuries of cultural development — these only render more tragic our present disarray. Today we find that science itself leads to conundrums. Faith appears to be ossified into hardened categories. Humanism is suspect. Even atheism is losing its credibility and the call to revolution has become an opiate for the people.

We find ourselves surrounded by problems we can neither fully understand, nor reject as unintelligible, observes J. T. Fraser *(Of Time, Passion and Knowledge)*. We are driven by aspirations whose goals we cannot hope to reach, yet cannot accept as unreachable. We teeter between belief and unbelief, between an almost limitless faith in our own abilities and a disgust at the pettiness, the stupidity, and the cruelty of a race enamored with destruction.

Do we not cry with the Psalmist?

"I am sinking in the deepest swamp, there is no foothold. I have stepped into deep water, and the waves roll over me. Pull me out of this swamp! Let me sink no further. Save me from deep water. Do not let the waves wash over me! Do not let the deep swallow me! In your great tenderness, turn to me. Quick! I am in trouble; answer me. Come to my side. Redeem me!" (Psalm 69)

It is to a world like ours that the Advent message is addressed. "Comfort, comfort my people, says your God. Speak tenderly to Jerusalem, and cry to her that her warfare is ended, that her iniquity is pardoned." (Isaiah 40:1-2)

Undeserved suffering has become so widespread in our world that it is commonplace. Violence surrounds us — the overt violence of terrorism and warfare, and the covert violence of hunger and poverty, of unjust social and economic systems that perpetuate human degradation. The reality of suffering humanity forces the question anew.

What is at stake is not a charming holiday irrelevance but the character of the universe and the meaning of human history. Shall we agree with Thomas Hobbes that human life is "solitary, poor, nasty, brutish and short"? Shall we reconcile ourselves to what Sigmund Freud once called the "normal unhappiness" of human existence?

Two months ago I listened as Dr. Hans Küng addressed a large gathering of clergy at Riverside Church. He spoke in moving terms about the Shoah, and the widespread spiritual desolation it engendered. Someone asked how anyone could believe in anything after the Holocaust. How could we believe in a higher vision, a nobler calling or a greater purpose for our lives?

Küng paused, and then he quietly responded. "I can understand those who turn away from God after this. But as for me, I can only say that I can only go on after this because I believe in God. Belief in God helps overcome such catastrophic events."

What difference does belief in God make to us?

It means, Küng added, that we may expect to know someday the answer to the question first posed by Leibniz: Why is there something and not nothing? It means that all of the suffering, pain and death that are so much a part of our world are not final, but refer to something wholly different. It means that our restless yearning for identity has an ultimate meaning that transcends our personal histories, that we will not be left empty. It means that our striving for absolute justice is absolutely justified, that truth will be known, that divisions will be overcome and that our warfare will be ended.

It means that the poor in spirit will receive the kingdom of God, the gentle will have the earth for their heritage, those who mourn will be comforted and those who hunger and thirst after righteousness will be satisfied. It means that the merciful will have mercy shown to them, the peacemakers will be called children of God, the pure of heart will see divinity. It means that we do not have to bear the whole responsibility for all of human history.

It means that we do not die into nothingness, but into God.

It means the fulfillment of the oldest, strongest and most urgently felt wish of humankind: It means that we can hope again.

The House

Bonnie and Duke were with us that day. We arrived in Shepherstown around 4:30 p.m. After stopping at the only stoplight in town, we drove past the college, the abandoned train station and the shanties huddled under hickory. We continued over a pocketed, dirt road until we could drive no further. With supplies in our arms, we walked the last half-mile through brush and bracken to a deserted mansion. The moist black earth hushed our eager tread. Squirrels heralded our arrival as they called their greetings from the limbs. Sparrows took note of us, but continued their more important work overhead.

According to townsfolk, a local man had built this house in the early 1900's for his young and lovely European bride. But soon after it was completed the house and its lady within — its soul, its *raison d'être* — were consumed by a raging fire. Only the shell remains — a home now for all manner of other than human life. They say the man despaired and never returned. It is clear that he never reclaimed this home that housed his dream.

Our Lady of Nature has dreams of her own. She has begun the slow, healing work of destruction. Scavengers have stripped the interior of its paneling, exposing red clay block walls. Trees have sent roots into beams and stone walls; saplings spring from the remaining sections of the roof. Rains are attacking the foundations. Pipes, cables and even nails, corroding under the coordinated assaults of wind and water, are returning to the dust from which they came. Vines have scaled the walls, exploiting every crevice.

Wildflowers now grow in fireplaces high above the foundations. Blooming roses poke their heads above the ferns. These are all that remain of once formal gardens overlooking the Potomac.

We approached deferentially. Soon the smells of burning wood and cooking hamburgers mingled with the honeysuckle and nearby river odors. We ate our bread and drank our wine in silence: the bitter-sweet Eucharist of friends too soon to part. We laughed at the follies of our childhood and grew pensive before the hopes those children entrusted to us.

We tried to see the future; the house loomed before us. Its enigmatic presence commanded our attention even as it commanded the landscape. Without its soul, it became the soul of the larger wilderness. Embracing earth and sky as one, it welcomed all into its sun-warmed cavities — to rest and peace, to the tomb and womb of life.

All too quickly the sun, that benevolent tyrant of our lives, hastened westward. Shadows climbed the walls to join the coming darkness of the skies. We turned away from this strange presence and retraced our steps to the car. Along the way we stopped to examine other half-hidden buildings. They also were beginning the long transformation.

We loaded the car and drove the last seven miles through the gentle West Virginia countryside — back to the towns, our homes and the ongoing busyness of our species.

La Convivencia

We are constructing bridges between the religions we inhabit, the races that would define us, the class interests that frequently divide us and the politics that distort our perceptions of one another. These bridges are essential if we are ever to know peace. When we cross these bridges we grow in our appreciation for the complexity of our planetary life. The breathtaking beauty at the heart of every culture humbles us. Paradoxically, we become more fully human as we discover how little we know about the great mysteries of love and life and the work of God upon the earth.

But there is another bridge that we also are creating. Some of us — like Imam Feisal Abdul Rauf — may be architects of important parts of it. Most of us are laborers who work tirelessly in anonymity, hardly aware of the significance of our efforts. I am not speaking of bridges between us, but of the bridge from the present to the future, from the "no longer" to the "not yet."

Last year, Atlanta's World Pilgrims traveled to Al-Andalus (the Arabic name for Islamic Spain) to unlock the secrets of *La Convivencia* — that fabled period between 711 and 1492 of the Common Era when three major religions shared most of the Iberian peninsula. During that era, often under Islamic governance and tutelage, a very high civilization flourished. Jews have called it their "Golden Age". While other Europeans were suffering through a dark and superstitious age, Iberians of differing faiths together were enjoying great advances in art, science, architecture, medicine, music, languages and literature, philosophy, commerce and the graces of living.

Sadly, this epoch in human history could not be sustained. When we look below the surface, we see that — then like now — our religions were divided against themselves as much as against each other — Muslim against Muslim, Christian against Christian — as well as Muslim, Jew and Christian against each other. Now as then we are learning that — even as we build bridges between our religions — we also must build, widen and strengthen the bridges within them. This is a very difficult task.

Al-Andalus — like our world today — really was a collection of tensions and tendencies — tendencies toward unity and unprecedented civilized advancement, and tendencies toward sectarian strife and the brutal deconstruction of these very advances. Both existed together simultaneously — respect and detestation, mutual commitment and fierce competition, cooperation and duplicity.

Nevertheless when the spirit of *La Convivencia* prevailed, it resulted in a succession of brilliant accomplishments. Flesh and blood human beings struggled against their lower impulses to create a civilization of enduring intellectual and spiritual excellence.

We who went to Al-Andalus on our interfaith pilgrimage learned that the *La Convivencia* we we,e seeking did not exist as a pristine moment in the past, as Luís Sánchez Nogales reminded us in Granada, but rather as a possibility for the future. It is not something we would discover as we visited sacred sites, but something we would fashion as we grew to know each other.

Each of our religions envisions a golden age of *La Convivencia* when there will be peace on earth, salaam among all peoples, and shalom within the planetary balances that sustain us. This golden age may be delayed, but it cannot be denied. It beckons to us by day, calls to us by night and summons us to respond. The future is invading the present through our dreams. It invites us to trust our highest aspirations.

Until this golden age is realized, God gives glimpses of it. Right now, in this room, we sit together at the table of unity. Jew, Christian, Muslim — we are the bridge builders. The future resides in us. Every time we turn away from fear or hatred, every time we cooperate in a creative endeavor, every time we take time to learn more about each other, the golden age comes closer.

Who Will Speak?

Jerry Falwell recently proclaimed that Jesus will return within the next decade. At a service attended by 1,500 followers in Kingsport, TN, Rev. Falwell explained not only that Jesus' return is imminent, but also that a false and evil Jesus will precede him. This Antichrist (who already is present on earth) must be Jewish according to Falwell. "The only thing we know is that he must be male and Jewish." He does not say that Jesus himself also must be a Jew.

Such words! Such heavy, wounding words! Though Falwell himself might never light a torch, his voice is heard around the world. He is tossing verbal grenades into volatile times. His remarks fan the fires of anti-Semitism. They contribute to the rationale of bigots who act upon their hatred.

Last month, anti-Semitic arsonists firebombed three synagogues in Sacramento. The library of one, B'Nai Israel, was completely destroyed; 5,000 volumes were reduced to soot. Blacks, Jews and Asians were shot in Chicago. homophobic, anti-Semitic and racist vandalism and violence is increasing at synagogues, churches, schools and in neighborhoods across our country. Is there any wonder that our friends are asking, "Is this the beginning of another reign of terror? Another *Kristallnacht*?"

Reflecting on the Holocaust, Pastor Martin Niemöller reflected, "In Germany they first came for the Communists, and I didn't speak up because I wasn't a Communist. Then they came for the Jews, and I didn't speak up because I wasn't a Jew. Then they came for the trade unionists, and I didn't speak up because I wasn't a trade unionist. Then they came for the Catholics, and I didn't speak up because I was a Protestant. Then they came for me — and by that time there was no one left to speak up."

In Sacramento, they are speaking up. The response from the larger community was immediate and resounding. At the next Sabbath gathering, thousands of people — Christians, Baha'i, Buddhists, Muslims, Native Americans, agnostics, New Age, others — gathered to worship and continue to work in solidarity with the Jewish community.

"We preferred to keep quiet," recalled Pastor Niemöller. "We most certainly are not without guilt; I ask myself over and over what would have happened if 14,000 Evangelical (Lutheran) ministers all over Germany had defended the truth with their very lives in the year 1933 or 1934, when there still must have been a possibility? I can imagine that we should have saved 30 to 40 million lives, for this is the price that we now have to pay."

Let us also not keep quiet. Not when synagogues and churches are burned.

Not when family planning clinics and gay/lesbian lounges are bombed. Not when Matthew Shepherd is hanged on a cold fence in a Wyoming field. Not when James Byrd is dragged behind a truck, beheaded and abandoned in Texas.

"If I am not for myself," asked Rabbi Hillel nearly 2,000 years ago, "who will be? If I am for myself alone, what am I? If not now, when?"

Victoria's Secret

In the mid-1970's, a shy but ambitious male graduate from Stanford University wanted to buy lingerie for his wife. But Roy Raymond was uncomfortable with the probing glances he received from department store clerks. The merchandise he sought was located discreetly away from public view, and what he managed to find was either excessively frilly or boringly conservative. Borrowing money from his parents, he opened the first Victoria's Secret in a shopping center near San Francisco. He decorated it to resemble a Victorian boudoir and began to offer the upscale merchandise for which the chain has since become notorious.

Soon his store was acquired by a conglomerate, and rapidly became the largest lingerie outfitter in America. Victoria's Secret catalogs began arriving in mailboxes across the country. The chain's success among primarily conservative and middle class shoppers reveals the extent to which our society has become decidedly un-Victorian. Now tucked between bookstores, kitchen wares and the food court, we have come to accept our sensuality as a normal part of everyday life. Reticence has gone the way of all flesh, if you'll pardon the expression. "Transparency" and "full disclosure" no longer apply only to politics.

To the degree that "Body by Victoria" represents our liberation from the musty, prudish oppression of olden times, thanks be to God. After all, while Raymond was creating his new boutiques of erotic apparel, mainline Protestants were crafting new theologies of erotic spirituality. *God As Eros* is everywhere. This is the title of a popular course now offered by the Christian Association at the University of Pennsylvania — hardly a bastion of permissiveness. Anne Bathurst Gilson's *Eros Breaking Free*, published by our own Pilgrim Press, is just one of many books worldwide that are contributing to this reappraisal of body, earth and deity. Erotic theology proclaims that God calls us to embrace passionately the world that God passionately has created. It encourages us to praise God with the fullness of our being, including especially our sexuality. It is no longer uncommon for churches like ours routinely to offer courses like *Our Whole Lives* for all ages — classes about healthy, life-affirming sexuality.

So far, so good. But is this what *Victoria's Secret* really conveys? Or is it — perhaps unwittingly — the agent of a different oppression? Look at their models. Do they look like us or people we know and love? They are not supposed to! We are supposed to want to look like them. We feel inadequate if we don't.

A quick romp through Victoria's catalogs reveals a depressing similarity in these women — all sleek, young and "beautiful." None are distinctively "ethnic." None are very dark, or even slightly "full-bodied." None are over 40. None are individuals — an essential prerequisite for genuine Eros and attraction. All the so-called "imperfections" that make us unique have been airbrushed away. We are left with a homogenized, Eurocentric, neoclassical, mythological and upscale consumer's notion of what is and is not appealing. In the end, this can be as censorious and life denying as the priggish morality it replaces. It beckons us to the lovers' nest, but it provides a Procrustean bed. Many of our children deny and deform themselves to fit preconceived and impossible notions of beauty and acceptability.

Another Victoria, a Columbia University professor named Victoria de Gracia (*How Fascism Ruled Women*), researched how young women came of age in Mussolini's Italy. "Their lives were a disconcerting experience of new opportunities and new oppressions," she says, and they were, "ignorant of being subject to constraints that were unprecedented in their absoluteness." Something like this can be said today. So many young women and men are made to feel worthless and unacceptable when they stand before a mirror. They are taught what not to wear, what not to be. A sculpted body is becoming a condition for worldly success.

Unlike this market driven exploitation of our sexual insecurities, incarnational and creation centered spiritualities want us to see and affirm the intrinsic loveliness of the natural world and of the bodies that we are. In this our faith is counter cultural. It summons us beyond superficial stereotypes and transient fantasies. It encourages us to celebrate true beauty and passion where it most truly exists — ultimately in you and in me.

That Desperate Winter Sea

Three hundred and seventy-five years ago an adventurous, desperate band of young adults and children assembled at Plymouth's harbor. All England was awash in violence. The monarch and parliament, Protestants and Catholics, and ever-changing economic classes were embroiled in shifting alliances and constant conflict. On the continent, the Thirty Years War was wracking the German states. New technologies were transforming the world. New discoveries in science and commerce were fundamentally altering all aspects of human society.

In and of themselves, our Pilgrim ancestors were quite unremarkable. Brewster, Alden, Bradford, Winslow or Fuller — their contemporaries had little reason to remember these names. Though they were young and entrepreneurial, they controlled no estates, administered no bureaucracies and possessed no claim to royalty. Indeed, they were oppressed by the powerful, hounded by the bureaucrats and persecuted by the king. Caught in a maelstrom of forces beyond their control, they launched their little ark into that "desperate winter sea."

They boarded two well worn shipping vessels, the Speedwell and the Mayflower. To their dismay, only the Mayflower proved seaworthy. Too many people with too few provisions crowded under its masts. For two months they precariously skimmed the surface of an icy sea. Finally they arrived at the brittle edge of a vast and unknown world. A winter more harsh than any they could have imagined challenged them. They were not prepared. They built temporary shelters against the raging New England storms. They tended their many sick; that first year they buried more than half of their community in unmarked graves.

As unprepossessing as they were, nevertheless they became the stuff of legends and tall tales. In fact they were quiet heroes in the face of extreme adversity. Confident in the purposes of a benign and mighty God, they were willing to risk everything for freedom and a new beginning.

Their struggle was personal and political, physical and economic. But even more, it was a moral and a spiritual struggle. They fought, Saint Paul would say, not only with flesh and blood but also with principalities and powers. Their moral imagination wrestled fiercely with the conventional practices of their time. In the darkness of their age they saw a great light; in a time of great darkness a light shined upon them.

Through them, future possibilities first invaded and then exploded the limitations of their era. Because they dared to dream of a commonwealth where individual dignity and freedom of conscience is honored, because they dared to commit themselves, their families and their resources beyond any reasonable measure, because they dared to enlist themselves wholeheartedly in the attainment of their dream, they called a new world into being. They bequeathed to us a new vision of human possibility.

But old ways die hard, and even our Pilgrim ancestors had their lapses. More than two hundred years later the nation they helped to create found itself engaged in another fiercely moral struggle. The dignity of the individual person was at stake again. This time the issue was slavery, an issue that was destined to test us, try us, and split us asunder. Because of it, our nation descended into the fires of fratricidal carnage. We depleted our wealth and exhausted our energy. We poured out the lifeblood of our children. But the stain of slavery was removed from our landscape. America received a new birth and a new challenge.

The New England poet James Russell Lowell saw within that American struggle evidence of a greater competition. The first editor of *The Atlantic Monthly*, he is best remembered for his famous poem, *Our Present Crisis*. (Garrett Horder adapted a few lines of it into our famous hymn, *Once To Every Man and Nation*.) I encourage you to read the original.

Lowell was a contemporary of Karl Marx. Like Marx, he believed that history is the arena in which universal forces are in conflict. For Marx, these forces were always economic, but for Lowell they were always moral. Marx thought that class warfare is inevitable, and the outcome predestined. Lowell believed that within every crisis lies a deeper moral challenge. Truth struggles with falsehood, light with darkness, courage with cowardice, "old systems" with "the Word." For Lowell, a "new truth" constantly is breaking into history making "ancient good uncouth". This new truth requires careful discerning and calls forth a courageous spirit. While it contains the key to a more fully human future, its triumph is far from inevitable. It waits upon us. Its incarnation depends upon our choice, our decision, our resolve and our willingness to sacrifice present good for a higher universal Good. But when any of us, anywhere in the world, acts nobly, unselfishly, courageously and for the ultimate good, the whole world trembles with joy.

James Russell Lowell looked to American history and especially to the voyage of the Mayflower for guidance in interpreting the moral crisis of slavery. The great message of the Mayflower, he believed, was not in the particular answers or dogmas that the Pilgrims embraced. Rather, he found it in the journey itself, in the courage, openness and willingness of our forebearers to risk all for the light that was dawning upon them.

Alice's Restaurant Revisited

I was reading William Bradford's account of the founding of Plymouth Colony on the icy shores of New England in 1620 around the same time that I was watching Arlo Guthrie's film, *Alice's Restaurant*. As strange as it may sound, I think these events are related: Advent, the Pilgrims and *Alice's Restaurant*.

My generation is far from monolithic. We were freedom riders and flower children, war veterans and war protestors, political activists and those who dropped out altogether. Some were committed to revolution, some to reform and some to defending freedom across the sea. Some believed in the greening of America and some in the psychedelic expansion of human consciousness. Some sought to invent new and liberated forms of human intimacy and community. Some sought a "whole earth" philosophy of gentle presence.

Our mental maps included Liverpool, Selma, Woodstock, Newport, Chicago, Dien Ben Phu, Jackson State, Kent State, Memphis, Haight-Asbury, Berkeley, Montgomery, Esalen, Hanoi and Saigon. We traveled easily from the *Green, Green Grass of Home* through *Strawberry Fields* on our way to *Scarborough Fair*. Whether we were easy riders or hard travelers we were sure a hard rain was gonna' fall. We were accompanied on our journeys of 500 Miles by Puff (our magic dragon), the Universal Soldier, and Sergeant Pepper's Band. Often our politics were no more sophisticated than our bumper stickers: "Make Love, Not War" on the Left; "America: Love It or Leave It" on the Right.

When I first saw *Alice's Restaurant* as a young man, I especially enjoyed Arlo's humorous iconoclasm. I liked his easy presence, gentle voice and what I took to be his celebration of the counterculture. Like many of us, I suppose I was a weekend hippy. I got to Woodstock, subscribed to *The Green Revolution*, wove belts on a homemade loom, wore long hair and an Amish hat, and met my future wife in a coffeehouse. I even bought a guitar and developed calluses in all the right places.

But I never could play more than three chords so my songs were kind of boring. I never "turned on" or "tuned in", much less "dropped out." I studied hard at Princeton, worked hard at weekend and summer jobs and stayed in touch with my parents. I walked out in disgust at an emotional

peace rally on the university campus and I protested the protestors who
locked old men (seminary trustees) in a library conference room. My
politics were more reformist than revolutionary. I worked for the Fellowship of Reconciliation, the NAACP, and Students for a New Congress.
When I had to choose between a campus rally and a Greek seminar, I
chose the seminar. Photographs show me at times with a beard and flowing white shirt, and at times with rimless glasses and a three piece vested
suit. I was, I guess, strongly ambivalent. *Alice's Restaurant* embodied
what a big part of me wanted to be, while another big part was absorbing
Edmund Burke's *Reflections on the French Revolution*.

Watching *Alice's Restaurant* again, now with the eyes of a grown man,
I see much more than before. Far from celebrating the counterculture,
Arlo's film is a true lamentation. It is a story about the death of his father,
and it may also be a lament for the reforming spirit that Woody Guthrie
embodied. Arlo walks a lonely road through the film. He walks between
two worlds. On the one side is his Dad's world of union organizers, traveling evangelists and down-home folks made strong by the challenges of the
Great Depression. On the other side is the world of his own generation.
His struggle with the authorities, which I originally thought was the point
of the film, was really only a humorous counterpoint to a much deeper,
and sadder, exploration of the failure of the countercultural dream.

The film begins with the deconsecrating of Trinity Episcopal Church in
Hasitonic, near Stockbridge, Massachusetts. In a very poignant ceremony, attended by few and aging worshipers, a bishop speaks lovingly of the
sacred memories attached to the building. With a solemn voice he then
declares that this historic white frame church "is hereby pronounced
secular and unconsecrated." Even as the worshipers are mournfully leaving, Ray and Alice are jumping with joy on the lawn. They bought the
church, and they intend that it now will house a new kind of social order:
a society based on love, caring and gentleness — a witness to Life in the
midst of death. As Ray shouts from the pulpit he just bought, "This is a
place to be what we want to be!" Alice adds, "What more do we need?"
And Arlo replies, foreshadowing the conclusion of the film, "A lot of
amazing grace."

Alice and Ray planned to support their community with a restaurant;
hence the name of the movie. The commercial that Arlo wrote for the
restaurant became the theme song for many in our generation: "You can
get anything that you want, at Alice's Restaurant." A crowd moves into

the church with colorful clothes, easy laughter and affections freely expressed. They banter and play. They celebrate a memorable Thanksgiving meal that becomes the centerpiece of the film's comedy.

Although it may not be obvious yet, this is already very close in spirit as well as geography to the Pilgrims at Plymouth. The idea of like-minded people separating themselves from a society they believe to be corrupt is common to both. The intention to establish a new community based on benign values is common to both. The thought that they represented not only an alternative to a world passing away but also a vision of a more beneficent future is common to both. Although the church of William Bradford was as puritanical as Alice and Ray's "church" was permissive, both thought of themselves in moralistic and Utopian terms.

There is something prototypically American in all of this. The refusal to accept the sin of history is part of our national identity. We were to be a "new world" unfettered by the hurts and evils of the past. These stories are set in New England. Our Puritan theologians told us we were the New Israel, where a new innocence would breed a new humanity. Although they would have been anathema to the Puritans, Ray and Alice were pursuing the same dream that began 350 years before.

There is another similarity in these stories. Death stalks both communities and asserts its awful prerogatives even in Utopia. But behind this similarity there is a world of difference. At Plymouth Plantation that first winter, as they lost their loved ones to fever and cold, they dug seven times more graves than they built houses. At Alice's, one of the young members of the community dies of an overdose of heroin. At Plymouth the deaths were a sacrifice accepted in order to establish the community. At Alice's, the death was a waste and even, perhaps, a consequence of the ethos of their community. At Plymouth, the deaths led to a deepened fellowship and a renewed commitment among those who remained. At Alice's, the death led directly to the disintegration of the community. When the community learned that their theme song was a lie, and you really can't get anything you want, there was nothing else to fall back on.

The final scene of Arlo's film is extremely moving. Sensing that something is deeply wrong, and that things aren't working out as they had hoped, Ray, Alice and the others attempt to re-consecrate the church. They do it in the only way they know how: with helium gas, a little hashish and dancing. But the magic is gone, the community dissolves, and the people go their own way. Only Ray is left saying that if they just had some land in Vermont everything would be all right. The others know it is over.

Though the Plymouth settlement was more successful, it wasn't too many years before they were beating Quakers, burning witches and running all who disagreed with them out of Massachusetts. It may be tragic when Utopian communities fail. It can be even more unsettling when they do not. The problem, as I see it, is related to the lessons of our Advent Season. During Advent we "prepare" our hearts and minds for the birth of the Christ spirit. We acknowledge the brokenness and pain not only of our world but of ourselves.

Arlo Guthrie understood this. He seems to be saying in this film, in his own gentle way, what Saint Paul was saying: "I do not do the good I want to do, but I do the evil I do not want to do." What we need, Arlo said, is, "A lot of amazing grace."

Our Congregational churches claim direct spiritual descent from those first Pilgrims at Plymouth. And at least some of our present members feel spiritually connected to Ray and Alice. Local congregations can be compared to intentional communities. We are not bound together by blood or creed but by our common pilgrimage and our desire to be part of a genuine community. If we live only unto ourselves, or if we are blind to our capacity to hurt one another, or if we ever think that our truth is superior to all others, then we will have failed to learn the lessons of Utopia.

There is more than one way to deconsecrate a church. By formal ritual to be sure, but also by a casual nonchalance or a non-committal attitude. By a timidity of faith. By a celebration of freedom at the expense of earnest searching. By a failure to see Christ at work in our midst bringing forgiveness and new life. By asserting our own agenda without thought of divine intent. By holding to old grudges and resentments. By placing our wants upon the altar before we bow to pray. By believing that we can get anything that we want without accepting the cost. By thinking that a church is merely "a place to be what we want to be" without first allowing God to shape and form our wanting. By wrapping the values of our secular society in the words of our traditions. There are many ways to deconsecrate a church.

And so it is with some fear and trembling that I engage in Christian ministry. I recognize that some of the most significant influences of my life also have been destructive. Some of the traditions that I cherish contain within them tendencies that can bring harm. Both good and evil intermingle in my heart and will. I know what it means to hurt, but also what it means to inflict harm on others. Isaiah's plea is mine as well: "Woe is me! I am lost, for I am a person of unclean lips and I dwell among a people of unclean lips." Yet he adds, "These eyes have seen the Sovereign God, the God of Hosts." I need — we all need — what Arlo said so well: "A lot of amazing grace."

Christmas

Into Our Emptiness

It was about this time of year, if there be years in heaven. The celestial beings had been celebrating for eons of time and their festivities were likely to continue for eons more. Heavenly celebrations are like nothing on earth. Even the most imaginative among us, blessed with the gift of gab and having visited the Christmas punch too frequently, even they could not begin to describe the joy, the rapture, the sensuous delights enjoyed by our untiring heavenly guardians. I won't even try.

Except to say this. The reason we cannot fathom the fullness of divine celebrations has nothing to do with our nature, as though we are mere mortals and they are angels, as though we are plastic and they are fine china, or any of that sort of thing. It is not because we are different that we can't understand.

It's not because we have forgotten our true natures as some Platonists would have us believe, as though somewhere deep in our psyche there is the fine china original, merely covered up and obscured by gross accumulations of dirt or dust. That may be true in some cases, but it has little to do with our inability to hear the ethereal music or dance in the heavenly ball.

The real reason, if I may be so bold, is that we love more than angels love. To be more precise: we love more desperately than angels love. Angels live blissfully in an eternal now, without thought of future or past, gain or loss, or any of those distinctions so important to us. What is theirs to enjoy, is theirs to enjoy forever. And all of it, without limitation, is always theirs to enjoy.

But hiding in our psyche, like a gremlin in a software program, is a little inerasable, irascible, irrevocable naysayer. However excited we are by our lover's touch, however moved we are by the lilt of a song, however sumptuous is the taste of our mother's bread, however comforting are the blended aromas of wood smoke and strong coffee, nevertheless, a small voice refuses to be silent. This voice has only one line that it dictates endlessly to us. It has only one line, but it is so insistent, so clamorous, and so imperious in its pronouncements that eventually we attribute it to the wisdom of the ages. This voice says to us — when we see the dawn breaking over the ocean, or rock the baby in our laps, or watch our child score her first soccer goal — this voice says to us, over and over, "This too shall pass."

"This too shall pass." These words erect a great barrier between the angels and us. Do we know joy? This too shall pass. Do we know happiness? This too shall pass. Do we know heartache, loneliness and pain? This too shall pass. Do we have longings so great and passions so grand that they sometimes consume us? These too shall pass. Beauty? Youth? Wisdom? Old age? All this shall pass. No celebration goes on forever.

These words have a paradoxical magic in them. When we first hear them, all the real, honest to God, full blooded, visceral existential meaning of our experiences is drained away. This will pass? Everything will pass away? Then of what value is it?

Although they can rob us of meaning, these same words also comfort us. I am bereft, but this too shall pass. I am alone, but this too shall pass. I am in anguish, but it will not last forever.

Amazingly, these very same words become bearers of a new kind of meaning, a desperate meaning, a peculiarly human meaning, a meaning not found anywhere outside the human psyche. If this experience must pass then it is unique, infinitely unique. It is therefore of infinite value. If this moment is unrepeatable then it is priceless. It is a pearl of great value, entrusted to me and to me alone for all eternity to enjoy or not to enjoy, to use or not to use, now or never. This child, this lover, this loved one, becomes infinitely precious precisely because the clock ticks and the time we share is passing. Humans understand this in a way that angels will never comprehend.

In contrast to the celestial celebrations of our guardians, our festivities are always touched with this poignant sense of passage. It is always there, in everything we do, behind all that we say or share or cherish. So when we love, we love desperately. Our affirmations are passionate. They are protests against time's passing. "Here!" we say. "Now!" we say. "This!" we say. Here, now, this moment, this place, this person, this is good, this is precious.

Still, in spite of our desperate attempts to squelch it, the little voice will not be silenced. In spite of our dance and song, we feel greedy and cheated. We want more. We need more. We are entitled to more. But the voice keeps saying, "This too shall pass."

But back to our story.

The celestial beings were playing and singing and dancing and romping through the heavens with nary a negative thought, not even one. Then several happened to look out upon the earth, very near and yet very far from them. They were startled by what they saw. Instead of rejoicing they saw grieving. Instead of dancing there was sadness. They looked into nursing homes, and urban apartments. Into prison cells and hospital emergency rooms. Into suburban living rooms where fireplaces cast shadows on the ceilings. Into farmhouse kitchens where weary farmers talked slowly over meager meals. They looked under bridges and by river-sides and saw women and men huddled around fires, stuffing newspapers in their trouser legs. And from everywhere they heard crying. Some were cries of grief, some of fear and some of rage. And in that moment, history changed forever.

The angels understood nothing of what they saw, but everything of what they felt. They made their way to the throne room and whispered in God's ear. Suddenly, throughout the heavens, everything became silent, so quiet you could hear a baby breathe. And all of the angels, and all the heavenly hosts, joined in one thought: what can we do? It is not right for any part of God's creation to fear, suffer or grieve. What God has created is good, and every part of creation is good. But how can the stroke victim celebrate, trapped in an unresponsive body, unable to make even the simplest wishes known? How can the prisoner celebrate, not knowing her fate or her family's, or the future? How can the parents celebrate when they don't know whether their son will ever leave the neonatal intensive care unit? How can the brother celebrate with the death of his sister so fresh in his mind?

The angels were naive at first. They tried to beam messages to earth, to let us know that there is more to life, infinitely more, than even the infinitely precious moments we cling to. We did not receive their messages. They tried to enter our dreams. We said, "They are only dreams." They appeared to us in visions; we thought we were hallucinating. Nothing they did could deprive us of our tightly clasped illusion that "this too shall pass." Sorrow covered the earth.

Then one of them said, "If we could just be one of them, talk with them, walk and work with them, eat hot stew and drink beer with them. If we could just raise children like they do, and paint pictures, and put up

Christmas trees. If only we could work in the mines, swim in the seas or climb the mountains. If we could worry with them about their aging parents, experience with them the progressive loss of function, know with them the terrors they face, then we might understand them better. Then we might communicate. Then they might trust the guidance we offer."

God, of course, witnessed all these vain attempts of the angels. God was aware of their frustrations. God was frustrated too. The divine celebrations came to a standstill while God pondered the situation. "You are right," God said. "It must be done. They must know me not through visions and dreams, not through brilliant intuitions and philosophies, but in their flesh. They must know me in their own bodies, in their waking and sleeping, in their laughing and weeping, in their joy and fear. It must be done."

Without another word, that divine, unspeakable, radiant, all creating, all enveloping energy we mortals call God collapsed upon itself. All the angels and indeed all the universe shuttered and shook. The stars in the sky blinked in amazement. Animals on earth awakened with uneasiness. Suddenly, there was no God in heaven, but only a vast and silent emptiness.

Then somewhere a baby cried.

A baby cried from a stable in Bethlehem and the angels rejoiced to hear it. Another baby cried in Sarajevo, and another in Santa Fe, and yet another in Circleville. Everywhere babies were crying. Some cried for hunger, some for thirst, some to be changed and some cried for sleep. Some cried from fear. And some just cried and cried because they liked to cry. But that one baby, in Bethlehem, that baby's cry was... well, if you listened closely to that baby's cry, you could hear all that was to unfold and all that had unfolded down through time.

In that cry God took flesh and filled our emptiness. Henceforth, there would be two voices to listen to. "This too shall pass," says the one voice. "Behold, I am with you," says the other.

That baby would grow up as all children do. That child would play, enjoy friendships, and suffer the slights and hurts of all flesh. That child would know terror and loneliness, unquenchable grief and enervating despair. Eventually that Child would experience the loss of strength and movement. Speech itself would depart from him. Even death would overwhelm him and suck him into its voracious maul. But first within that Child, and then around the Child, and now in every corner of the world a new message was proclaimed: "Behold, I am with you."

Meanwhile, the celestial party was completely suspended. The angels gathered anxiously, wondering about the mystery that had transpired. What if earth-wisdom is right? What if everything passes? Would God return to them? Would they also pass away? Anxious about what was happening, first one and then another and then all the heavenly hosts made their way to the skies over Bethlehem. Hiding behind the darkness of the night, they looked in wonder at the child whimpering in the manger. How could this be?

Heaven itself had been mortgaged for earth's redemption. All creation would henceforth groan and grow together. Touched by earth's anxieties, the angels themselves became more human in their understanding. But oddly, as with humans, this was a gain as well as a loss. Their joy became more intense, and a bit more desperate, but each moment became more precious for them as well.

After God became flesh, and entered into our earthly festivities and our struggles, God changed as well. The realm of timelessness and certainty seemed to disappear. In its place came a realm of possibility, of flesh longing for transcendence and transcendence seeking incarnation. No longer would "matter" and "spirit" be divorced from one another. Hereafter the soul would embrace them both so that to know one means to know the other. "God became flesh," the ancients eventually learned, "so that flesh can become divine."

Henceforth, heaven and earth would be eternally joined, each infused with a new rhythm and dance. Conscious now of both the inevitable passing of time, and the undeniable presence of Eternity within it, heaven and earth both would become exponentially the richer for it. As the significance of this sank in, the angelic hosts could not help but burst into song. But their song was monotonously eternal no more. Now they sang with enthusiasm and earnest desire. They sang with a love they had never felt before. They sang out over the countryside, growing louder and louder, rousing shepherds from their sleep.

And you and me? What is to become of us? With our hopes and fears, our pleasures and pain, our strengths and failings — who are we to become? Not fleeting shadows against a kaleidoscopic universe of unfeeling matter, nor celestial beings above the passions of our flesh, we bear within us all that is of worth in heaven and on earth. In our bodies, minds and spirit, God and humanity have found a new identity. God and humanity are giving birth to new possibility. God has become flesh and filled our emptiness so that we might indeed become God.

No Human Author

Last spring Eduard Shevardnadze was in town to deliver the Carlson lecture at Northrop Auditorium. He was the Foreign Minister of the former Soviet Union. He is, I believe, one of the moral and visionary leaders of our century. It was my privilege to meet and talk with him and his wife at a reception that preceded the lecture. During the reception, I also talked with several of his staff members. One of them told me a story that I want to share with you this evening.

Prior to his arrival in Minnesota, Mr. Shevardnadze spent a few days in Washington, D.C. He attended a cultural event at the Kennedy Center for the Performing Arts. Following the performance, Jacqueline Kennedy Onasis and Ted Kennedy took him downstairs to the Center museum. He was shown gifts and presents from Nikita Khrushchev, Charles DeGaulle and other world leaders of that era. He was escorted to a video booth where he sat to watch a tape of the Kennedy years. On the screen was John F. Kennedy speaking in front of the Berlin Wall. Kennedy's words were memorable and prophetic: Human nature is the same on both sides of the wall, Kennedy said. Someday, leaders will emerge with a new vision of a new world and the wall will come down.

There sat Shevardnadze, thirty years later, in the Kennedy museum, listening to the prescient words of our young president. There sat he, one of those very leaders who had arisen, who had helped bring down that wall less than a year before. In that one room, at that singular moment in time, modern history met itself. And how utterly different our world has become.

Two years ago we could be jubilant because the Berlin Wall was coming down. A year ago we could celebrate the transition to democracy in the heart of the Soviet Empire. But tonight we look out upon a world that is restless and fearful; tonight we face a future that is improbable and uncharted. Tonight we understand how "time makes ancient good uncouth." Now that the enemy seems to have vanished, we are left to face ourselves.

What are we to say? How can we begin to describe our world?

Before he became President of the newly democratic republic of Czechoslovakia, the playwright Václav Havel spent years in jail for his human rights advocacy. He wrote to his wife from prison: "Imagine a world with no firm center, no fixed identity, no past and no future, no coherence or order, a world where all certainties are disintegrating and where, suspended above this disintegration like a melancholy mist, hangs the memory of a different world where things were themselves."

It was not just the world of prison life he was describing; it is the world he, Olga, you and I have inherited. We have memories of a different world, but old "verities" have vanished. Many of us feel as though we are adrift in a threatening and chaotic sea.

This is a moment full of pain and promise, danger and opportunity, hope and fear, warning and possibility, good news and troubling tendencies. Into this world the Christ Spirit is born. Too many Christmas pageants and Christmas cards, too much candy and tinsel, have obscured for us the real nature of our celebration.

Christ comes not to be romanticized in the stable of a small town inn, but to be welcomed in the middle of the noise, the technology, and the rush of the stressed-out professionals in the emergency room of a major urban hospital. Christ comes not to shepherds tending flocks in a bucolic hillside scene, but to overworked social workers in a sterile office building trying to make decreasing resources serve rapidly expanding case loads, trying to appease harried supervisors, trying to keep up with the paperwork and do justice to their clients. Christ comes not to kings, magi, or astrologers bedecked in sartorial splendor, but to attorneys and doctors who have decided to leave business as usual behind them to search for a new way to give meaning to their lives.

Christ comes not only to poor Palestinian Jewish folk, but to Palestinians and Jews, to Syrians and Lebanese, poor and middle class. And to Iraqis, Kurds, Turks and Iranians, to Vice Lords and Kiwanians, pro-lifers and pro-choicers, to paupers, princes and prostitutes and to all who must share this earth together. Not only to innkeepers but to gatekeepers, those who guard the access to privilege and power. To young women and men in prison, and to children who grieve. The little town of Bethlehem no longer can contain this miracle; the earth itself has become Bethlehem tonight. The alleys of Detroit, the power station called Chernobyl, the rain forests of Brazil, the corridors of government in South Africa — these have become the manger, the stable, the fields, and the inn for the Christ Child born to us.

There is much to learn from the story we recall tonight. For this is the story of a world in massive transition. It is about a homeless child, born into poverty, whose life began in a little backwater of a global empire in almost impenetrable obscurity. It is the story of one who lived under brutal conditions, whose destiny seemed controlled by corrupt institutions and whose very life ended prematurely. "Born poor, died young." Why do we worship him tonight?

We worship and welcome him tonight because of our deeply felt conviction that God's Spirit was upon him, and God's message was given through him. He is a peaceful prince, come in a world that has yet to understand his peace.

He introduced "agape" to the world — a self-giving, unconditional and affirming love. His was a style of paradoxical reversals: the first shall be last, and the last first... the greatest of all will be the servant... earthly wealth is vulnerable to losses, but spiritual wealth is attainable and secure... our greatest investments are not in property, T-bills or municipal bonds, but in the Community of Life that unites us all... seek God among the humble folks...

If there hangs above our head this evening the memory of a different world, an "Eden vision" of life before the fall, there also stands before us the vision of a babe wrapped in swaddling clothes and lying in a manger, a child who grew to young adulthood, and who carried with dignity what Havel calls "the burden of Being" just as each of us must do. He is the one who goes before us even now, in spite of all uncertainty, and who calls us to follow him.

Tonight we affirm with generations who have gone before us that we are not alone. We who would do what is right, we who would enlist in the struggle for justice, are not alone. Though the earth shakes and the seas roar, we are not alone. Though the world trembles with anticipation, we shall not fear. God has come to us, and will be with us, whatever may be our circumstance.

A last Havel story. Several months ago Havel was asked to comment, as a writer, on the chain of events that catapulted him from prison to the presidency.

"No human author could have conceived it."

Quotidian Angels

Sometimes, perhaps, they crowd the night sky; I never have seen them. It has been said that they blow trumpets, play harps, and sing with ethereal beauty. My ears have not heard this music. People tell me that some carry swords. I know nothing of this. In every religion, there are those who profess to know a great deal about angels and celestial hierarchies. I am not one of them. I confess to you that I have never seen an angel. Not the winged kind. Not yet, anyway. I reserve the right to be skeptical.

It has been almost impossible to get the more orthodox representatives of our various religions into serious interfaith dialogue. But one day the London Inter Faith Centre announced a dialogue on angels. To their amazement, the most conservative leaders of every tradition showed up, and those who came connected respectfully with their counterparts in other faiths. Interesting.

I remember visiting an archeological museum in Athens (Greece, not Georgia) where I was surprised to learn that ancient cities had street-lights, and that ancient men wore belts with buckles like mine. But what really struck me was the statue of a human figure with wings — an angel. I thought we invented that! We receive our tradition in bits and pieces from other human beings who were here long before us. Though cultures and religions change, many images endure. Do they persist because the experiences to which they point persist as well?

On the last day of a sabbatical in India I boarded a train in Madurai for the long ride to Delhi to catch my flight home. I sat alone watching the passing Indian landscape. Soon exhaustion overcame me and I fell asleep. I had slept for hours when a young Indian boy poked me sharply on the shoulder. "Sir! Sir!" he shouted. "I think this is your stop!" I rubbed my eyes and saw that he was right. I had only a few nanoseconds to bolt through the closing doors. I made it to the platform. The doors shut behind me and the train took off on its northward expedition. An angel? Perhaps. A very observant little boy? For sure.

A young woman from Bogotá was sitting on a London curb during a miserable rainy night. She was desperate, despairing and perhaps suicidal. An older woman in unpretentious clothing approached her, put an arm around her and assured her — in perfect Columbian Spanish — that things would get better. The older woman left; my friend got up and began her life again.

There are thousands of these stories, and just as many explanations for each one. There is something quotidian (ordinary or commonplace) about them all. I can relate to Spanish speaking grandmothers and young Indian boys more readily than to winged sword bearers and flying trumpeters.

I follow a quotidian Savior — a persecuted Jew, a refugee, a teacher, a healer, a storyteller, a prisoner condemned to execution. I worship a quotidian God who eschews esoteric truth and mystifying spirituality in favor of straightforward and unshakable compassion. I believe in quotidian angels — not winged creatures, but people sitting next to me on the bus, or maybe even reading this essay right now.

•

Lloydia Lives Here

Lloydia lives here. In Atlanta. Maybe you've seen her. She rides the bus. She shops at the mall. She goes to school. But at 13, she probably knows more about Atlanta — or parts of it — than you or I ever will know, or ever want to know. At an age when many girls anxiously are waiting for their first period, Lloydia knows pimps and johns and other shady characters. She sees our world through the eyes of a child. She sees it also through the eyes of a prostitute. Danger, fear and violence — these have been her companions. Betrayal, cynicism and hopelessness — these have shaped her spirituality.

Lloydia actually dreamt of getting pregnant, of delivering a baby who would love her without abusea and love her unconditionally. She wanted an infant whose very neediness would justify her life and whose dependence would make her feel important. She hoped for a child who would miraculously deliver her from the hell of her present life. At the same time she dreaded getting pregnant after every encounter. She was horrified at the possibility of delivering a child whose very existence might seal her into a way of life she wanted desperately to escape. Lloydia knew of nowhere to run and no one to whom she could turn.

What does all this Christmas talk mean when translated into Lloydia's world? How does she understand the young woman at the center of the story, the one who so strangely conceives? Who is this baby born to her? Who is this runaway young couple, Mary and Joe, crossing international borders to escape the reach of the law? Who are the fearful men in the fields and why are they afraid? How smart, really, were the wise men in the story — decked out in silks and fine woolen clothing, carrying hockable valuables into hostile turf? Did Lloydia ever wish upon a star? Does it matter? When was the last time she really enjoyed the night sky? Has she ever heard the angels sing?

Yet I suggest that Lloydia may understand this familiar story with a clarity that is denied to you and me. For Christmas proclaims an impossible hope emerging from the despairing cry of our world. It points to an impossible beauty within the most sordid circumstances. It declares to Lloydia that she need not walk the streets alone. She must not depend on her abusers to protect her. God has heard the cries of her heart. The Most High God has come to her.

Not, as you might suppose, in an ecstatic vision. Not even in the form of a baby. Christ doesn't always come wrapped in swaddling clothes, and sleigh bells don't always accompany Christmas. Christmas came early to Lloydia this year in the form of an aggressive, no-nonsense, investigative reporter named Carol Hanson, and later in the form of friends, counselors, teachers and family members. Because Ms. Hanson cared enough about Lloydia's story to tell it to the world (The *Atlanta Journal Constitution* Nov. 12, 2000), Lloydia has been given another chance at life.

The Holy One came into our world, endured in flesh the worst our world could deliver, and is delivering us. God sees and cherishes Lloydia's innate and intrinsic loveliness. Beneath whatever calloused or calculated toughness she may have assembled into her self-protective armor, beneath any brutal hardness she may believe herself to have become, God sees her "original face" and the pristine purity at the center of her soul. God looks into Lloydia's heart as one looks into a disregarded masterpiece, ready to gently clear away the accumulated dust and dirt — and hurt — so that her original beauty may once more be revealed.

As I was researching this piece I discovered that Lloydia's name means "Alp Lily." The Alp Lily, it turns out, is a delicate flower that survives in harsh and forbidding wintry climates. It blooms in granite crevices where nothing else seems able to grow. Its very existence testifies not only to the strength of the life force on our planet, and also to its beauty. Lloydia. Alp Lily. Determined loveliness.

Lloydia has returned home this Christmas. She and her family are starting over. They have learned a great deal from her exile in Atlanta's version of hell. Now they are beginning to learn a great deal more. They are seeking help. They have a long way to go.

Christ comes to Lloydia tonight, and she is born anew. Her innocence has been restored to her: "… the purity of a lily unstained." The baby she once wished for — and dreaded — is herself. She is learning to see and treasure the luminous loveliness she is. She is learning to hold her head high, and to treat herself with the tenderness and respect that have always been her rightful due. She is learning to give as much care to herself as she once imagined she might give to another. Christ comes tonight as both the greatest gift and the greatest giver, offering to all who accept it a glimpse into our true nature and our ultimate destiny.

Lloydia lives here. In Atlanta. Maybe you've seen her. Maybe she has seen you. She rides the bus. She shops at the mall. She goes to school. At 13, she is just beginning to appreciate who she truly is, and what she might become. She is Lloydia. Alp Lily. A sacrament of determined loveliness. Lloydia has come home this Christmas.

Traveling in Style

It was 1968. The brochure described it as an elegant way to travel, even for those of us who can't afford sleepers or roomettes. For weeks we had anticipated the pampering by kind attendants, the relaxed comforts of a plush coach, the delights of leisurely dining as the train wound its way southward on Christmas Eve. My family planned to meet us at the station in Washington.

We had gotten to the crowded Vermont depot about twenty minutes before the train's scheduled departure. Carrying a huge, heavy box of presents along with our suitcases, we checked with the ticket agent. "I can check your things, if you really want me to. Nobody does, though. If you want them to get off at the same place you do, you'd better just carry them with you."

Well, the box made a good seat. We struck up casual conversations with our travel companions. As we waited, a group of four fine feminine vocalists sang and played (on recorders) medieval carols, ballads and rounds. Another group of swaggering collegian rock musicians unveiled their guitars, but they all compromised with blue grass and native folk. The concert was unexpected, superb, and free.

No formal announcement was ever made, but we learned that the train would be two hours late. There had been some difficulty with customs inspectors at the border who chose this night to be unusually thorough. After it arrived, we lined up in the station but we were not allowed to board for another forty-five minutes. The heating systems in a number of cars had failed and they were trying, unsuccessfully, to fix them.

When the conductor finally shouted "All Aboard!" the crowd swarmed to the platform. (Rumors had circulated that some of us might have to stand all the way to Washington.) The cars were icy, and ours looked (and felt) like a collector's item from New York's subway system museum. Even after we got settled, the train failed to move. We had been "slightly derailed" according to the conductor. Another half-hour passed before we began our journey.

Without blankets or pillows, we passengers huddled together as closely as decency permitted through the cold hours of that New England night.

The club car was jammed, and dry. The "elegant" dining car had no food, and it was difficult to get even half a cup of coffee.

One of our passengers was a Scot who was touring North America with his mother. "It's not as bad as it seems," he tried to reassure us after valiant but vain attempts to secure some tea. "In India, if they fail to get you a seat although you've made reservations, they simply tell you that it's yesterday's train."

Another exhausted pilgrim with two weary children at her side related how she had left Nova Scotia three days before. Due to late trains that caused her to miss important connections, she still was traveling. "I expect to be three-and-a-half days late when we finally arrive in the District of Columbia," she said. "If we arrive."

With the next day's sun came a little warmth, and we crowded around windows. Meanwhile, down in Washington, niece, nephew, cousin, sister, mother, father — all six — climbed out of the red Rambler station wagon at Union Station, a little early for the anticipated homecoming. "What time is the train from Montreal due in?" my father asked the woman at the Amtrak information booth.

"Oh," she stammered, "that train." She swallowed. "We don't actually know, sir, just where that train is right now." She told him of a bottleneck in New York City. "Maybe," she speculated hopefully, "they've got it in some kind of holding pattern around Grand Central."

That was nearly true. Taking advantage of an enormous traffic jam, we had been sidetracked for repairs. The heating system was fixed and we were again on our way. (It was fixed so well that after New York, it couldn't be turned off!) Sandwiches were brought on board and sold for $1.75 each. The toilets were restored to order.

We arrived hungry, sweaty, and exhausted. We felt like veterans of a Siberian campaign, but we knew that we had experienced history. Someday we will be able to tell our grandchildren that we remember Amtrak when... and they will listen in disbelief.

Epiphany

Esther's Sea

Esther Schnoes was a remarkable woman. She committed the energy of her life to a vision of reconciliation. From the days of her work in Chinatown and Spanish Harlem in New York City, through her work with the Twin Cities International Program, from her days of teaching and tutoring children with disabilities through the opening of her home to more than seventy international guests from all over the world, she lived what many of us merely talk about. I think of her as Waldo Williams thought of his mother:

> She was anxious for many
> at evening, and the weary knew
> the entrance to her court.
> She would rejoice with the joyful,
> sense the pain, join the feast.
> In the ocean of her heart there was a cherishing.
>
> (Angharad)

If, in the ocean of her heart there was a cherishing, perhaps it was because the ocean had instructed her heart from a very early age. For Esther loved the sea. In her apartment there are photographs taken by her father of the sea. There are rocks and clefts along the Atlantic coast, with names like Purgatory and Camel Rock that shaped her childhood consciousness. Her retreat for years was among the sheltering rocks near the top of palisades by Purgatory, near Newport. Indeed, it was her wish that her cremated remains be scattered on the ocean from that very place. Listen to Esther's own words, from her book of recollections:

> "How I pity those who have never had the opportunity to fall in love with the sea. Even at its most peaceful moments there is movement and rhythm and a tremendous tranquility that can put at ease even the most disturbed frame of mind. But when it is at its wildest, whipped by winds of hurricane force, with waves and spray flying high above the cliffs and rocks, then the sea is its most thrilling self."

Esther loved the sea, and her love of the sea mirrored her love of life: its tumultuous and powerful forces one moment, its serene and gentle presence the next. As she was an enthusiast of the sea, so was she an enthusiast of life: family, genealogy, children, education, community, friendships, gardening, international understanding, the reconciliation of peoples distanced by conflict. For her, to be alive was to be engaged passionately with life, to love life, not to accept it passively but to make a positive contribution wherever she went. Even when she battled the ravages of cancer, and through all the ups and downs of the recent months, she did not give in to negativism or despair. She had an unbridled optimism about life, and a wonderful faith in its possibilities. Now that she has gone away from us, like a sailor returning to the sea, we take comfort in the memories she has bequeathed us.

> *As the moon sinks on the mountain edge*
> *the fisherman's lights flicker*
> *far out on the dark, wide sea.*
> *When we think that we alone*
> *are steering our ships at midnight,*
> *we hear the splash of oars*
> *far beyond us.*

The sea is a wise teacher. Esther was a discerning student. She came to know intuitively what the sea was eager to teach: the web of life is seamless and complete and divine reality encompasses all in a loving embrace. Esther came to know that nothing of true value is ever lost. In the ocean of her heart, there was a cherishing.

The Ladle and the Sea

Rikyu was one of the great masters of the tea ceremony in Japan, a character of legendary proportions in Zen literature, a man renowned for his wisdom and highly refined sense of beauty and aesthetic judgment.

There are many promontories in that island country. Each has a unique vista of the ocean. One excelled all the others in the view it gave of the sea. This particular piece of land, high above the water, was most coveted through all of Japan. When Rikyu acquired it, there was much excitement. Here was a marriage made in heaven — the most exquisite land, the most beautiful perspective, and the greatest artist and gardener of his generation. Everyone was eager to see what Rikyu would do.

Months passed. There was much activity. Materials for the teahouse were carried up the slope. Whole trees passed through the neighboring villages. People speculated about what must be happening. Finally the day came when Rikyu issued his invitations to tea. Only a select few were invited. They prepared themselves for what they were sure would be the most memorable moment in their lifetimes. They fasted. They meditated. They cleansed themselves until the day arrived.

Rikyu met them at the base of the hill, and they walked up a simple path. As they approached the crest of the hill they were stunned. Anticipating some unique view of the sea, instead they entered a wooded enclosure. A veritable wall of tall trees blocked even hint of the ocean below. As small stream trickled at their feet.

Their minds were perplexed and their souls were disturbed. Still they followed their host unquestioningly toward the simple teahouse where the ceremony was to take place.

There is a cleansing ritual in the Japanese tea ceremony. One by one, they knelt before the stream, and lifted a simple wooden ladle full of the cold and clear water. And one by one, as they looked up from that humble kneeling position — and from that position only — they could see the vast and shimmering sea beyond the trees. They could see the rain from distant clouds touch the water at the horizon.

In that instant, they understood. The small dipper of water in their hand and the vast ocean beyond them were one. They understood that they —

like the drops upon their fingers, like the flowing stream beneath them, like the boiling water for the tea awaiting them, like the falling rain, like the movement of the seas — they were all but parts of one reality. One reality teeming with life. One reality alive with breath-taking beauty. One reality eternally transforming itself into its opposites, reconciling in itself all the conflicting tendencies we encounter. One reality reuniting in itself all that might seem lost, broken or forgotten.

As each one stood to continue their approach to the teahouse, their vision of the sea was again obscured. But each would always remember the gift of awareness that had been granted as they knelt beside the stream.

Epiphany At Sunrise

I am a confirmed "morning person." I bid good night to the moon when I go to bed, and good morning to it when I arise. I get up early each day — before the family awakens, before the dogs begin to stir, before the newspapers are delivered. I make coffee, say Morning Prayer, do chores, answer e-mail, and perform my ablutions before the sun rises in the east.

If you are a "night person" you may find this admission incredible. If you wait until midnight to come to life, if you prefer to sleep until noon, then we definitely inhabit different time zones. But please don't get me wrong: I like your world too. Even at 60, I can "pull an all-nighter" if I must. You don't have to convince me that good jazz starts late. I too savor the nocturnal life of many cities. I can enjoy a late night party with you, and good conversations that stretch into the wee hours. But, truly, my preferred time of day is early morning.

Sometimes I go walking in the morning moonlight of my sleeping neighborhood. An amazing moment often comes just before sunrise; every sentient being should experience this epiphany at least once in its lifetime. For a few minutes everything becomes absolutely silent, and then a single bird begins to sing. Although the sun itself has not yet risen, its faint first light illumines the eastern sky. Soon I hear two birds, then five, and then a veritable chorus singing nature's version of Lauds. Especially in the summer this symphony intensifies for an hour or more and then, just as mysteriously, subsides. In this singular moment when night gives way to day, I am transfixed between two worlds.

As the rising sun lifts it bald pate above the distant horizon, light and life return to the earth. I feel the rhythms of creation awakening in my body. Night people who are returning home and morning people who are rousing from their beds experience the same exhilaration. The sun is rising; all shall be well.

With nary a thought or nod from us, radiant and life sustaining sunlight gently awakens and enfolds our planet. House lights come on along my street. Drivers crank up their motors. The roaring and buzzing of machines overwhelm the chirping harmonies of nature. I continue walking, certain now that I have seen a miracle.

Thoreau wrote in Walden, "Only that day dawns to which we are truly awake." My early morning routines are my ways of awakening to each dawning new day. What more can I do to awaken to the dawning of the new creation?

A Civil Peace

On this feast day of Saint Martin of Atlanta, it is appropriate to give thanks for many of the changes in the racial landscape of America. Our neighborhoods, schools and most of the institutions in our communities are beginning to reflect Dr. King's dream. Stereotypes are falling; prejudices lie exposed for what they are.

To be sure, a great deal of work remains. Every demographic statistic reveals glaring inequities along the fault lines of race, gender and handicapping conditions. Gay and lesbian people continue to experience legal and illegal persecution. The demons of prejudice and discrimination have not been exorcised completely. There is much pain and suspicion. "Multicultural" fragmentation is as likely as multicultural celebration. The politics of rancor threaten.

In today's world, civil manners may be as important as civil rights in our progress toward the "Beloved Community." Ralph Wood suggested in *The Christian Century* that, at their best, manners maintain a civility and cordiality among people who otherwise may feel antipathy. Manners protect us from heedlessly intruding into others' privacy. O'Connor believed that justice without civility and courtesy inevitably leads to codes of speech and behavior that are as oppressive as the injustice they seek to correct.

To Dr. King, the "Beloved Community" meant more than tolerance; he worked for a coming together of hearts, minds, spirits and aspirations. He called for us to bear each other's concerns and embrace each other's hopes.

Although Martin King was confrontational, he also was unfailing in his civility. Not to defeat one's enemies, but to convert them into friends was his primary intention. "Hatred is too great a burden to bear," he said. Nonviolent resistance depends upon the gracious affirmation of our common humanity as well as the candid recognition of all that stands between us. It seeks to discover common ground, and build community where none existed. It lays the groundwork for trust and mutual effort toward common goals and purposes.

On this 66th anniversary of Dr. King's birth, is it asking too much of our politicians and policy makers — and of ourselves as well — to continue to speak candidly about the problems that beset us, to continue to "speak truth to power" prophetically, but to do so respectfully, trying to find the common ground on which enemies may become friends?

Let us rededicate ourselves to this effort, so that our children, and our children's children, may know a just, lasting and civil peace.

Forest Light

For so long he had been alone. He walked the forest alone. He climbed the trees alone. He slept under the starry vastness of the night, alone. There were others, of course, others like him. Sometimes they walked and climbed with him and slept under the starry skies with him. But that never changed the fact that he was alone. Sometimes he would lead, and sometimes follow, but always he was quite alone.

One night as he slept, when the moon was flooding the forest with its light, she came to him. As though in a dream, guardian owls announced her. Bats darted through the branches with excitement. Crickets heralded her arrival with a ringing heard through the entire forest. She came on gossamer wings made of dreams and pixy dust. She came to him, he knew not why. She blessed his eyes with gentle fingers. He opened these eyes to the moonlit thicket where he lay, and everything was as it had always been. Nothing was amiss. Except.

Except behind (and within, beneath and around) everything he saw, quite distinctly, a light. 'Light' isn't what he saw, but amber, violet, emerald, azure, crimson and a thousand other gently pulsing colors, each one attached to (or part of) an object in the world he thought he knew. The forest was aglow. Connecting the forms of every forest object were glowing strands of energy. They ran in every direction over great distances, into the past and the future too. Some even ran to the stars. His familiar forest became a vast, complicated and ever-changing interweaving of light and energy moving instantaneously and constantly from form to form to form. He saw that he himself was enmeshed in this weaving and connected to these forms. He was frightened. He tried to shake off the illumined cords that bound him to the forest. Dull yellow fear quickly spread from his center to others. He could not break free.

"Why?" he asked.

"You are too much alone," she answered. "We are worried about you."

"Who is we?" he asked.

"We are the Forest and the Field, the Mountain and the Sea. We are you, and others you know, and others you know nothing of."

"Have you bound me to you?" he said, indicating the multicolored pulsing strands that flowed through him.

"Oh no! We have changed nothing. Everything is as it was. You were alone, but you were never separate. We have given you the gift of seeing. But I will remove this gift if it discomforts you."

"No. Don't. It's all so ... astonishing, and I didn't know. It's all so... new. I know how to be alone. I don't know how to be 'with'. It's difficult."

She paled. "Being 'with' can be very difficult when your heart wants to be alone.

"Can I be 'with', and still walk and climb among the trees and choose my own breakfast?"

She laughed. "Of course you can! You must be yourself. But when you are most yourself, you will not be alone."

"There is more," she said. "When you are separate, I grow smaller. My energy grows weak and my light grows dim. When you are alone a part of me must die."

"How can that be?" he asked. "That's not fair! Who are you?"

"I am the song of the turtle dove. I am the perfume of the honeysuckle. I am the breeze that cools you in summer, the rain that quenches your thirst. I am the fire that warms you on winter nights. I look up at you from the lichens and down upon you from the stars. I would love you with all the magic of my being and give you everything my powers can call forth. I would awaken you softly with the first sun and bathe your body with the sweetest oils. I would walk with you on all your explorations, share your discoveries and privations, and accompany you even to the last and greatest portal through which all must pass. All these years I have awaited you and only you but you would not open your soul to me."

He looked at her. His heart leaped within him with tenderness. Could this be true? Could she be real? Could a creature of such love exist? She sat quietly, smiling a sad smile, waiting for his response. There was no guile in her, no ambition, no possessiveness, nothing at all to fear. He looked at her features; they were remarkably similar to his own. He looked into her eyes. (This is something he never allowed himself to do.) They drew him into a different reality. He felt most unworthy.

Through her eyes he passed into a continuum of time and space hauntingly familiar yet alien to his soul. Through her eyes he beheld a shimmering passion for all things beautiful and good. In her eyes he perceived a love so great, so strong, so full of resolve and fury that it raged like a flooding river against the closed door of his soul. In her eyes he saw himself as a being of light and energy with gossamer wings made of dreams and pixy dust.

Sphinx like, she waited. He fidgeted. He wanted to fling open his soul's door to her and invite her to stay. But he was afraid. He was afraid he would drown in this love, afraid he would be crushed against the confining walls of his own construction.

"What is pixy dust?"

She was infinitely patient. "A small measure of pixy dust can move a mountain, and almost everybody has some," she responded, teasing him. "But it isn't easy."

"Where does it come from?"

"Most people don't know where to look. It's usually under their feet. It's the dust that falls when hopes are dashed, when bodies are violated, and when spirits are crushed with impunity. It's the dust of neglect that falls from the bed of the lonely child. It's the dust of despair that collects on the feet of those who are abused. These things are horrible, but without this dust we will never be able to heal the forest. Most people sweep it away, but I have learned its power. You must gather it up, hold it in your hands before you and not turn away. You must honor it and offer it to the Great Spirit as a gift. You must add to it the salt of your own tears. When you do all this, the dust becomes powerful. It opens hearts and minds. It opens your eyes to what is real.

She waited. She exerted no pressure; more than once she offered to go away.

But at every hint of her leaving he shouted, "Please stay!" Still he held tightly to the door of his soul, half pushing it open and half pulling it closed, trying to defeat the patterns of a life-time. She was amused and saddened by his struggle. Though her soul hung with his in the balance she did not interfere in his struggle against himself.

He grew weary and sleep overcame him.

The next morning the sun rose in the sky, bringing the forest to wakefulness. He stirred and felt its warmth renew his body. He opened his eyes; everything was as it had always been. Nothing was amiss. Except.

Except that sunlight was flooding the recesses of his soul as never before. Its radiant energy penetrated him. He heard pigeons cooing a new song. A gentle breeze carried the strong scent of honeysuckle to his nostrils. Squirrels chirped above him and jumped from branch to branch; he looked with wonder at the lichen covered rocks. He felt alive as if for the first time, and part of everything. He was alive and in love with all creation, and he was not alone.

Baptism of Jesus

Dizzy's Delight

As always, I was trying to digest the latest world crises with my coffee and muffins. But my eye was drawn to the lower corner of the front page. The announcement of the deaths of two of our century's greatest artists, Dizzy Gillespie and Rudolph Nureyev, stunned me. A great sadness remained with me all of the day.

My "background task" that day was to reflect on the text and subject for Sunday: the baptism of Jesus. My "foreground tasks" were to counsel with a suicidal parishioner, plan a statewide financial drive, and keep to a daily round of appointments and meetings. But the sadness wouldn't go away. Although I never knew Gillespie or Nureyev personally, each had contributed to the world I inhabit. Each had lightened the burdens I carry. Facing the world without them seemed like cruel and unusual punishment from a God too grim for words.

Nureyev was born on a train puffing along the shores of Lake Baikal in southeastern Siberia in 1938. That was the year, you may recall, when Neville Chamberlain returned to Britain from Munich announcing "peace for our time." It was the year of *Kristallnacht*. Nureyev grew up to become the world's most famous performer and choreographer. Although he was a stickler for classical technique, he brought a contemporary approach to Nineteenth Century ballet. According to one obituary, he "taught dancers to jump an extra measure higher, and not be afraid of the grand manner." To contemplate a world without Nureyev was to contemplate a world grown prosaic, humdrum, and less hopeful.

It also was around 1938 that a young jazz trumpeter with Teddy Hill's band began to receive international acclaim. Dizzy Gillespie, of course, was the archetypal "bad boy" of jazz. He was thrown out of work in the Depression because of his rebellious temperament. Hill called him "the frantic one." He was a "headlong player, a risk taker, who flung phrases with abandon," a musician who "poured out cascades of notes," a horn player who produced "a full, clean sound with long, rolling lines." But his rebellious nature was controlled by his keen intelligence, his disciplined character, his mastery of musical theory and his innate good sense. He was smart, intentional, good-natured and methodical in his revolutionary approach to jazz.

Diz — along with others like Charlie Christian, Charlie (Bird) Parker, Kenny Clarke, Thelonius Monk, Nick Fenton and Max Roach — became the new wine in the old wineskins of the swing era. Gillespie and friends joined African Americans in other fields (like actor Canada Lee, singers Paul Robeson and Marian Anderson, and writers of the Harlem Renaissance) to challenge and reconstruct the American experience. They embodied a new assertiveness of the African American spirit. Their contribution was as much social revolution as musical innovation.

The bop rebellion of the late 30's was a wholly black invention. It was created by young black musicians who came of age in the golden 20's of segregated, racist America. When they toured, they were paid less than whites of lesser ability. They were forced to stay with private families instead in hotels. They were fed from the back doors of restaurants, and could not invite their own families to their performances.

They grew ironical, resentful and scornful of white reality. Where African American jazz performers of previous eras — like Louie Armstrong, Cab Galloway and Duke Ellington — understood themselves to be primarily entertainers, bop musicians turned this upside down. Their "cool" style in language, dress and behavior as well as in music challenged their audiences. They had the courage to insist that they were right. James Lincoln Collier called the music that came out of Minton's in Harlem a "core set of social ideas" that initiated the modern age. It was, he says, a "Declaration of independence."

The bop musicians fashioned a new order out of the chaos of racism in pre-war America. By challenging and transforming an older and established musical form that had degenerated into mere entertainment, they attained a new level of musical integration. They were the precursors of a new way of experiencing reality.

Jazz commentator, Joachim Berendt said that the challenge faced by artists in every generation is to bring order out of the chaos of their times. It is only possible to order chaos by getting close to it. Perhaps this is why many artists live such turbulent lives. Process theologians teach that "order" is constantly in danger of falling back into a primordial chaos on the one hand, or degenerating into a stifling triviality on the other. The order won by one generation becomes the triviality that must be demolished by the next.

Gillespie's colleague Charlie Parker seemed intuitively to understand that a new music was being born through him. "I could hear it sometimes," he recalled, "but I couldn't play it." Then, by using higher intervals of a chord as the melody line, and playing increasingly away from the beat, he found it. "I could play the thing I'd been hearing, and I came alive." He came alive. He imposed a new order that transcended chaos and overcame triviality. He created a new reality.

The sadness I felt began to dissipate as I tuned in my local jazz radio station. They were playing Diz's music all day long. There was nothing sad, bluesy or trivial in what I heard that day. To the contrary, there was energy; a tremendous, tumultuous, effervescent, *joie de vivre* was flowing through that horn. Diz may be dead, but that music gives life to the weary soul.

I went on to talk with my suicidal parishioner. Our talk turned to music. Her face brightened when we discussed her favorite classical composer, and his sheer delight in exuberant sounds. For a while, this delight pushed back the foreboding chaos of living and dying for no apparent reason. Although Diz was not explicitly in the conversation, I felt his solemn clowning presence at my shoulder.

I kept to my appointed rounds; I meditated on the baptism of Jesus in the River Jordon those twenty centuries ago. Gradually it became clear to me. For what was baptism in that ancient, desert world? It was a ritual act to frame and interpret an ambiguous reality. That river baptism represented a descent "into the depths" to wrestle with Leviathan; Leviathan is the symbol in the Hebrew Bible of all that is chaotic in human life. Christ's baptism offered a framework to order the chaos of that time. It was after he descended into the depths, after he faced the chaos and rose above it, that Jesus was claimed by God as the beloved child. The voice said God was "well pleased." God's claim was an affirmation of God's pleasure.

Pleasure? The end result of all this struggle is pleasure? Is that the significance of Nureyev's immense contributions? Delight! Is that the meaning of Dizzy's life? Yes, but authentic pleasure and delight — pleasure poised precariously between chaos and triviality, and delight in eternal need of renewal.

The world my newspaper describes is chaotic, and the solutions we mortals imagine often seem so trivial. In our personal lives too, chaos overwhelms us, and trivial concerns suffocate our spirits. So I thank God today for Gillespie and Nureyev who point us in the right direction.

I imagine that heaven must have become a far more delightful place this week. In one corner Nureyev is teaching the angels to jump a measure higher than they have ever jumped before and not to fear the grand manner. And in another Diz has joined Monk and Bird (and maybe Saint Peter) for a glorious jam session that will never end, ceaselessly expanding the vocabulary of joy.

Pleasing

This is my beloved child in whom I am well pleased.

(Matthew 3:17)

We stood in a circle holding hands. The deacon asked us to bow our heads as he intoned his prayer. He concluded: "… and may all that we say or do be pleasing in thy sight, O God. Amen." It was comforting to hear this familiar phrase as we said farewell to our friend, Gleason Glover. My father had ended many a table grace and family prayer with exactly these words. Yet something the deacon said felt different. What was it? I pondered this as I drove home.

Then it came to me. Pleasing! My father didn't say pleasing. My father said acceptable: "May all that we say and do be acceptable in thy sight, O God." Between "acceptable" and "pleasing" there is a world of difference. Is this difference reflected in the attitudes we bring to worship, I wondered, or indeed, to life itself? Does it explain why Gleason lived every minute so fully, and radiated such a healthy and vital energy? Does this help explain the exuberance of so much African American worship? In so much of Black life, for so many generations, being "acceptable" to white folks was a matter of survival, but "pleasing" God and each other was a matter of grace and style. And it went both ways. As Alice Walter wrote, "Any fool living in the world can see it (God) always trying to please us back."

My childhood religion, on the other hand, was severe and austere. In all its forms, pleasure was suspect. God was a cosmic Scrooge, keeping accounts against a fateful day of reckoning. God tested and tried us to see if we could "endure" to the end. In this religion, life itself was a burden to be borne, not a treasure to be enjoyed. "Acceptable" was the most we could hope for. "Pleasing" was beyond the pale.

But perhaps, as Paul Tillich believed, God already accepts us unconditionally. By virtue of our being, we already and irrevocably are "acceptable" to God. Or as Jesus taught, God already cherishes each and every one of us. Not "keeping accounts", but "pleasing a loving God" becomes the essence of our faith. Not "enduring to the end", but "growing in love'"becomes the goal for our spiritual journey. If so, then delight must take its place beside duty in the lexicon of our spiritual disciplines. And we in the more Stoic traditions may learn the value of pleasing the God who is always trying to please us back.

Ordinary Time

A Moist Heart

In the grand scheme of things, it might seem a small thing, not worthy of the evening news. Two men from Colorado's Department of Fish and Wildlife drove up to a bend in the Colorado River to stock it with rainbow trout. Linda Hogan, a Chickasaw poet and University of Colorado professor, happened to be standing with a friend nearby. They decided to watch the silver sided fish find their way in the water to freedom. They stood quietly as the men climbed into the truck bed and opened the tank that held the fish. To their dismay the men did not use the nets they had brought with them. Instead they poured the fish into the truck bed and then kicked them out and down the hill into the water. The few fish that survived were motionless and shocked, their gill slits barely moving, their skin hanging from their wounds. At most, she said, it would have taken the men a few minutes longer to have used their nets, to have treated the lives they were handling with dignity and respect, to handle life with what she calls "caretaker's hands."

Although the act itself was brutal enough, for Ms. Hogan it has become a symbol for much of what is wrong with modern life. These actions, she wrote,

> "… must be what Bushmen mean when they say a person is 'far hearted.' This far hearted kind of thinking is one we are especially prone to now, with our lives moving so quickly, and it is one that sees life, other lives, as containers for our own use and not as containers in a greater sense." (Hogan, "What Holds The Water, What Holds the Light," *Parabola*, Winter, 1990.)

We see this attitude everywhere — in the streets of our cities, the board rooms of major corporations and the halls of government. We feel it in our twisted relationships to the earth. It permeates our assumptions about so many great issues that affect us all. Far Hearted. Cold. Cynical. Hard. Distant.

But we are searching for a new heart that is spiritually alive. Our search for authenticity reflects a deep and pervasive hunger. The old order is passing away and a new order is emerging. We are caught in a nether land. Old absolutes are failing. Old mores fail to restrain our most brutal impulses. Personal crises overwhelm us. Relationships meant to nurture have become barren or even destructive. We are disoriented at best and, at worst, disillusioned.

Spiritual quests often begin in situations of grave social and personal dislocation (A. C. Robin Skynner, *Psychotherapy and Spiritual Traditions*, 1983). What kind of person do I wish to become? What do I want my life to mean? To what or whom do I belong or intend to be loyal? In what community am I most at home? These are fundamentally spiritual questions. When we ponder the meaning of death, the presence of beauty or our relationship to the universe, we are moving into the spiritual realm. Even questions about the nature of justice, the dignity of persons or the distribution of wealth open our hearts to wider vistas.

Within the traditions of the Abrahamic faiths, the spiritual path often is called "finding one's heart." The heart, metaphorically, is the most inward part of us, and the center of all consciousness. It is the dwelling place of God. In this sense, to be "far hearted" is to be far from the Divine.

The 14th Century Saint Gregory Palamas wrote that to find the heart is to overcome the fragmentation present in every life. Finding the heart involves a reconstruction of the human person and a rediscovery of a lost part of the self. To find the heart is to be possessed by a divine love in a way that is of profound benefit to others and to the larger world. It is a "coming home." (Andrew Louth, *Knowing the Unknowable*, 1994).

As beautiful as this sounds, the first step in many spiritual journeys involves grieving. Jack Kornfield, a clinical psychologist and Buddhist teacher, thinks that meditation is almost synonymous with grief work, and that grief is the precursor of enlightenment:

> "Opening the heart begins by opening to a lifetime's accumulation of unacknowledged sorrow...The Buddhists describe this as an ocean of human tears larger than four great oceans... We grieve for our past traumas and present fears, for all the feelings we never dared experience consciously. Whatever shame or unworthiness we have within us arises, much of our early childhood and family pain, the mother and father wounds we hold, the isolation, any past abuse, physical or sexual, all are stored in the heart... Meditation is primarily a practice of grieving and letting go... Out of our grief work comes deep renewal." (Kornfield, *A Path With A Heart*, 1993.)

The Papago Indians of the American Southwest tell the story of an Elder Brother who was killed. After a few days he struggled to come back to full strength and renewed life. To gain this he searched for a moist heart. He made many stops for there were enemies along the way who tried to prevent him from finding new life. But with each victory he grew stronger and his heart became more moist. Finally he stood alive, in full vigor and with a very moist heart. The Seminole Franciscan Sister, Mary José Hobday (*Seeking a Moist Heart: Native American Ways for Helping the Spirit*), underscores the importance of this story. She reminds us that "it takes a moist heart to walk with our brothers and sisters, a moist heart to be at peace in ourselves, a moist heart to serve the people well."

In the world's great wisdom traditions, *samsara* or *maya* (the misleading world of appearances), the "shadows" of Plato's cave or various temptations lead us astray. But we want to leave behind everything that is lifeless and illusory. To find and nurture the living heart is the motivation of all spiritual quests. To encounter the Life that lives in us is our ultimate vocation. Deep feeling, great generosity and spiritual living are the qualities that help us overcome our far heartedness and moisten our hearts.

One of the most important ways to moisten our hearts is the practice of silence. "Silence," wrote Hobday, "gives the soft distance between spoken words. It yields a poetry spoken without sound. To live with Indian people is to discover a beautiful enhancement of the spirit through silence."

An appreciation for silence is nearly universal among the wisdom traditions. By the practice of it, wrote Nikephoros in the 13th Century CE:

> "…the intellect descends into the heart. When that happens, there is a joyful sense of homecoming. The intellect becomes luminous. The finding of the heart by the mind is the attainment of simplicity and the recovery of the fundamental unity of the human person."

Sister Hobday also celebrates the traditional practice of living and talking with the dead. Communion with ancestors keeps the heart moist and vulnerable. So does the cultivation of one's personal relationship with the land and all the creatures who inhabit it. The land itself is a living teacher and a benevolent provider. Openness to its wisdom renews and refreshes the heart. She speaks of the willingness to seek a personal and communal vision, and attending to the many stories life has to tell.

To these native practices I add those from our Christian tradition: spiritual counsel with a trusted advisor, singing, chanting, public worship and private devotion, repentance and forgiveness of self and others.

These are practices that help us to overcome our far heartedness. They moisten our hearts and open us to God.

To separate the wheat from the chaff, to discern truth in the midst of illusion, to penetrate beneath the surface of a sometimes tawdry existence and find there a more luminous reality — this is the essence of the spiritual quest.

Martha's Feast and Mary's Portion

Martha, Martha, you are worried and distracted by many things; there is need of only one thing. Mary has chosen the better part, which will not be taken away from her.

(Luke 19:41)

When Jesus entered Bethany, Martha opened her house to him. In the time-honored traditions of her people she busied herself to make his stay comfortable. She arranged a room and drew cool water. She began preparations for a feast. She invited many guests. She assembled foods, spices, flowers and beverages. She cleaned, cooked and set the table. The dictates of centuries of hospitality compelled her to busyness. She was honored that the Teacher had consented to stay with her; she wanted this meal to be memorable.

While she worked her sister sat with their guest. Mary listened to his stories and engaged him in conversation. With so much work to do and so little time, Martha grew resentful of Mary's indulgence. Had not both Father Abraham and Mother Sarah jointly prepared the feast for the strangers at Mamre? Did Mary think she was better than they?

With irritation in her voice Martha tried to enlist Jesus in her cause. "Good sir," she said, "don't you care that my sister has left me to do all the work? Please, tell her to help me!" How surprised she must have been by his response. "Martha! Martha! You are anxious about many things, but only one thing is necessary. Mary has chosen the better portion, and it will not be taken from her."

Many commentators, both ancient and modern, fault Martha for not being "spiritual" enough. Mary is seen as the paradigm of the intelligentsia and the patrona of those who value mind over body, spirit over flesh, and the contemplative vision over the requirements of practical life. Mary had chosen the "better portion" of conversation while Martha chose mundane preparations for the meal.

There is a gloss on this story that comes from the sixth century writings of the Desert Fathers. A visitor once approached the monastery of Abbot Silvanius. When the traveler saw all the brothers working in the fields he said to them, "Do not labor for bread that perishes. Mary has chosen the better part."

The elder instructed one of the brothers to show the guest to a room. The ninth hour, which was the normal hour for dinner, came and passed and no one came for him. More hours passed. The guest watched the door eagerly, waiting to be summoned to a meal. Finally he left his room to find the abbot. When he found him he asked, "Are the brothers fasting today?"

"Oh, no, they have all eaten."

"Why wasn't I invited?"

"Oh, sir! You are so spiritual. You have no need for bread and material substance. You read and pray all day and do not need nourishment. You have chosen the better part."

Then the guest prostrated himself. "I beg your pardon, abbot."

The elder pardoned him, and then said, "This is how Mary herself stands in need of Martha. It was because of Martha that Mary could receive her praise."

Whatever else Luke's story intends, this clearly is a story about hospitality. It poses a conundrum for all of us who are Marthas in the world, all of us "practical types" who want to do what is right according to the customs we have learned. But there is no less a conundrum for the Marys among us, all of us who seek mysterious paths to spiritual truth apart from the practical aspects of our lives. The story begs us to ponder the nature of true hospitality and, within that, true spirituality as well.

Hospitality is one of the universal values that make us fully human. In every nation traditions of hospitality run deep. Practices of many kinds have developed to guide us in being proper hosts and guests to one another. Sometimes hospitality becomes high ritual as in the bread-and-salt ceremony of the Ukraine or the Tea Ceremony in Japan. To knowingly violate the norms of hospitality is to be rude and insulting, and has been known to lead to wars. How a people receives its guests reveals its fundamental values.

The Plains Indians of North America developed traditions of a generous hospitality that are astonishing to peoples of European descent. The "Giveaway" is one such Indian custom. At funerals, naming ceremonies, weddings and other major events, but also when there is no special occasion at all, the hosts give away their most prized possessions as a way of honoring their guests. They give away even essential household items. People make beautiful objects such as colorful bead work and finely woven blankets. They hold competitions to see which are the most beautiful, and then they give them away.

"Things are made to be given," wrote Ella Deloria, expressing a view of the world quite foreign to many of us. The Giveaway focuses on "the ultimate need of people to care for each other. Out of that comes all etiquette," explained Lakota artist, Arthur Amiotte. "You are a finer person not by having… but by using what you have as a means for ennobling the human spirit. When you give, it becomes an act of love."

I have been touched by the unanticipated hospitality of others. Even in the midst of great scarcity, I have eaten more than my fill from overflowing tables, knowing well the effort and costs to my hosts. Others have invited me, a stranger with no claim on them, into their homes and work places, into the sacred spaces and intimate moments of their lives. So many people of other races, cultures and backgrounds have shared the substance of their lives with me. They became my tutors in the fine art of being human.

I always will remember an incident in Saint Petersburg (then known as Leningrad). It was the Soviet era; people were wary of strangers. One evening, our group of American volunteers with the Fellowship of Reconciliation was seeking a shelter for homeless people. We were told we would find it in a certain abandoned apartment building. We found our way to the right address, but the building was not abandoned. It obviously was not a shelter. We knocked on an apartment door. In our limited Russian and English we said, "Homeless? Homeless?" The woman at the door was distraught. She quickly counted us and threw up her hands. "Five of you!" she exclaimed, "I only take three. I call my neighbor."

When she understood that we ourselves were not homeless, she still made a table of foods, vodkas and sweets. We enjoyed a long evening of limited conversation and much music in the overheated apartment of this stranger who befriended us. Can you imagine this scene being repeated here?

We don't have to strain to recognize the high value of hospitality in Jesus' teachings. The observance of ceremonial forms was important to him. On the last night of his life he knelt before his disciples to wash their feet.

He harshly judged members of the privileged class who failed to offer the proper hospitality prescribed by the etiquette of his culture.

Yet the observance of outward forms was not his central concern. The rituals of hospitality had developed over centuries to facilitate human interaction but they were merely "outward and visible signs" of an inward and spiritual attitude toward others. Jesus could be as severe toward those who observed accepted canons as he was of those who didn't. He justified ignoring conventions when circumstances warranted.

From his parable of the Good Samaritan and his description of the last judgment to his last words from the cross, Jesus expanded the ancient Semitic affirmations of hospitality. He saw within a generous welcome a deeper ethical imperative. He advocated a radical hospitality that carries us beyond ethnic, class, political and gender boundaries. For Jesus, it is not enough to serve those who come to our door or to welcome or feed our guests. We must actively seek the hungry, thirsty and sick. By serving the lonely, imprisoned and despairing, we are serving Him.

All of this leads back to our original conundrum. If Jesus so valued hospitality, why did he not acknowledge Martha's selfless generosity on his behalf? What is missing from this story?

Ivan Klima is a contemporary Czech writer whose works were circulated only as *samizdat* during the "Stalinist darkness" in what was Czechoslovakia. Since the collapse of communism his international reputation is growing as his works are translated. In *Waiting for the Dark, Waiting for the Light* he explores how ordinary people dealt with the demands of an oppressive state. He describes how the need to compromise and adapt created a paralysis of the soul, a suspended animation and a spiritual constriction. At one point he asks, "What is tedium?" His answer is, "Time filled with encounters that leave no mark on us."

"Time filled with encounters that make no mark on us." Martha is at spiritual risk at just this point. She is anxious about many things. She has an abundance of tasks but one thing is lacking.

She fulfills every conceivable expectation of the generous host. Her guests will be impressed. They will talk about the Teacher's visit for months. But she is in danger of reducing this encounter into an occasion, and this meeting of hearts into a merely memorable event. When the dinner is over she will be unchanged. Perhaps her generosity is not as selfless as it seems. Perhaps, unknown even to herself, she is using Jesus' visit to earn praise and admiration for herself. But in getting what she wants she will miss much more.

The "better portion" chosen by Mary lies in this and this alone: She remains present to her guest. She listens, inquires, reveals, asserts, defends and allows his spirit and hers to engage. She receives and gives, challenges and appreciates. In this, her spirit grows. This kind of hospitality can never be prescribed; it grows from a wise and caring heart.

Were this all the evangelist intended, it would be sufficient. How often have we wasted such moments? How often, out of fear or foolishness have we allowed encounters to become mere occasions and forever lost the promise of the moment?

This kind of tedium is the opposite of spiritual fulfillment. Here is where the dead bury the dead. But Christ came that we might have an overflowing abundance of life. He came to Bethany bearing the promise of transformation.

"In the Bible," wrote the Latin American theologian, Gustavo Gutierrez, "'to live' always means 'to live with,' 'to live for,' and 'to be present to others.'" To live always involves the fine art of hospitality. The spiritual challenge for us is not whether we are a Mary or a Martha. We are both — always and inevitably. We are flesh and spirit, mind and body, infinite longings and practical limitations. The challenge is how to be fully alive in the moments given to us. How can we be open to encounters that bring renewal and transformation.

The key to Luke's story is that Martha's and Mary's visitor is not just another friend or even a renowned teacher. He is a "sacred visitor," or more strongly, "the Lord." The reader is supposed to know what the sisters do not: that in this visit the "Word" is becoming flesh. This world belongs to Him. Though very much their guest in Bethany, He also is their Host — and the supreme Host who welcomes all. Martha and Mary are as much His guests and He is theirs.

Jesus bears within himself the image and likeness of God, which is our true image and likeness too. He is the divine messenger seeking to lead us back to our own divinity. He calls us into the fullness of life God intends for us.

If we are both Martha and Mary we are also, in a terribly important way, "sacred guests." We are guests upon the earth, guests in our era, and guests within our communities. We are always hosts and guests to each other.

What if this knowledge becomes our spiritual practice? What if we invest our energy and resources into fashioning a welcome for others? What if we conduct our businesses and go about our jobs with this host-and-guest vocation? Would not our politics and economics change dramatically? What if the Bosnian Serbs, Muslims, Croats and others thought of themselves as guests and hosts to each other? What if Irish Catholics and Protestants assumed responsibility for each other? What if Newt Gingrich and Bill Clinton tried to live out a tradition of deep hospitality toward one another? Is it not possible to understand "affirmative action" as a kind of radical hospitality?

On a more personal level, what if I am both host and guest to my partner or spouse? Or to someone with whom I have a troubled relationship? Or to my child or aging parent? Would this not banish tedium from our lives, and open us to new possibilities for grace and life?

The Beloved Community

At his best, Martin Luther King, Jr. was the mouthpiece of his God. God had a controversy with this nation, a controversy about race and power, a controversy about economics and opportunity, a controversy about where the meaning of human existence was to be, but most of all a controversy about the nature of our community.

Tonight we honor this man who was a mouthpiece; tonight we would amplify his message throughout the state of Minnesota. It was a message about the interrelationship of love and power, about brotherhood and sisterhood and fellowship.

But most of all it was a message about community. Dr. King challenged us to become worthy of one another and to fashion what he came to call the "Beloved Community."

After all the dinners have been consumed, after the holiday breakfasts have been digested, after all the words of all the speeches have vanished into the winter air and found their way into the hearts and minds of listeners everywhere, after the children have finished their recitations, painted their pictures and sung their songs together, after the musicians have gone home from their concerts and the dancers have returned to their studios, then the birthing of the Beloved Community will begin.

It will begin in the homes of our community, and in our neighborhoods. It will begin in our churches and synagogues, in our mosques and sweat lodges, in our courtrooms and prison cells, and in a thousand classrooms throughout the nations.

The Beloved Community will begin when police officers care enough to treat young black males with the same respect that they show to me. It will begin when those who are alienated, those who have given up on education or employment or those who have embraced violence and intimidation, discover that life is more than money, more than sex, more than drugs, more even than power.

And when they are encouraged by the whole community, by all of us, politicians, employers, teachers, preachers and those who have power and money, when they are encouraged by the whole community to find a new life, a new hope and a new reason for living.

The Beloved Community will begin when all of us acknowledge together that none of us is God, that God is not white, that God is not black. God is not male and God is not female. God is not gay and God is not straight. God is not the mascot for any religious community.

Yet, though none of us is God, God resides in all of us: in every child born in every land this night, in Somalia, Soweto, Sarajevo or Saint Paul, in every teenager without exception.

God resides within us, between us, among us.

Whether we live alone, in a nursing home or in a condominium high above the city, whether we live on a farm or in a prison cell, whether we wear black leather, pink polyester or gray pin-striped wool, whether we like jazz or classical, new age or country, rap or gospel music, we are cherished by God. God looks upon each one of us and all of us with the eyes of a wise, proud and saddened parent. God looks on our city and our state tonight, and on our country and our world, with the greatest tenderness and compassion.

It is God who raised up Martin, God who pricked the conscience of a nation with his words, God who sent an arrow of loving shock into the heart of our people, God who shaped a vision to shape a world where we might live together peacefully, lovingly, and with hope in our hearts, a world where we might forgive and be forgiven, teach and learn from one another, love and be loved into wholeness.

After all our words and all the speeches of this weekend have been spoken, it will be time, it will be time to begin to live the dream of the Beloved Community.

A Crisis Overdue

When I first came to Maine, I wondered why Maine people were so acutely interested in the weather. New Jersey had always been overcast, its weather rarely spectacular. It possessed a kind of sameness that pleased only the bureaucrat. I never liked it and consequently never developed a taste for weather, although I could taste it when pollutant-laden winds blew my way.

I never knew the bewildering rascality and playfulness of weather until I came to Maine. Our weather is for disciplined aesthetes, and Maine people have become its connoisseurs, paying close attention to its finest shifts and the nuances of change.

But why? As we face this winter, I begin to understand. Weather brings more than pictorial beauty or cathartic rage. It dictates to nature, and nature to us, the patterns of our lives. When it threatens, we take note.

The president, the governor and our local oil supplier are telling us it will be a cold winter, and the truth is sinking in. Wood burning stoves are hot items. The price of wood has been jacked up even as the cords have been stacked up. Unwary buyers are likely to get burned.

You know by now that I grumble and complain. I like to swap tales with my friends of our miseries and our woes. I am perversely enjoying the one-upmanship of the "I'm sacrificing more than you" discussions to which we are all lately prone. Indeed, I'm even a bit eager for Christmas to come and pass and to plunge into the hardships that lay ahead.

All of which calls for an explanation. First, there is you. If I must face a winter crisis, I would rather be here, in a small community of friends and neighbors, than isolated on the sixth floor of an apartment house in downtown Newark.

Not that all of you are the principled citizens you'd like to be. I know that some of you already have begun to hoard gasoline and oil. Some of you refuse to turn your thermostats back, or drive more slowly, or pack away your snowmobiles. And perhaps life for the rest of us will be a little more difficult because of your rashness. Sooner or later, however, you'll join us.

This "crisis" is projected for three to five years. Have you prepared for that? Meanwhile, the rest of us are relearning something of vital importance in America: pulling together in a time of peril. That means being together more, and that means getting to know each other more, and that means... so many wonderful things.

A second reason I'm not scowling at the weather just yet is that some sort of crisis like this was long overdue. For me, I mean. I've been needing an excuse for years to slow my life down, to attend fewer meetings, plays, concerts, and parties. I've spent far more personal energy than I've been able to manufacture.

I knew that a day of reckoning was not far away. It has arrived. I'll have long winter evenings to reassess my life — where I've been, who I am, in what direction I wish to move. I expect to learn from it, to be happier because of it, have more time to read, reflect and enjoy my friends.

What can we learn from the trials ahead? We will learn of the limits to our lives which nature imposes. We will learn where we may resist and where we must cooperate. "Nature sustains itself through three precious principles," wrote Lao-Tzu: "gentleness, frugality and humility." We would do well to embrace them, and follow.

So Many Books

Across the street from the post office in the town where I grew up was a two story white masonry building with dark green trim. An archway on the right side led to the local police headquarters. I would go there to register my bicycle every year.

On the left side of the building were two large doors that led to a stairway. On the second floor was our local library. It was very small. I would go there as often as I could.

I spent many an afternoon wondering through the stacks and reading the newspapers and magazines. I signed out books every week, and I eagerly devoured them. Somehow I developed the idea that I if I could read all the books in the library, I would become a wise man. That was my ambition.

When I went to high school I was shocked to discover another library, and this one was slightly larger than the second-floor public library downtown. Still, it did not seem unreasonable to imagine reading all of those books before I died.

The day came when I went to college. It was a small state school, but its library took up three floors, with lots of stacks packed very closely together. Undaunted, but realizing now that my task was growing exponentially more challenging, I resolved to burn the candle at both ends to see it through. To make matters worst, I discovered bookstores.

But I especially remember that day in September when I walked onto the Princeton University campus to begin my graduate studies. Entering the Firestone Library, I was stunned by this cavernous building and its vast collections. From outside, I could see three floors, but my heart broke when the librarian told me there were three more below ground. There were over fifty miles of shelves in that library alone, all heavily laden with books. Every level was so big that they had embedded tile compasses in the floors to help you find your way. But wait! I was absolutely crushed when I learned that this was only one of Princeton's libraries, and there were fourteen more on campus. I was completely defeated as I tried to adjust to the fact that surely I would die before I could read all the books I needed to read.

An Ambiguous Visitor

Today is an in between kind of day. I sit huddled next to the radiator in our living room, leisurely typing away on the 1944 portable Royal Aristocrat typewriter on my lap. Odors of drying pine permeate the room. The howling lament of the wind is punctuated by the steady ticking of our firehouse clock. The house groans and rattles. My coffee cup is cold.

Outside, our neighbors' youngest, bundled like big balls of yarn, are pulling and tugging at their stubborn Saint Bernard. All over town the presents have been exchanged, the meals have been consumed, the reunions consummated.

Perhaps it is too soon to say that it is over, too soon to re-box all the ornaments and trimmings for their storage in the attic, too soon to let go of the fleeting holiday moments. Anxious and eager youngsters are still underfoot; cookies and candies remain in the bowls. Occasional Christmas songs can still be heard on the radio.

Yet it now seems slightly out of place. A subtle melancholy haunts this Christmas season; today it chooses to reveal itself. It stalked us silently through the streets, the stores, the shopping centers, through the bus terminals and Christmas visits. It lingered uninvited at the Christmas dinner. And here, in my post-holiday living room, it has become my companion.

I suppose I could banish it with a flick of my television switch or by making myself busy in any number of favorite pursuits. Later, perhaps. But for the moment, I am weary of smiling. I rather welcome my ambiguous visitor.

Melancholia is not nostalgia, though they are kin. When one is nostalgic, one longs to recapture the inner peace, joy or excitement of a previous time when Christmas was a Lionel train around a tree, a church pageant and my father's cream pie. Because the past cannot be recovered directly, nostalgia leaves us restless and unsatisfied.

Melancholia is a bit more profound. It is a natural, probably useful, element of the human psyche — a kind of metaphysical grieving for the changes that the world continually throws upon us. It slipped in with the Christmas cards this year, with all those little notes telling of the changes and events in the lives of our friends. New babies are expected by friends in Massachusetts and in Africa; an ocean house was acquired by other friends near Boston. A favorite uncle died, a cousin was transferred, another couple separated after only four years. And what of the cards that didn't come?

The present is ever slipping from our grasp. Our fondest dreams and our thwarted opportunities alike are swallowed up in the swiftly moving stream. However full our joy, however deep our sorrow, however intense our anger, however sacred our trust — it all seems to pass away. While the future is ever the basis of hope and hope is badly needed, its arrival strips from us too soon the moments that we treasure.

Today I do not wish to smile. I grieve. I grieve not only for the obvious losses of friends with whom I once shared this season, but also for the many changes in the world which have changed me. I grieve for the doors that have been closed, the paths that may have ended. Yet the past is past, and that too, is as I wish.

In a short while I will freshen up a bit and put on another pot of coffee. But for the moment I am content to watch the children play with their dog and listen to the ticking of my clock.

Silent Places of the Past

Martinsburg, West Virginia. For the most part, most of us can function pretty well wherever we find ourselves on this growing-smaller planet. Unlike our peasant forbearers, we are not chained by circumstance to any certain plot of ground. Our visions are not limited by its horizons: our consciousness is molded by more than its particular contours. We are free to fly above it and away, to escape the shackles that enthralled generations before us.

Those of us who bother at all to return to the place of our childhood find that it has changed as much as we. Stranger to stranger we converse, seeking the lost or hidden thread which once bound us so closely. Like a face from the past, we eagerly search for telltale clues to unlock the memory, the context, the moment.

We walk the alleys, revisit the playing fields, and seek out the sidewalks on which we died a thousand deaths. How small and shoddy they seem now — these battlefields of the past — hardly capable of holding the vast armies that marched across them in the chilly gray of those January evenings.

Where are the swarms of supermen who leapt from garage roofs at unwary passers-by? In supermarkets and suburban malls, no doubt, still a danger to the unsuspecting. Where are the hopscotch patterns on broken pavements — that chalk art of yesterday's children? On canvasses now, lining the walls of galleries, or on greeting cards, websites and packaging. Where are the platoons of hiders and seekers, of sledders and sliders, of rock throwers and magic show-ers? Where are the Indian Chiefs in brightly colored plumage, the creatures from outer space, the phantoms from the deep lagoon? Where are the feet tangled in jumping ropes, the full-throated threats to go tell Momma, the bouncers of balls in busy streets?

Some have remained, keeping alive the continuity of the community. One finds them occasionally in the factories, the stores, the churches, the banks. They speak slowly, secure in the knowledge of their roots and probable destinies. Yet occasionally one detects a certain restlessness in their manner, a certain yearning for that which will not be.

Others have carried their childhood memories with them to far away places, contributing to the cross-fertilization and rich mixing of our global village. Usually in a hurry, they walk confidently in the world beyond their homes, the world of their own choosing. Yet, on their occasional sojourns home, one sees them wistfully seek out and savor the silent places of the pasts.

•

Praise in a Minor Key

Religious faith is a universal phenomenon. Doubt also is universal. There resides within each of us an impulse to believe and nagging questions that undermine our confidence. These are two poles of a single continuum; we need both in order to mature spiritually. But is it possible to honor faithfulness and doubt simultaneously?

In every culture there are rituals and behaviors related to some conception of the Sacred. In every language, women and men have evolved words to describe their experiences of a divine reality. Psychologists acknowledge that a receptivity to the concerns of faith is a vital part of human maturation. Neuroscientists and anthropologists are exploring the importance of religious faith for brain development and species evolution. Physicists, poets, philosophers, attorneys, engineers, doctors — people from all walks of life — have testified to the reality and importance of their religious experiences. Coming to terms with God is an essential component of our growth toward wholeness.

Recently Turkish and German archeologists under the direction of Klaus Schmidt made an amazing discovery. In Southeastern Turkey they have found an extensive temple complex called Göbekli Tepe; it predates Stonehenge, the Pyramids and all other known monumental construction. At 11,500 years old, it is the oldest place for worship yet discovered. It contains large T-shaped stone pillars, fine artistic carvings and abstract pictograms. Before this discovery, prevailing scientific orthodoxy had it that religion and art developed after we had settled into agricultural villages that made specialization of functions possible. But given the new monumental evidence to the contrary, anthropologists are revisiting this hypothesis. They are beginning to speculate that the creation and maintenance of places such as Göbekli Tepe required our hunter-gatherer ancestors to settle into communities nearby. Then they began to develop agriculture in order to sustain themselves and these massive establishments. In other words, we used to think that religion and art were the later products of human social evolution. Now it is suggested that human settlements and social evolution were the products of our species' need to sustain religious practices. An intense devotion to the Sacred has been a part of human consciousness from the beginning.

In today's world, to have faith means to make a basic affirmation that life is worthwhile. Keith Ward said it well: "To believe in God is to believe that at the heart of all reality... is spirit, consciousness, value, reason and purpose." (*Holding Fast to God*). Wonder and awe form the basis of our faith. Most of us, I suspect, have encountered evidences of a Divine Presence. We have known life-changing experiences of mystery, forgiveness and blessing. Within the serenity engendered by a breath-taking view from a mountain, or in the midst of a struggle for direction and meaning, we have been moved to say, with Jacob at Beth-El, "Surely God is in this place." Upon this bedrock of human experience religious communities have been formed. They are stewards of the possibility of religious experience.

Yet sometimes faith does not come easily. There are times when belief in God or God's goodness is difficult to sustain. There are moments when we cry out but Heaven seems empty. "Deep calls unto deep" but we hear no reply. We experience crises of faith in which we feel the world giving way beneath our feet. In these times of need, many of us turn to the religious communities in which our faith was nurtured. Sometimes we are helped. Sometimes we are disappointed by the response. I can think of a number of responses that, although common, are potentially destructive to the seeking soul.

Some churches and religious leaders trivialize our doubts and questions. I remember when I was a teenager and John Robinson's first book, *Honest To God*, arrived in the bookstores. Having been raised in the fundamentalism of a small town, I was both deeply impressed and deeply disturbed by this book. I went to a pastor whom I greatly respected to discuss it. He responded, "Robinson doesn't have a leg to stand on!" When I pressed for reasons, he said that he had only read the first few pages before he threw the book down in disgust. In truth, I felt dismissed as well.

On other occasions we encounter appeals to orthodoxy, tradition or authority. There are some who would stifle all discussion of evolutionary theory because it doesn't fit into a preconceived religious orthodoxy. Others insist that our beliefs about Jesus fit a particular norm. Many are the churches that say you must believe this doctrine or that in order to achieve true salvation. Many are the pastors who impress upon squirming confirmands the tenets of their own "one true faith", without giving the young people space to arrive at their own formulations. Many are the religious counselors whose only response to the thoughtful questioner is that "you have to believe".

Another response that I think is particularly modern and peculiarly

American, is an appeal to hype. In these churches, we must always be successful, always happy, always above our problems. Recently a clinical psychologist I know transferred her membership from an affluent suburban church that was bursting at the seams to an inner city church. The minister asked her why she was changing her affiliation. In her former church, she replied, everyone had to smile all the time. There was no place for her tears, questions or pain. In her new church, she said, she felt that she could be a human being.

A look at the American religious landscape indicates that these responses convince and comfort vast numbers of our fellow citizens. But there are others for whom these answers are more alienating than healing. They do violence to our most profound religious sensibilities. Although their faith is real, they also need the space to explore their questions.

The contemporary theologian, John MacQuarrie, recently said in his Gifford lectures that

> "... There are minds which cannot rest unless they have inquired, as far as there powers allow, into the very foundations of belief. They would consider it irresponsible not to conduct such an inquiry." (*In Search of Deity*)

I must confess that I am one of these. With the Psalmist I am one of those who thirst for God "as the hart pants for water". We seek a religious faith which is deep, meaningful, comforting and true, but which also responds to our deepest questions.

This is a matter of some urgency. In many mainline churches one senses a growing impatience with the openness and diversity which questioners inevitably require. In the new "uniting" church envisioned by the Consultation on Church Union, there is a subtle emphasis on authority, dogma, tradition and discipline. I fear that such an attitude will drive thoughtful and sensitive people away from the very institutions charged to be the trustee of the possibility of religious experience.

Is there another way? Of course there is. We can learn something from our sisters and brothers in the Jewish community. In the prayer book of Reform Judaism in America there is actually a liturgy on the subject of doubt. Far from castigating our questions as unacceptable, they are celebrated as essential equipment for one's spiritual journey:

"Cherish your doubts, for doubt is the handmaiden of truth. Doubt is the key to the door of knowledge; it is the servant of discovery. A belief which may not be questioned binds us to error... (But) doubt is a testing of belief. Truth, if it be truth, arises from each testing stronger, more secure. Those who would silence doubt are filled with fear; the house of their spirit is built on shifting sands. But they that fear not doubt and know its use are founded on a rock. They shall walk in the light of growing knowledge; the work of their hands shall endure. Therefore let us not fear doubt but let us rejoice in its help. It is to the wise as a staff to the blind; doubt is the handmaiden of truth." (*Gates of Prayer*)

Our doubts and questions reflect a deeply Biblical sense that our relationship with God is a living relationship. Living relationships involve not only belief and confidence, but struggle, wrestling, restlessness, doubt, laughter, anger, bargaining, argument and sorrow. The stories of Abraham, Sarah, Hagar, David, Ruth, Moses, Jacob, Peter, Mary, Paul and even Jesus, are stories of the "long, dark night of the soul" as well as tales of that "joy which comes with the morning".

The phenomenon of doubt is a necessary condition for growth in faith and spiritual maturity. It dispels illusions and unmasks superstitions. To the degree that it is thwarted, we are prevented from casting aside outgrown conceptions and beliefs in order to more fully appreciate the depths and the wonders of divine reality.

The psychiatrist, Ana-Maria Rizzuto, in a far-ranging study found that most of our images of God are formed during our pre-adolescent period. Even atheists have definite images of God, which they reject. These pre-adolescent images generally go unchallenged and unrevised until we are faced with a major crisis later in our lives. (*The Birth of the Living God*) On those occasions, unfortunately, we find that our "Sunday School God" of childhood may fall victim to the catastrophe. We are left with a void precisely when we need the strength and sustenance that faith provides.

It has been my experience over the years that most people have at least one profound and basic question of faith, a question that defies easy solution, a question that nags and gnaws at our consciousness and leaves us unsatisfied. For some of us it is a question about the suffering of obviously innocent people. For others it is a question about the existence of so much evil in our world. For still others it is a question of how to live responsibly in a world overwhelmed by need and pain. For one friend of mine, it is the sheer violence of God as depicted in the Bible. For another it is a question about the nature of prayer. I have come to believe that these questions are actually gifts of God. By keeping us unsettled and seeking they keep our minds and hearts open to dialogue with the living God.

From this point of view, the fear of questioning reveals a more serious lack of faith. If God is real then God does not need to be protected from our questions. God does not need to be propped up by our support. As the Scottish theologian, John Baillie, once said, "God must run the risk of honest inquiry," and he added thoughtfully, "God is glad to do so."

The Psalmist of course knew suffering, doubt and questions. Nor did she hide her anguish. "Day and night tears are my food." "I pour out my soul in distress." "How deep I am sunk in my misery, groaning in my distress." But she does not end in despair. "The Lord entrusts me to his unfailing love alike by day and night." "God's praise on my lips is a prayer to the God of my life". "Yet I will wait for God."

Her cries were rooted in a deeper and abiding faith. Although she raised a cry "out of the depths", she was confident that God has the power to lift a person out of "the miry bog" and to set her feet upon a rock. Her lament, said Old Testament scholar Bernard Anderson, was really an expression of praise — "praise offered in a minor key". She had confidence in the faithfulness of God. She anticipated a new lease on life. Her cries were motivated by a deep certainty that Yahweh is a compassionate God — the God who hears, who is concerned, and who is involved with people. The God to whom the Psalmist cried was "not characterized by apathy, but by sensitivity to the human condition". (Anderson, *Out of the Depths*)

The end of doubt is not despair, but growth. It is based not in cynicism but in confidence. The way we deal with our doubts and questions is a measure of the seriousness with which we treat our relationship with God. It is an affirmation, not a denial, of the reality of our own religious quest. Doubt is like a staff to the blind. Questions asked of faith are really praise offered in a minor key.

Lent

Virtual Racism

Edwin Perkins, a distinguished African American ambassador, was addressing a gathering of mostly business professionals when the moderator interrupted to announce the O. J. Simpson verdict. Although we had shared a meal together, we really didn't know each other. So when the announcement was made, there was an awkward moment. A restless, ruffled silence descended as people looked for cues about the proper way to react. Should we applaud? Hiss? Boo? Mostly we were confused. Republican and Democrat, liberal and conservative, young and old — in our confusion, we turned to each other. There was something very tender, very real about that moment. Before our positions had congealed into defended rigidities, we were gentle toward each other. We were downright human.

In the aftermath of the trial, I look back on that moment as a reference point, a reality check on all the analysis and rhetoric that has followed. I have talked with many people: African American and European American, female and male. Rarely have I encountered the strong and polarizing opinions that the media assures us now characterize race relations in America. There is anger, but there is also hope. There is still much to say about racism, and about battering, the power of money, racial bias in policing, and justice in America. There also is much to say about the common threads that bind our lives together.

The following Sunday the Mayflower choir and the choir of Saint Peter's African Methodist Episcopal Church came together for a musical festival. Nearly a hundred musicians joined in song; members from both congregations filled the sanctuary. We called the newsrooms of the local newspaper and major television stations. We suggested that two celebrated choirs — one Black and one White — and a church full of diverse people together might be newsworthy. At the very least we offered another image of race relations in our city. We were met with yawns of disinterest. What we were about — joyfully sharing traditions and finding common ground — was a nonevent to the always ambitious reporters. Another reality check? You bet.

The media and the marketers have created a virtual reality of race relations. They seduce, strong-arm, and overwhelm us with their analyses and perspectives. They manipulate and distort as much as they reveal.

It doesn't take long for the confused among us (i.e., most of us) to take our cues from the newspapers and the broadcasts. When we (of all races) react to the images they present, we all lose.

"Don't believe everything you read," my mother always said. Look for reality checks along the way.

Too Many Funerals

A voice is heard in Ramah, lamentation and bitter weeping. Rachel is weeping for her children; she refuses to be comforted for her children, because they are no more. Thus says the Lord: Keep your voice from weeping, and your eyes from tears, for there is reward for your work… there is hope for your future… I will turn (your) mourning into joy. I will comfort (you), and give (you) gladness for sorrow.

(Jeremiah 31: 15-17, 13b)

In his book, *My Name Is Asher Lev*, Chaim Potok reports this conversation between a young Jewish boy and his father as they were walking home from synagogue. The boy saw a dead bird on its side against a curb near their house.

"Is it dead, Papa?" I was six at the time, and could not bring myself to look at it.

"Yes," I heard him say in a sad and distant way.

"Why did it die?"

"Everything that lives must die."

"Everything?"

"Yes."

"You too, Papa? And Mama?"

"Yes."

"And me?"

"Yes." Then he added, "But may it be only after you live a long and good life, my Asher."

I couldn't grasp it. I forced myself to look at the bird. Everything alive would one day be as still as that bird?

"Why?" I asked.

"That's the way the Lord made his world, Asher."

"Why?"

"So life would be precious, Asher. Something that is yours forever is never precious."

We gather now to pray, to grieve, and to affirm the preciousness of life. All life. Each life. Every life. We bring to this moment our fear and frustration, our anger and anguish, our confusion and conviction that life is too brief, and life is too precious, to be wasted on our streets.

Too many lives have been sacrificed on the altars of community violence: Jerry Haaf. Mary Foley. Tycel Nelson. Rhonda Fairbanks. Margaret Marques. John Chenowith. Lloyd Smalley and Lillian Weiss. Richard Miller. Estelle Flaherty. Earl Craig. James DesJarlait. Corinne Erstadt. This roll call names but a few. Numerous others were as anonymous in death as they were in life, but each was precious and unique. They were Black and White, Indian and Hispanic. They were able-bodied and they had handicapping conditions. They were children and adolescents, middle-aged and elderly. They were straight and they were gay. They were homeless and they were prosperous. They were citizens of our city, and they were refugees. The one thing they shared was the way they died: violently. Each was a friend and family member. Each had a story to tell, a life to live, and a future to anticipate. There have been too many funerals. There is too much grief to bear. There are too many grudges to settle. Rachel weeps for her children and refuses to be comforted, for they are no more.

Complex as it is, we are interpreting our present crisis in an all-too-familiar pattern. We want there to be bad guys and good guys, victims and perpetrators. Depending upon our point of view, the bad guys or the good guys are the police, the so-called "gangs", the African American community, or the politicians and community leaders. But this is no game of cops and robbers. This is no fight between Robin Hood and the Sheriff of Nottingham.

The violence we condemn today is happening within as well as between our various and diverse communities. This violence is tragic for many reasons but most of all because it ultimately destroys even those who perpetrate it. From Sarajevo to Soweto, we have learned that guns can win battles, but not wars. "Hatred," as Dr. King once said, "is too great a burden to bear."

The word, "violence" comes from the Latin word meaning to violate, to break, to disregard, to do harm or desecrate. Anything that violates, desecrates or does harm to the preciousness of another life is a violent act. Violence may be perpetrated brutally, "in cold blood," with knife or club or gun. Violence may be inflicted covertly, over great distances, with the mere stroke of a pen. We know that we have been violently treated when we have been broken, when the value of our lives has been disregarded, when our core identities have been desecrated or profaned.

African Americans in our community often suffer from a violence far more pervasive and destructive than police harassment. This is the violence of continuing racial discrimination in employment, union access, and the awarding of contracts. This is the violence of substandard rental housing and insensitive landlords. This is the violence of banks and lending institutions that red line whole neighborhoods, shifting the monetary investment needed to vitalize or revitalize our communities. This is the violence inflicted by faxes and phone calls, by well-tailored executives, sometimes in suburban offices, who are convinced that they are merely following sound business practices. But this violence contributes to the hopelessness that is destroying our community. Red lining is inevitably followed by "blue lining" — the use of police power to control discontent.

Frontline police officers suffer from this violence as well. They become the most visible and immediate representatives of a failing social order. They are caught between a society unwilling to seriously and consistently address the needs of its minority citizens, and the restless despair of those who refuse to accept the status quo.

African Americans do not suffer violence alone in this community. American Indians have become strangers in their own land. Violence against Indian people not only includes brutal physical attacks but racial discrimination and daily insults to their sacred heritage. Their cultural creations become souvenirs; their cherished names become mascots for the entertainment of others.

Gay and lesbian members of our community are not safe in their own neighborhoods. Women fear for their lives in parking ramps, on public streets and sometimes in their own living rooms. Refugees who come to our city seeking safety cannot be certain they will be secure.

What about our children? A four year old watches the news, and greets her father with the question: "Daddy, what is murder?" A nine year old asked the whereabouts of Jacob Wetterling. Children now must be taught to distrust strangers, store clerks, parish pastors, family friends, and — sadly — even other family members. Children must walk past drug deals to board school buses. They are sometimes greeted by anti-Semitic or racist graffiti when they attend worship at synagogue, *masjid* or church.

Several children in my congregation talked with me about community violence last week. Andrew, a first grader, volunteered that the way to end the violence was to put signs all over town saying, "Stop It!" People would read the signs, he thought, and stop killing one another. But I'm afraid, Andrew, that as long as we are afraid of each other we won't stop. And why won't we stop?

Our present crisis reveals something very disturbing about us. We have become addicted to violence. We may decry street violence today, but we do not hate violence. We are saturated by it. It entertains us at home, on the movie screen and in the arena. We use it to sell products. We lace it with sex to titillate our fantasies. We use it to define our manhood.

Visit a toy store, and look at the veritable arsenals we sell to our children. Operation Desert Storm has given rise to a whole new generation of children's fashion. Transformer toys bespeak a world where even the most benign appearances mask lethal power. Cartoons and commercials reinforce a world where intimacy is alien and gentleness nonexistent. Even Disney now takes peaceable, non-violent stories — like *Beauty and the Beast* — and gives them an angry, nasty, murderous twist. Violence pays big bucks. We are teaching children that conflict can only be resolved in a final, furious and violent cataclysm.

We want to believe that all our violence is caused by something else. Poverty causes it. Profiteering causes it. The breakdown of community institutions causes it. The erosion of some preexistent moral consensus causes it. If only we can find the cause outside ourselves — in our social or economic conditions, in our upbringing, in the provocative behavior of other people toward us — then we can find the answers to our concerns. But the answers are elusive.

Aleksandr Solzhenitsyn, in his reflections from the Gulag, once wrote:

> "Gradually it was disclosed to me that the line separating good from evil passes not through states, nor between classes, nor between political parties, (nor between the races,) but right through every human heart and through all human hearts... ."

If there is violence in my community, then I must look deeply within my own heart. How have I knowingly or unknowingly contributed to this violence, to the desecration of one person by another? Have I been so concerned with my own well being, with the safety of my family, my neighborhood or own community that I have allowed others to sink beneath burdens too heavy to bear? Have I been too fearful? Too passive? Too preoccupied? How have I turned away?

The Catholic theologian, Jon Sobrino once defined sin as a willingness to offer anything and everything to God — except my own security. He writes, "God calls into question the only thing that real sinners are not disposed to give up — their own security." Sin involves turning away from the future that God offers us because we cannot control it. This sin, I believe, resides in my heart, in every human heart, and in all human hearts. It is this sin that stands in the way of our reconciliation. Until we are willing to trust our security into God's keeping, we will be afraid. As long as we are afraid, we will count the wrongs of others and ignore our own. We will accelerate the endless spiral of self-justification that feeds our community's violence.

To the police officers who are gathered here I want to say that we respect you and support you. We grieve with you. We condemn the atrocity of the slaying of your fellow officer. We acknowledge the stresses you are feeling. Some of us have ridden with you in your patrol cars and walked with you on your beats. We are grateful for the real and personal risks you and your families assume on our behalf. We expect you to keep the peace. But you know better than anyone that peace is more than an absence of violence. It is the presence of wholeness and shalom. When the life of each one of us is valued and precious, then your job will be safer. Then we shall have peace.

As peace officers, you work to keep order in our community. To do that you need our help. Keep lines of communication open to all of us, whoever we are. Let us know how we can help you. Remember that any lasting order must be built on the solid foundation of mutual trust. To achieve order, let us work together to restore trust.

Our civic order depends upon more than communication and trust. It depends upon the depth of our commitment to inclusive justice. Let us come together as a grieving, wounded, yet hopeful community. Let this day mark the birth of a new spirit in Minneapolis.

Today we turn from violence to shalom, from fear to forgiveness, and from a vengeful spirit to a contrite heart. Today we dream dreams together. Today we embrace a compassionate, just and inclusive vision for our life together. Today we affirm our unity against all violence. Today we anticipate with Jeremiah the time when our mourning will be turned into joy, and our sorrow transfigured into gladness.

Let today mark a new day in our community. Beginning today, we promise to put aside business and politics as usual. We affirm the absolute value and unconditional preciousness of every life we encounter. We place our security in the hands of Almighty God, who is infinitely wiser than we. We pledge ourselves to find new ways to bridge old divisions. In words Terry Waite recently spoke to us at Northrop auditorium, we commit ourselves "to make the weak strong, the strong just, and the just compassionate." We shall begin to rebuild trust, restore order, seek justice and pursue peace in all areas of our lives.

In closing, a story:

A wise rabbi once asked her students: "When does the night become the dawn?"

"When I can look at a distant form and distinguish a tree?" responded one.

"No," said the rabbi.

"When I can tell that the moving form is a dog running across the field?" asked another.

"No," said the rabbi.

"When does the night become the dawn?" a third student asked.

"When you can look into a stranger's face and see your own brother or sister. This is when the night becomes the dawn."

Wales forever, Amen!

When the train doors opened, a veritable sea of excited sports fans flooded toward Cardiff Arms Park. Like small figurines in a swift current, we were swept with them through narrow lanes of vendors hawking fish and chips, beer and leek soup. Leek soup? Yes, the aroma of leek soup wafted over us in the damp March air, as pervasive and enticing as the smell of sizzling bratwursts at a Vikings opener. The Welsh National Union rugby team soon would take the field against their vaunted English rivals. Two of the greatest players of all time, Gareth Edwards and Phil Bennett, would lead the charge. Spirits were unbelievably high. Little did I know I was about to witness one of the finest games in what later came to be called the "second golden era" of Welsh Rugby.

The rivalry between the Welsh and the English is especially deep-seated and arouses the most intense emotion. It is rooted in the long and unfortunate history between these two nations. Just before the match, I later learned, Bennett rallied the team with words that became iconic throughout the country: "Look what these bastards have done to Wales. They've taken our coal, our water, our steel. They buy our homes and live in them for a fortnight every year. What have they given us? Absolutely nothing. We've been exploited, raped, controlled and punished by the English — and that's who you are playing this afternoon."

Rugby occupies an exalted place in the Welsh consciousness. It is said that one Sunday morning worshippers entering their chapel were confronted by a huge sign on the communion table. *Cymru am byth!* (Wales forever!) The minister was perturbed and had the Deacons remove it because it lacked religious significance. But when he returned that evening he found an even bigger sign that now read, *Cymru yn oes oesoedd. Amen!* (Wales forever and ever, Amen!)

Indeed, in Wales rugby approaches the status of a national religion. A Welshman in Hong Kong, Gareth Thomas, declared that Twickenham (England), Stade Français (France) and other national stadia, "Are great fortresses of the game, but its cathedral is in Cardiff." He observed that anyone who has experienced the unique atmosphere in the Welsh capital on the day of an international "cannot but subscribe to this notion." Comedian Max Boyce said that the roof over the new Millennium Stadium is pulled back when Wales attacks, "so God can see us play". It was even suggested that a church be built on the spot where Edwards once scored a "try" over Scotland in the mud.

The two other great passions of Wales are poetry and choral singing. Although the "Chairing of the Bard" is perhaps the grandest annual ritual in the country, it is for their music that the Welsh are justly famous. Every Sunday afternoon in chapels across the land they gather to practice their four-part singing of sacred songs. *Cymanfa Ganus* (Singing Festivals) are held in towns throughout the year, and annually at their great cultural event, the National Eisteddfod. Throughout the world, wherever two or three of Welsh descent are gathered, there are Cymanfa Ganus.

Oh, and I forgot to mention one other favorite pastime: the pub! Many a Welshman — and woman too — repair often to the pub for a good time and good conversation. In Pontardawe even the local A.A. meets in the pub. ("Recovery means drinking less," I was told.) The Welsh insist on distinguishing between "chapel" and "pub" folks — you are one or the other — but many households have a foot in both. The proof of this soon will become obvious.

We entered the stadium and found our way to our places. Cardiff Arms Park was built to hold 53,000 people, more or less. The announcer told us the crowd that day numbered in excess of 60,000. Among the throng of people were many of the rich and famous. The announcer even welcomed Frank Sinatra. There were no seats or bleachers to be seen. Sinatra et al. may have had seats but the rest of us stood through the game. (That's why they are called stands!) Forget any sense of personal space. We were a single collective mass who raised a deafening roar when the Welsh players ran onto the pitch.

Though we were packed elbow-to-elbow and front-to-back, somehow vendors made their way to and fro, up and down among us. Beer was abundantly available, and abundantly consumed. As my fellow standmates began to drink, they also began to sing.

They sang in four parts, and they sang the great hymns of their great tradition. The more they drank, the more they sang. They sang and drank and cheered and sang some more.

How gloriously they sang! They sang the sweetest of lullabies, *Ar Hyd y Nos*, with an unimaginable tenderness, and they sang their stirring national anthem, *Hen Wlad fy Nhadau* with patriotic fervor. Imagine

60,000 Welshmen, with no apparent concern about designated drivers, singing in practiced harmonies: *Cwm Rhondda. Aberystwyth. Bryn Calfaria. Llangloffen. Ton-y-Botel. Hyfrydol, Calon Lân.* Raucous cheers punctuated their singing when Wales scored or made a play, and indignant boos when England did the same. (Now I understood Vernon Davies' comment about his son's decision to play for England: "I knew he would never play for Wales," he said. "He's tone deaf.")

The Welsh triumphed over the English, 14-9, in that well-contested match. I had gotten to see Gareth Edwards and Phil Bennett at their peak, even as they were nearing the ends of their storied careers. In high spirits when the match was over, my friend and I sang our way out of the stadium with the boisterous crowd, down the narrow streets and back onto the train.

I always will remember that day — not as much for the match as for the music. Not as much for Gareth Edwards or Phil Bennett (or even Frank Sinatra) as for the thousands of anonymous Welsh men and women under that gray March sky who sang of their homeland in the language of their ancestors. I have been to many cathedrals in the UK and elsewhere, but never have I been so stirred. Leek soup and Welsh hymns were not what I expected when I left Pontardawe that morning.

Mourning by Bumps and Band-Aids

I was in a hurry. Bending forward to pick up a shoe, I banged my head on the corner of a shelf. A huge and bleeding bump — my friend called it a hematoma — immediately rose from my skull, bringing pain to me and horror to my children. No serious injury occurred, but the wound remained for days. I covered it with a band-aid, more to spare others its unsightliness than to protect my head. I soon discovered that the band-aid and the bump served a purpose I had not anticipated. They signaled the world that I was hurting, vulnerable and tender.

My mother died a week earlier, after a painful and progressive disability. Her death left me with a deep psychic wound. There was a rawness and immediacy about my pain. Sometimes I needed to talk about it, and at other times I couldn't. The business of my life continued relentlessly, whether I was prepared or not prepared, whether I felt strong or weak. Healing had to be squeezed in between the carpool and the church meeting.

However, this band-aid stopped people. "What happened to you?" they asked. Sometimes I responded, "I bumped my head." At other times I said, "My mother died." I wanted the world to know of my loss but I didn't always want to talk about it.

Every member of my family experienced injury or illness after my mother died. While most people would attribute this to "stress", I suggest a different explanation. It may be the psyche's way of declaring its need for special consideration.

Grieving is neither well understood nor accepted in our culture. Many thanatologists (death specialists) seek to tame its wildness by describing a predictable "process" with inevitable "stages". We are told to "work through" our grief as we "let go" of our loved one. There is, it seems, a "right way" to grieve.

I long for the days when grieving was more mysterious, and when we who grieve were given time and (psychic) space to allow the inevitable transformations to grow within us. To burn a candle, to gather after a month (or forty days or a year), to ritually observe the loosening of the bonds — these make more sense to me. They are public ways of honoring private grief without dictating the form or content one's healing should take. The black armbands or head coverings, the crepe hung over doors —

these were the bumps and band-aids of past generations. They discreetly informed the public that here were individuals in a special condition of vulnerability, who were adjusting to a world that had been made unacceptable by their loss. Here were individuals who carried within them a need for special care.

In our fast paced modern world, crowded with commitments and obligations, crepe no longer hangs over our doors; neither do arm bands nor head coverings protect us. We are left to heal as best we can in the spaces we create. Bumps and band-aids will have to do. I thank God for friends who understand.

To Justify a World

Abraham said, "Suppose ten (righteous ones) are found there (in Sodom)?"
The Lord answered, "For the sake of ten, I will not destroy it."

(Genesis 18. 32b)

There is a Jewish tradition of the *Lamed-Vov*. According to this tradition, the continued existence of the world depends on the presence of thirty-six just or righteous individuals in every generation. They are called the "Thirty-Six" *(Lamed-Vov* or *Lamed-Vovniks)*. They are anonymous, indistinguishable from any of us. Often even they are unaware of their calling. If but one of them were lacking, the suffering of humankind would poison the souls of all newborn infants; humanity would perish with a single cry. The world itself would vanish.

The *Lamed-Vovniks* are the hearts of the world; into them pour all our griefs. Thousands of popular stories have developed about them, and their presence is attested everywhere. An old text of the Haggadah tells us that the most pitiable are the *Lamed-Vov* who remain unknown even to themselves. For them, bearers of the suffering of all humankind, the spectacle of the world is an unspeakable nightmare. In the seventh century, Andalusian Jews venerated a rock shaped like a teardrop. They believe this to be the soul of an unknown *Lamed-Vovnik* petrified by suffering. A Hasidic story, told by Andre Schwarz-Bart in *Le Dernier des Justes*, goes like this:

> "When an unknown Righteous One rises to heaven, he (or she) is so frozen that God must warm him for a thousand years between God's fingers before his soul can open itself to Paradise. And it is known that some remain forever inconsolable at human woe, so that even God cannot warm them. So from time to time the Creator, blessed be the Holy Name, sets forward the clock of the Last Judgment by one minute."

Why 36? Rabbi Stacy Offner of our neighboring Shir Tikvah congregation offers this explanation: 36 is 18 doubled. Hebrew characters for the number eighteen also form the word L'Chaim, or "Life." In a profound sense, the existence of thirty-six righteous individuals preserves life for the rest of us. Their reason for being, their reason for suffering, is to preserve life. If even one of them is missing, life itself will cease.

113

The world in which I came of age was a world of catastrophic expectations. Martinsburg was no Sodom or Gomorrah. (Trust me!) But adults seemed obsessed with the global wars in which they had participated, and the great depression they had survived. The Korean War was underway, the Cold War was engaged, and huge arsenals and armies were massing in various parts of the world. Cameras panning the carnage of the Nazi death camps provided some of the first footage for our new black-and-white televisions. Carl MacIntyre, the radio equivalent of today's Pat Robinson or Jerry Falwell, spewed a hate-filled gospel of pseudo-Christian righteousness into the airways. Expressing a deep-seated paranoia in white America's psyche, Joseph McCarthy used the House Un-American Activities Committee to bully people of good-will and sensitive conscience. The Klan was vigorous in my part of the country. We were told to fear international communists, the Yellow Peril, the international Jewish conspiracy, uppity Negroes, Catholics and just about everybody else.

The first nuclear bombs fell on the port cities of Hiroshima and Nagasaki just months before I was born. Even as a little boy I knew that nuclear weapons technologies were spreading. Bombs were being detonated regularly in North American deserts, Chinese hinterlands and on Pacific atolls. "Atom bombs" gave way to hydrogen and then to neutron bombs. Sophisticated and vicious biological and chemical weapons were described in the nation's press. We studied radioactive fall-out and global dispersal patterns. Underground shelters were developed in public buildings and private backyards; we wrestled with such ethical dilemmas as whether to admit friends, neighbors or strangers in the event of a real attack. Even the youngest were taught useful "survival skills" to get us through. ("Turn your eyes away from the blast!") Radio and television programs were regularly interrupted to test the "emergency broadcast network" that would be used to instruct us after the bombs had fallen.

Churches, for their part, fueled the fires of national hysteria. Russia and China were identified as agents of the Antichrist. Biblical texts were graphically interpreted to reveal that the end of history was upon us. Armageddon was imminent. The second coming of Jesus Christ was but the blink of an eye away. All of us soon would be gathered, judged, and on our way to hell. Indeed, God willed the destruction of the world. God wanted it to happen, because we were so bad.

A few of us questioned the theological underpinnings of such a world-view. What kind of God would both love us and hate us enough to destroy so much that we — and presumably God — considered valuable? But this was a world of double messages and moral schizophrenia: Work hard, but the end is near. Do you best, but there is no future. People questioned the value of struggling to do right when the collapse of the world was imminent.

The world in which I came of age teetered on the edge of the abyss. Like the ancient cities of Gomorrah and Sodom, its coming destruction was nearly certain, and certainly soon. Prominent people openly wondered about the value of insurance policies, estate planning, career development or formal education in a world that soon would be no more.

Although this particular "age of anxiety" has passed, the abyss remains. The world for many today remains a world of much fear, little hope and no confidence in the future. Some of today's youth, we know, are planning their funerals instead of their futures. Why should they strive for anything worthwhile or struggle to be good?

This is a fundamental question. Why be righteous? Why be just? Why be good? To be good involves struggle, demands sacrifice and requires courage. Particularly in eras or situations of moral confusion or corruption, in Gomorrah and Sodom, why struggle to know and do what is good?

We say we value goodness, but we often value success more. Good deals more than good deeds seem to make us happier. Competition is one of the great engines that drive our society but many times it drives us into ethical dilemmas. How often have we heard someone say, "Good guys finish last?" To be called a "do-gooder" is not the highest compliment.

Yet there are reasons to do good.

Down through the centuries, many of our spiritual forebearers believed that righteousness was a prudent and calculated investment resulting in tangible rewards in this life. Prosperity was a sign of God's blessing. Even today popular preaching implies that by living virtuously we will receive and enjoy the "better things" of life.

Another reason to seek goodness is the "press" we will receive. People whom we respect will respect us. We will earn acclaim for our virtuous commitments. Although righteousness may be costly, others will see what we do and appreciate us more.

Another reason involves keeping our "eyes on the prize". Many believe that our life in this world is but a part of a larger journey of the soul. There will be a moral reckoning when all our sins and good deeds will be tallied up. If we want to enter paradise or nirvana, if we want to be free from the wheel of suffering or receive eternal bliss, then we must earn the result through an increasing virtuousness. Though the world may cause us harm, the universe will reward us with infinitely greater gifts.

Yet another, and perhaps a higher species of reason is that embracing virtue gives intrinsic pleasure. The moral life is the good life. Good deeds become ends in themselves, apart from any and all other rewards or punishments. "The reward of a mitzvah is a mitzvah," said Rabbi Offner. It may not yield prosperity, success, fame or fortune, but we can sleep "the sleep of the just."

Sometimes the answer to our question, "Why be good?" may well be, "to justify the world." I am convinced that the existence of the world depends on the presence of good people. When there is so much corruption, cynicism, stupidity and self-seeking, how could it be otherwise? Is this not the great lesson of the collapse of corrupt and totalitarian empires in our time? Within the Soviet empire there was Solzhenitsyn and Sarkov. Within South Africa there was Mandela. Beneath the radar of all oppressive regimes are the countless people who live courageously, giving themselves generously for others. No society can survive when its social capital of virtuous commitment disappears altogether.

Every day I read reports of judges, prosecutors and police in Columbia who have the guts to tackle the drug cartels, and I am encouraged. I read of law enforcement officials in Italy who take on organized crime, and I am encouraged. I read of efforts in this country, often heroic, to diminish the power of big money in our politics, and I am encouraged. If there were no Mother Teresa, no Father Dudko in Siberian exile, no Martin Luther King, Jr., no Li Lu of Tiananmen Square, no Václav Havel, then would our world continue?

Do I have their courage to do what they are doing? Behind these notable examples are countless anonymous people who are committed to the moral high ground. They go quietly about their lives and yet, each day, they sow seeds of faithfulness. Because of them the world continues.

Sociologists recently concluded a study in Boston. They identified neighborhoods that were identical in every respect except one. Half the neighborhoods had populations of which 80% or more participated in religious communities. Less than twenty percent in the other neighborhoods were so involved. They documented that children growing up in the first set of neighborhoods, even if they themselves were not religiously involved, were much less likely to become involved in serious trouble.

Some of us may do good deeds because we hope for rewards, but most of us know better. The sun rises on the just and the unjust together, Jesus said, and it rains on the righteous and the unrighteous alike. Benefits are not distributed in a morally predictable fashion. Gunfights, car crashes, suicides, fatal cancers, economic disasters and even crucifixions claim the best and worst among us.

Whether *Lamed-Vovniks*, moral leaders or just ordinary folks, good people everywhere are the anchors of the world. They are leaven in the loaf, the salt of the earth. Jesus said that even a cup of cold water given to a thirsty person would not be overlooked. The smallest act of kindness can change the world forever.

Cost-benefit analyses do not work. We strive for goodness because anything less betrays our essential nature. Paul says it well: The reign of God is, "Not for food and drink, but for righteousness, peace and joy."

The 36. *Lamed-Vov*. The goodness of a few. And the world receives another chance.

One Man's Integrity

We believe in no man's infallibility but it is restful to be sure of one man's integrity.

(Charles Spurgeon to William Gladstone, January, 1882)

The Book of Job (known as the Prophet Ayub in the Qur'an) is one of the most celebrated compositions of all religious literature. It contains some of the most moving poetry in the Bible and dialogues that rival Plato's best creations. It is profound, searching, subtle and fiercely honest. It exposes the shallowness of almost all religious responses to human suffering. Like all works of true genius and art, it does not preach. Indeed, its very ambiguity drives the dogmatists crazy.

As we all know, Job was the paradigm of the righteous and upright individual. He was prosperous, kind and generous. He was a family man and a community leader. He lived in harmony with the earth. He was a blessing to all who knew him.

But Job's faith in God was tested through a series of undeserved, grim, cruel and severe deprivations. First his wealth and his personal belongings, then his beloved family and his reputation as a good man — all these were stripped from him. Sores were inflicted upon him. Nightmares tormented his sleep. His very life became an open, aching wound, until he came to curse the day he was born:

> "I will not restrain my mouth. I will speak in the anguish of my spirit. I will complain in the bitterness of my soul… I would choose strangling and death rather than my bones. I loathe my life. I would not live forever… ."

What is the central theme of the Book of Job? Most people would say that it is a book about suffering, about the meaning of human suffering. Job, the good man, suffers unimaginable torture at the hands of a Tempter. His would-be friends advise him to "Curse God, and die," but Job remains faithful.

In my humble opinion, the book of Job is not about suffering, or not only about suffering. Surely it is one of the greatest of all texts that attempt to deal with the meaning of human suffering, but I do not think this is its central theme.

To me, the central theme is about relationships. More to the point, it is about living with integrity at the intersection of three primary relationships: Self, God and World. It is about mental and spiritual health. Job was not just righteous; he is the exemplar of that virtue we have come to know as "centeredness". He was profoundly self-aware. Job is the prototype of personal integrity. He is the epitome of a courageous honesty. Job is so certain of his core identity and so certain of his relationship to the Divine, that no temptation or torment could unsettle him. Job simply is.

Job was no ascetic. He did not denounce the flesh and praise the spirit. Job loved life passionately, and the life he loved is the life of flesh, flowers, flocks and families. When these were stripped away, he protested vehemently the pain of loss.

Job did not inhabit an eternal universe where the wrongs of this world would be righted in the next, or where loved ones taken here would be reunited there. Though in a controversial epilogue he was "rewarded" with new possessions and a whole new family, Job bore physical and psychological scars the rest of his life; he carried memories and grief until he himself passed away.

Job was no Stoic. He was passionate about everything. He did not rationalize. He never went "into his head" to explain away the reality of his pain, or its basic unfairness. He was no mannered gentleman. He did not protect his friends or even God from his scorn or his anger. He did not suffer quietly. Job was a fiercely honest man.

He was honest with himself. He listened to the arguments and advice of his counselors and friends, but in the end he kept his own counsel. Against all evidence, he maintained his innocence. He protested even against God. He knew himself well, and he honored what he knew.

Job also never wavered from his trust in God. God was as real for Job as Job was real for God. The two had a lifelong relationship. Job's relationship to God had nothing to do with whether Job prospered or suffered. His personal holocaust never, not even once, became an occasion to doubt the reality of God. He knew himself, and he knew God. The relationship was profound and trustworthy: Job even said at one point, "Though he slay me, yet will I trust him."

Finally, Job understood — as few of us understand — his proper relationship to the world. The world sheltered and nurtured him. The world was familiar and comfortable. The world presented him with unimaginable beauty and pleasure. The world also brought surprises and tragedies, losses and hardship. When Job had lost all his possessions, and all his children as well, even then he was moved to say,

> "Naked came I from my mother's womb. Naked shall I return. The Lord gave, the Lord has taken away. Blessed be the name of the Lord."

Is this not an incredible statement to modern ears? Whether in plenty or want, he turned to God. The Sacred was the central and primary fact of his life, the North Star by which he navigated through all the years of joy and suffering. Job embodied, in the words of the philosopher, Walter Kaufmann *(The Faith of a Heretic)*,

> "... the most admirable attitudes possible for humanity: to be able to give up what life takes away, without being unable to enjoy what life gives us in the first place; to remember that we came naked from the womb, and shall return naked, to accept what life gives us as if it were God's own gift, full of wonders beyond price, to try to fashion something from suffering, to relish our triumphs, and to endure defeats without resentment... ."

All of this is to be celebrated and emulated so far as we are able. We want deeper, better, richer, fuller, more meaningful, more mature, more honest relationships to ourselves, to God and to the world. But if the book of Job is any indication, this wanting is not for the foolish or the faint-hearted.

One Wish

About now the daffodils are blooming in Wales. If you ever travel there, you may come upon Saint David's Cathedral, an 11th Century church situated in the western extremity of that tiny country. The British government has spent an enormous sum to renovate this masterpiece of Norman architecture. In recent centuries it had fallen victim to neglect and pollution. It also sat in the flight path of the Concorde and, until a short time ago, was shaken regularly by sonic booms.

The hills around it now are turning from brown to green. If you spend time there you will feel its quiet antiquity. You may hear the echo of an ancient chant, the baaing of sheep, even chisels and hammers striking stone. You may see commoners and gentry arriving for services. You may even see stonemasons on scaffolding made of rough hewn boards and heavy ropes. You will smell the salt in sea-laden breezes, and imagine the faint sweet frankincense near the altar. Pungent odors of raw mortar and stone will mingle with acrid smoke from peat fires in a hundred valley hearths nearby.

Waldo Williams (in "Ty Dewi" in *Dail Pren*) captured this timeless mystery in his great national poem on *Dewi Sant* (Saint David). Williams himself was a gentle man, a poet and pacifist. His compassionate heart was fired by a mystical vision. He described life in and around the church as it flowed from one generation to the next. Most moving to me are the words he puts into the mouth of a medieval stonemason.

> "...Un dymuniad a aned I minnau
> I ddal yr aing oni ddel y angau.
> A naddu rhes fy nyddiau yn fywyd
> I deml yr Ysbryd yn nhud fy nhadau."

James Nichols translates these words in his little book on Williams (*Writers of Wales*):

> "One wish was born to me,
> To hold the chisel until death comes
> And to carve the row of my days to be a life
> Unto the temple of the spirit in the homeland of my ancestors."

The beauty of this verse lies for me in its first line, "One wish was born to me… " The stone mason does not say, "I have many goals to accomplish before I die," nor "I need to get my priorities in order," nor "I just don't have enough time to do all the carving I want to do!" She doesn't talk about the ten things in her "bucket" to do before she dies, nor does she grumble about those who have more or do less. "One wish," she says. She wants her life to become a temple of the spirit in her homeland.

What is our wish?

In our world not far from this cathedral, troubled teenagers take guns to recklessly wound and kill. Intolerant extremists use religion to destroy, terrorize and kill. Success is identified with acquisition, money is worshipped, children are prostituted, officials are corrupted, and the young are intentionally addicted. What is our wish?

In our world, nations consume their capital to acquire weapons and the poorest citizens live without hope. Sharing — whether of bread or sex — has lost its sacramental dimension. We are entertained by violence. We prosper by the ceaseless exploitation of our planet. What is our wish?

Williams himself chiseled hard at life. He carved the row of his days into a soaring cathedral of the spirit but we too are craftsmen and craftswomen. What will we carve with the row of days? What wish was born to us?

Golden Boy

When I was younger I dreamed that my family and I were going to a pot-luck supper in the basement of my childhood church. I wore a beautiful suit of golden armor, rode a great white horse, and carried a magnificent lance and shield. The shimmering helmet enclosing my face was topped with a huge scarlet plume. My family walked alongside wearing clothes that were plebeian, functional and boring. I rode the steed, they walked, and everyone whispered in admiration as I passed.

When we got to the church I discovered that, in this armor, I could not sit down. I could not easily talk to other people. The gold was so soft that, when I bumped into a pillar or a table, it would dent and ding my armor. I leaned carefully against the wall.

As the room warmed up, so did I. I sweated profusely. But beneath this armor I wore nothing else. I could not remove the armor and I could not bear the heat. Soon everyone forgot about me. Turning their attention to food and fellowship, they talked and laughed and sang. My friends ran playfully around the hall. They invited me to join them, but how could I? I was stunning to look at, dazzling in appearance, unique beyond words, but I was completely alone. I was hot and hungry, and unable to talk, sing, eat or play. I was miserable.

Do I want to be the "knight in shinning armor?" If so, this is the price I must pay.

Minor Key Angst

The impeded stream is the one that sings.

(Wendell Berry)

You might not think that the child of so many revivals, the little guy who grew up with Sunday School attendance pins that hung to his shoes, the one who continued to earn merit badges even after Eagle Scout, you might not think that this boy would become so deeply enamored of everything melancholic, of old sad songs and tragic stories. You might not think this, but I did. As a defense against all the hype and hyperbole that passed for religion in my little corner of the universe, I early began to listen to voices that sang in different, and quite often, minor keys.

If you put two books in front of me, say, Unamuno's *The Tragic Sense of Life* and Peale's *The Power of Positive Thinking*, I would reach for Unamuno. If you invited me to a concert of either African American spirituals or Handel's *Hallelujah Chorus*, I would seek the *Balm in Gilead*. The world as mediated by Norman Vincent Peale seemed disconnected from the real pain in my world. The universe of Handel was too tightly controlled, too dogmatically certain and just too perfect to include me.

When I became a little older I was drawn to an album of Jacobite ballads sung by Ewan MacColl. I knew nothing of Britain's bloody battles or brutal history, but the music went straight to my heart. *Such a Parcel O' Rogues in a Nation* is a very sad drone filled with bitterness and despair. It is a black hole of melancholy from which no light escapes. It sucks all life into its dark lament. Perhaps for that very reason it became my personal anthem. I liked it so much that I wrote a hymn to fit the music. Though the music already was a dirge, my verses took it many notches lower. Have you ever sung a hymn where "pathos" and "bathos" were paired?

Was I a melancholiac, addicted to the dark side of human experience? Or was I simply compensating for the relentless cheer around me in the face of a world gone awry? To this day I have a visceral distrust of preachers, politicians and salesmen who proclaim only the good, the true and the beautiful without acknowledging the shadows they themselves are casting. And in a universe as vast as ours, I distrust anyone who claims to have a corner on the "truth" (by revelation or discovery) or to possess exclusive access to divinity. I have always preferred, with Wittgenstein, to "take the bloody hard way."

Those who live and preach in a major key are probably more successful than I. They are bright, cheerful and energizing. People are attracted to them. But I have chosen to live my life and conduct my ministry with a tilt toward the minor. I find the minor key to be a richer lode, capable of more subtlety and refinement. Actually, I find it more true.

Let's talk about the music for a moment. There are many "modes" in music; major and minor are but two. Each has its own sound. Within the minor mode there are three different scales and they each have their distinctive sounds. A friend, a professional musician, suggested that we think about the difference between major and minor keys in this way: Imagine that a major scale is an ascending staircase; the first step is the 'home' key — for example "C". The next step is "D" and the third is "E". If you can walk normally, it is easy to go up these steps. They are single steps or "tones". Now imagine that you suffer hip pain. You can't lift you leg high enough to get onto the third step, so you make a half step (semi tone) — a smaller, more painful step. This, she said, is the defining characteristic of a minor: a contracted and shrunken step. The steps of a major scale are open and free, but on the minor scale the third step is a smaller interval; it is the note in the gap that usually gets stepped over, the thing that is avoided in the major scale.

It is remarkable that this shift of only half a step (semi tone) can change the quality of a song so dramatically. In *Les Misérables* by Claude-Michel Shöenberg, both Valjean and Javert are given much of the same music to sing, but Javert often sings it in a minor key. These two characters are bound to one another existentially and musically, but they are fated to pursue opposite objectives. The major distinguishes Valjean as the hero while the minor sets Javert apart as the obsessed pursuer.

In western culture especially the idea is deeply rooted that the major key is the music of light, joy and power while the minor key is the music of anguish, loss and desperation. But songs written in a major key are not always happy. *Yesterday* by the Beatles is quintessentially a sad song, yet it was composed in a major key. Likewise, songs in a minor key are not always sad. *Moondance* by Van Morrison is a good example. The same can be said of jazz, country music and Christian hymnody.

We know that a great deal more than key determines the "feel" of a piece of music — rhythm, tempo, loudness, instrumentation and many other factors. In addition, many songs shift constantly from major to minor and back again. Even so, many people agree that the minor key conveys feelings of longing and great beauty intertwined. Minor keys can be as haunting in their loveliness as the dying leaves of autumn. Another musician friend said that songs in a minor key are, to her, among the most poignant and beautiful in the world.

> "It's not unlike the feeling I had in Norway when seeing the fjords for the first time; the beauty was so deep and exquisite and overwhelming that I cried. A very minor key feeling. However, the Alps! They gave me a major key feeling when I saw them...so sparkly and bright!"

R.E.M. writes nearly everything in the minor key, and its music defies easy classification into happy or sad. *Everybody Hurts*, for example, is a deeply compassionate music video. Everybody hurts, but everybody walks away from a street corner evangelist who is preaching a one-way-fits-all salvation. The preacher seems to have answers to all but the most important questions: his own isolation and the unanswered questions in his own soul.

The "blue note" in the blues and jazz introduces yet another voice: the blues scale. This scale has a minor tonality forced over major key chord changes, or in conflict with the minor key scale itself. The resulting sound is as "bluesy" as in *Stormy Weather* by Harold Arlen. The blues originated on the plantations of the American South among African slaves, ex-slaves and their sharecropper descendents; it evolved from African chants, spirituals, work songs, revival hymns and country-dance music. The Mississippi Delta is the true home of the blues, as it is of jazz, but it has morphed into many different genres. Whether with swampy guitars and wailing harmonicas, or the sophisticated orchestration of Count Bassie, the blues are songs about troubles, trials and tribulations. Yet the music is far from morose. Ed Kopp (*A Brief History of the Blues*, 2005) writes:

> "While blues lyrics often deal with personal adversity, the music itself goes far beyond self-pity. The Blues is also about overcoming hard luck, saying what you feel, ridding yourself of frustration,

letting your hair down, and simply having fun. The best blues is visceral, cathartic, and starkly emotional. From unbridled joy to deep sadness, no form of music communicates more genuine emotion."

While the blues were surfacing in North America, another bluesy idiom was developing in the poorer *bairros* of Lisbon: *fado*. Not nearly as familiar to us as the blues, my heart melted the first time I heard Amália Rodrigues sing. If the blues came of age on the Southern plantations, fado — Portuguese for 'fate'— grew out of Portugal's long and bittersweet relationship with the sea. It has been called the Portuguese blues — mostly minor-key ballads about lost sailors, broken hearts, sad widows and lovers left behind. A twelve-string *guitarra portuguesa* or other stringed instruments unique to Portugal often accompany the *fadista* (singer). "Fado singers typically crescendo into the first word of the verse, like a moan emerging from deep inside. Though the songs are often sad," observed Rick Steves, "the singers rarely overact — they plant themselves firmly and sing stoically in the face of fate." (*Portuguese Fado — The Fisherwoman's Blues*) Fado always has felt strangely familiar to me; I think of Ms. Rodriguez as a Portuguese Patsy Cline.

In Sevilla (Spain) I first encountered flamenco. Technically, flamenco is neither major nor minor but Phrygian, but many of its tunings are minor, and its sound certainly is. I was traveling with a jazz musician who knew how to avoid the crassly commercialized versions produced for *touristas*. One evening we attended a show in the Santa Cruz district, at Los Gallos. A guitar player, a dancer and a vocalist filled the small stage and the whole room with the passionate energy of *cante jando* (deep song). Around midnight we went over to La Carboneria where, for the price of a drink, we sat amidst improvisations by local flamenco artists, some just returning from gigs around town. Flamenco, by the way, is not confined to the young, the lithe or the athletic. It is sung by children, old people and everyone in between. Flamenco has a rough-hewn rawness about it, an in-your-face integrity that begins somewhere deep in the gut of the performer and rises up in cries of intensity and passion. Guitarists and dancers add their aggressive rhythms and assertive energies from the center of this *jondura* (deepness).

The Spanish poet, Federico García Lorca, called this "black sound." He examined its compelling energy through the concept of *duende*.

"Everything that has black sounds in it, has duende... The duende, then, is a power, not a work. It is a struggle, not a thought. I have heard an old maestro of the guitar say, 'The duende is not in the throat; the duende climbs up inside you, from the soles of the feet.' Meaning this: it is not a question of ability, but of true, living style, of blood, of the most ancient culture, of spontaneous creation... The duende's arrival always means a radical change in forms. It brings to old planes unknown feelings of freshness, with the quality of something newly created, like a miracle, and it produces an almost religious enthusiasm." (Federico García Lorca, *Play and Theory of the Duende*)

Duende lives "in blue notes, in the break in a singer's voice, in the scrape of resined horsehair hitting sheep gut," observed Jan Zwicky (Royal Ontario Museum: *The Culture of New Music,* 2005). We hear it in jazz and the blues, and often in other music when performance and composition are not separated. It can be recognized in the works of classically oriented composers and performers, and in naïvely traditional music. Whenever we hear it, Zwicky asserts, "It insists that we honor the death required to make a song."

Here lies the explanation for my minor key angst. The composer, the performer and even the listener must "die" if music is to have life. When any one of us refuses, the music itself lapses into a kind of deadness. It becomes predictable, familiar and acceptable. We are entertained but not engaged, pleased but not challenged, confirmed but not transformed. This can be true for music in any key. But the black sound, the blue note, fado and the minor key — these remind us to honor the death required to make a song — and the dying in all life, the darkness in all light, and the loss in all salvation.

Akathist of Thanksgiving

During or before the Second World War, it is beleieved that Gregory
Petrov, an Archpriest in the Russian Church, was sentenced by Communist authorities to exile and hard labor in a Siberian prison camp.
or he may have gone of his own accord, a missionary to the internees.
In either case, he remained there until his death in the 1940's under
circumstances we can barely imagine. The details of his life and death are
not accessible to us, but we know much about Stalin's oppression of the
Russian clergy, the harsh conditions of the camps, and the brutal treatment of prisoners.

Before he died, he wrote a remarkable composition, *Praise God for
Everything*. Smuggled out of the gulag and beyond the borders of the
Soviet Union, this text made its way through Belgium to London. There
Mother Thekla translated it into English. Mother Thekla is the latter
day John Tavener's spiritual director. In 1988 Tavener set the poem to
music. Called now *Akathist of Thanksgiving*, I heard it recently when the
Plymouth Music Series brought together an ecumenical multitude of
instrumentalists and vocalists at the Cathedral of St. Paul.

Although it is written in the liturgical style of Russian Orthodoxy, the
poem and music have an immediate and universal appeal. Indeed, this
work may be our century's quintessential affirmation of life. It is a long
and quietly moving paean to the intrinsic loveliness of all creation; it
affirms the goodness of life in all circumstances. There is not a hint of
bitterness or rancor. There is no weeping or lamentation, no longings
unfulfilled. Instead he wrote this: "O Lord, how good it is to be your
guest," and "You have led me into this life as an enchanting paradise."
Petrov gives thanks for God's unceasing care, for chance meetings and
for friends, for thought, labor and creativity, for colors and seasons, for
scents and textures. He declares that God "restores their pristine beauty
to souls who hopelessly have lost it." There is nothing irreparable in all
creation. God is all love.

That such a life-giving prayer arose within the gulag conveys Orthodoxy
at its best. *Akathist* reveals the power of faith to sustain us, but it does
much more. Petrov points us to the very heart of being where we joyfully
discover that we are a welcomed part of something wonderful beyond
our measuring.

Holy Week

Die Fahne hoch!

Someone recently asked me if Horst Wessel's rousing *Die Fahne hoch!* could be considered a spiritual song. It was the Nazi anthem from 1930 until 1945. Promising an imminent end to "servitude" and "a day of freedom and bread" it became the stirring battle hymn of a desperate people. Singing it, they emerged from the smoldering ash heap of defeat to ignite a conflagration across Europe and North Africa.

The Third Reich itself was a spiritual phenomenon, albeit grotesque in its negativity. It arose to fill a void in the heart of a spiritually exhausted Europe. It became a surrogate spirituality that imposed order, created meaning, provided identity and inspired commitment to its own demonic vision. It was idolatry grown to horrific proportions.

Like all idolatries, the Reich united one people at the expense of others. It demanded the subordination, not the expression, of the unique gifts of every person it touched. It created a false and destructive community based on a false and destructive premise. Although its power derived from authentic spiritual sources, it twisted and deformed them into deeply anti-spiritual purposes.

It is the essence of idolatry to oppose God in the name of God, to destroy life in the name of life, to deny freedom in the name of freedom and to turn all that serves humanity against that same humanity. Though *Die Fahne hoch!* ("Lift High the Flag!") is energetic, animating and passionate, yet it called forth the worst and empowered the demons in those who sang it. The enormous popularity of *Die Fahne hoch!* is sobering evidence that, indeed, millions of people can be catastrophically and tragically wrong.

Hatred

If anyone comes to me and does not hate his father and mother, his spouse
and children, his brothers and sisters — yes, even his own life — he cannot be
my disciple. And anyone who does not carry his cross and follow me cannot
be my disciple... none of you can become my disciple if you do not give up all
your possessions.

(Luke 14:26-27, 33)

Imagine, if you will, that the reading from Luke today was actually a
reading from the Qur'an. "If anyone comes to me and does not hate
his father and mother, his spouse and children, his brothers and sisters
— yes, even his own life — he cannot be my disciple. None of you can
become my disciple if you do not give up all your possessions." How
would we perceive this text if it had come from the *Hadith*, from the
sayings of Mohammed? Surely the recipe for fanaticism, we would say.
Hatred enshrined in Holy Writ. But these are not Islamic words. They
are Christian words. They are thought to come from the mouth of Jesus.
In a world so filled with hatred, fanaticism and violence, what are we to
make of such words?

The first day of school began with an assembly in the schoolyard. Children were streaming in with their proud parents, brothers and sisters as
they did every year. The much anticipated moment arrived for the first
graders to be introduced. This had always been a tender moment. But
the ceremony this year was interrupted before it could begin. The people
heard shouting. They saw a band of 30-or-so masked and heavily armed
men and women running into the yard. They were shouting, "Allahu
Akhbar!" "Allahu Akhbar!" "God is greater!" "God is greater!" With
ruthless efficiency they herded more than 1,200 children and townspeo-
ple into the school gymnasium.

Thus began 52 hours of unspeakable horror. 52 hours of calculated
cruelty that ended in the deaths of more than 330 children and adults.
52 hours that devastated the community of Beslan, Russia, and assaulted
the moral consciousness of the entire world.

Not much is known yet about the captors, about their origins or their
purposes. One told the hostages that he himself had a wife and five children. Whatever their ages or life situations, they had come to this school

to kill and to die. They had sealed off those parts of themselves that are compassionate and humane, that link them to the larger human family and the earth. They had allowed deep resentments and grievances to fester and poison their minds and corrupt their spirituality. While they chanted the great affirmation of Islam and indeed of all monotheistic religions that "God is greater!" in truth they had reduced God to a small, narrow, harsh and vengeful tribal deity.

American theologian Howard Thurman, reflecting on the experience of African American people during segregation in his classic, *Jesus and the Disinherited*, observed that hatred is one way that oppressed people are able to maintain their sense of self worth. When they are downtrodden and powerless, when they have no hope, when they have little control over their own destiny, when all the world treats them as worthless, or simply as objects to be scorned or manipulated, then hatred rises up like fire within their breasts. Hatred of the oppressor becomes an assertion that one's essential dignity and humanity have been violated. Hatred, paradoxically, is a passionate affirmation of worth and being. "I hate, therefore I am."

The problem with this, Thurman came to believe, is that the person who hates becomes the hatred. Resentment and hatred literally consume him or her. It is a demon that takes over. Ironically, it robs the oppressed of whatever shred of humanity is left to her or him. In an extreme form she or he becomes a vortex of seething resentment. This negativity turns inward against the self, or outward against others. In either case, it destroys any basis for community, reconciliation or relationships. As Desmond Tutu once said, "Justice without reconciliation can be a very hard thing."

Hatred does not, like Aphrodite, spring full-blown from the head of Zeus. It takes time to develop. It requires the necessary conditions to grow. "The best of us, if left unlived, can be as poisonous as the worst of us, if left unhealed," wrote Ann and Barry Ulanov. The existence of such hatred in our world points to conditions that are unbearable. These desperate acts of desperate men and women point to desperate conditions that cannot be ignored. People harm others when their own wounds are unhealed. We do not reduce the harm by enlarging the wounds. To overcome fanaticism and terrorism, we must first of all become healers.

How then, are we to take these words of Jesus: to follow him we must hate those near and dear to us? Even given the excuse of Semitic hyperbole or exaggeration, how can we possibly interpret these words today?

Do these words represent Jesus' real attitudes toward his own family and friends? Well, on one occasion he seemed to ignore his mother and sisters. He told another would-be disciple to choose between following him and burying his father. On the other hand, Jesus showed consistent care for his mother throughout his life and even as he was dying. He lived with a tender regard for everyone, young and old, ailing and healthy, weak and powerful. He taught a doctrine of love, unconditional love, love even — or especially — for one's enemies.

Rather, using the rhetorical hyperbole characteristic of his time, Jesus wanted to demonstrate the high costs of Christian discipleship. To follow him means to put a "greater love" above concerns for wealth, power and privilege, above even family ties. This is not unlike young soldiers going off to defend their country, not unlike Olympians who put every ounce of their energy into their athletic practice, not unlike musicians and dancers who spend their waking hours passionately developing their arts. Christian disciples are challenged to put Christ first. Count the costs before you begin, Jesus said but, once you begin, don't look back. The Christian life is more consuming than soldiering, swimming or playing the violin. It is not necessary to choose between following Jesus and being a violinist, but the passion, the energy and the motivation will be the same.

Love the Lord your God with all your heart, mind, soul and strength, proclaims the *Shema* of Israel and Judaism. That is our first priority, Jesus said. God has first claim on our life and energy. To love God this way requires a willingness to give up what we think may be most important to us, in order to gain an even greater good. This requires a sober assessment of who we are and who we want to be, of what we are committed to and what matters most. It involves an honest appraisal of where we have succeeded, where we have failed and where we need to start over.

In his response to the enormous tragedy in Beslan, and to other recent terrorist attacks, Russian president Vladimir Putin seems to begin to grasp the larger context that spawns such violent hatred. He spoke yesterday to his nation. Oddly, his remarks were not devoted to "homeland security" in any narrow sense of the word. Instead he reflected on the corruption in the Russian judiciary and the inefficiency of law enforcement. "We have to admit that we failed to recognize the complexity and danger of the processes going on in our country and the world," he said. He did not speak of Chechnya, but I was impressed by his sober realism, his lack of bravado, and his self-effacing confession: We do not understand "the complexity and danger of the processes going on... in the world." I am impressed by this leader's willingness, in such a moment of vulnerability, to be introspective about his own country's failings. I am impressed by his willingness to say, "We don't know... " and "we don't understand... " He suggested that to overcome terrorists, Russia itself needs to develop, and to work toward becoming "an organized, united civil society." Not only "homeland security," but the quality of life, the meaning of citizenship and the nature of community within the homeland are his concerns.

Jesus did not advocate hatred, but a careful setting of priorities. For Christians, to love Jesus expands the heart so that it embraces and transforms all other loves. Our love for God is the only love that deserves to be at the pinnacle of our priorities. This love leads to freedom from the tyranny of our ego and manipulation by others. It is a love above patriotism, family, business and our desires for recognition or accomplishment. This is not the love of an abstraction. It leads us to cherish our world and it embraces our other loves and loyalties. It is a love for all other people, whatever their ideologies, politics or nationality. It is a love that seeks to include even when we have been excluded, and to reconcile when we have been rejected. It is a love that seeks to create a just and nurturing civil society in which all are safe, and all may flourish. Only such bold, generous and sacrificial love will eradicate hatred from the earth.

Acquainted With Sorrow

I had the opportunity to be a tour guide for Atlanta. The family of a friend had come from Zimbabwe for his wedding. As we walked around the King Center, they described the terrible AIDS pandemic in their country. As many as a fourth of the children have no parents, they said, no one to look after them, supervise them, teach them or care for them when they are sick. It is heart wrenching. One of the women in the group had lost her husband to death. She began to take an interest in these children — first one, then another, until she had gathered approximately a dozen children around her. She sewed clothes, cooked food, and taught them academic subjects and the skills of living. More children came. Soon there were too many.

At the same time other women, also widows in the community, sought her out. They complained about their losses, their hard lives without their husbands, their grief. She encouraged them to look beyond their own hardship to the crisis of the children in their community. She organized "widows clubs" for women in similar situations. Each woman now accepts responsibility for eight to fifteen orphaned and homeless children. Unheralded and unacknowledged in the larger world, this movement is growing in Zimbabwe. Out of their devastation, new bonds are woven, communities are repaired, and women and children are regaining dignity, purpose and hope.

This Seeing Faith

So when they had finished breakfast, Jesus said to Simon Peter, "Simon, son of John, do you love Me more than these?" He said to Him, "Yes, Lord; You know that I love You." He said to him, "Tend My lambs."

(John 21: 15)

Barry Lopez wrote the story of Crow and Weasel's journey of discovery into the far North. When they came to Badger's lodge, she welcomed and fed them. A wise forest creature, she gave them this advice:

> "I would ask you to remember this one thing. The stories people tell have a way of taking care of them. If stories come to you, care for them, and learn to give them away when they are needed. Sometimes a person needs a story more than food to stay alive. That is why we put stories in each other's memories. This is how people care for themselves."

Hunger, food, care and stories — this is the stuff of ministry.

What happens when we lose our stories? Paul Ricoeur wrote that the people most on the margins in our society are those without stories. How do we lose our stories? It happens when the people around us become too busy or impatient to attend to our frequently troubled narrations. But, Ricoeur insisted, "We must tell our stories because, in the last analysis, human lives need and merit being narrated."

Ruth once was a concert pianist. Although verbally animated, she finds it impossible now to converse coherently. She is the victim of Alzheimer's rapid advance.

Hulda is a German immigrant, living without family in a nursing home, confined to her wheelchair. Hearing is difficult, but she loves to sing her favorite hymns when she is wheeled into worship.

Marie lives in Connecticut. Although she suffers a host of health problems herself, she is caring for two elderly and dependent parents. Sometimes she is desperate and alone.

Margaret is animated, brilliant and free spirited. Approaching 90, she still maintains her independence. She's concerned about her brittle bones; she feels increasingly at sea in the fast-paced world around her.

Jack is hungry to talk about Bach, the universe, time, and his notions of infinity on this, the last day of his life.

Jacqueline was an Ivy League university librarian. Multiple sclerosis has robed her of her ability to care for herself. She still relishes stimulating conversation, good books and intellectual engagement. She too is lonely.

The residents of the care facility are strapped upright into wheelchairs. They line up at the elevator after lunch, waiting to return to their rooms. Cardiac, pulmonary and circulatory disorders have taken a great toll, restricting the ability of these men and women to define themselves, assert themselves, declare their basic wants, and affirm their own intrinsic dignity. Who will listen to their stories?

Except for their families and a few friends, and the dedicated staff members who care for them, they have become invisible. No one sees them. With time's passing, their isolation increases. Loving and life giving ties to the community are gradually pried loose. The spirit-in-this-flesh begins to crumble under the staggering losses the flesh-containing-spirit must endure.

Even the kindest among us sometimes turns away, especially when people no longer speak coherently, no longer interact in ways we deem appropriate or no longer assure us with their waning vitality that all is well. Though they may not be despised, yet they are acquainted with grief. Too many of us do not esteem them.

To these "marginalized" members of our community, what is the meaning of this evening's ordination? What must our ordinand carry within her soul? How shall she guide others successfully through the valley of the shadow into which they have entered so reluctantly? What kind of ministry is being called forth? I suggest three characteristics: a profound faith that God is good, a cheerful reverence for the created order, and an ability to see with the eyes of love.

"Live as though you believe in the goodness of God," instructed Julian of Norwich. Some call this unrealistic and those who embrace it naive. Instead, many of us wrap ourselves within the protecting veil of a cynicism that demands little stretching of our souls. As our holocaustic century draws to its close, its philosophers increasingly disparage such statements as Julian's as a mere platitude of impractical piety. How can this modest instruction cope with the severity of suffering, oppression, isolation and despair so evident in our modern world?

"Human life is not accidental," wrote Rabbi Abraham Heschel:

> "... It is a gift from a mysterious and loving source. Its purpose is twofold. First, it is an end in itself — loving, enjoying, creating, and reflecting the nature of the source. Second, it is directed loving, bearing, and creating aimed at unfolding the essential lovingness wherever it is closed off in a wounded, partially blocked or hostile nature."

God already and forever loves us. In Alice Walker's memorable words, "Any fool can see (God) is always trying to please us back!" God our Beloved leaps like a gazelle in the springtime. The Hound of Heaven pursues us down all the years. Nothing we do can make God love us more or less. We are relentlessly embraced by God's infinite and active love.

But do not mistake this faith for a shallow optimism. In her best-selling book, *Dakota: A Spiritual Geography*, Kathleen Norris, a Presbyterian elder, brought the spirituality of the Plains to the world's attention. In the vast, windswept empty spaces of the Dakotas "we learn to live with a hard reality: nothing lasts. Dakota wisdom teaches us to love anyway, to love what is dying, to love in the face of death, and not to pretend that things are other than they are." There can be no denial of pain's reality or suffering's harm in a faith that is centered in the Exodus and the Cross.

We have come to believe that even in the midst of our greatest tragedies God tirelessly walks with us and presents us with new possibilities. As we pass through valleys of deep darkness, God prepares new and brighter joys. "While you won't be given more than you can bear," advised Tilden Edwards, "you may be led by a way you do not know to become a channel for grace in ways you cannot predict." *(Spiritual Friend)*

Our ordinand is anything but naive. One would think James Forbes was describing Casey when he listed the marks of a mature spiritual director. She profoundly understands the movement from despair to grace. She trusts in the "healingness of the universe." She delights in the freedom of others.

Casey is an Oblate with the Sisters of Saint Benedict. Wisdom accumulated through centuries of contemplative life and generations of active service throughout the world informs her spiritual development. In guiding them, the Sisters hope that their Oblates will realize one thing: they have no reason for being other than to be loved by God and to love God in return. In her "continual conversion to Christ," an Oblate develops a deepening reverence for life. She comes to "respect life as a precious gift from God, and she seeks to defend and serve those who, because of age, health or race" are most vulnerable.

You noticed, no doubt, that Casey chose the classic text of pastoral (shepherding) ministry for her ordination. "Do you love me?" Jesus asked three times. Three times the disciple replied, "Yes, Lord, I love you." Three times Jesus answered, "Feed my sheep."

There is confusion about how to interpret the verbs "to love" (*phileo* and *agape*) in John's text. Let me add to it! What if Jesus really was asking Peter, "Do you see me?"

"The finest act of love," wrote the Indian Jesuit, Anthony de Mello, "is not an act of service, but an act of seeing. When you serve, you help, support, comfort and alleviate pain. But when you see me in my inner beauty and goodness, you transform and create."

Casey, we who know you are not surprised that God is leading you to pastoral ministry. Ministry is a place of deep hungers: fear, grief, disorientation, isolation, confusion and hopelessness. But it also is a place of deep gladness. Through your gladness Ruth, Hulda, Marie, Margaret, Jack, Jacqueline and, yes, even Budd Friend-Jones, have come to know and experience the goodness of God.

You see us. Your gladness lies in your seeing, and in your love of our stories. You see us realistically. You see us with love. You see us with imagination. Although you are capable of seeing us with an eye trained in the clinical and social sciences, you see more. In treasuring our stories, you help us treasure ourselves. In discerning the movement of the spirit within our lives, you open us to a more vast and exciting story than we ever could have imagined.

Love begins with seeing. One of the world's most famous "seers" is Mother Teresa of Calcutta. She sees many people at the margins of our world, people who have lost their stories altogether. A caregiver to the least of the human family, she has written a daily office that includes these words:

"Lord, may I see you... in the person of your sick and, while nursing them, minister unto you. Though you hide yourself behind the unattractive disguise of the irritable, the exacting and the unreasonable, may I still recognize you... O Lord, give me this seeing faith... "

How many of us long to be seen in just this way? How many yearn for someone to see, amidst the flotsam and jetsam of our lives, an intrinsic and sacred core? Each of us is a mystery calling for unique attention. Sometimes we need to be seen more than we need food to stay alive.

So assume for a moment that Jesus really is asking, "Do you see me?" If you truthfully can answer, "Yes, Lord, I see you," then Casey you are eminently worthy to be ordained, to tend Christ's flock, and feed our deepest hungers.

O Lord, give us this seeing faith! Amen.

God's Ujamaa

And this God made from one ancestor all the nations to live on the face of the whole earth... for we are indeed the offspring of God.

(Acts 17. 26,28)

Outside the lovely city of Kiev a towering and stark monument rises tragically from the depths of a vast pit. Tangled human bodies reach upward into the weeping sky. Some are strong Ukrainian sailors. One is a defiant young woman. They are Jews and homosexuals. A mother raises her child in desperation as she is pulled downward. An old man — dead — slides back into the pit. Clinging to him is another woman, not comprehending the magnitude of this savagery. She too is being sucked into the muddy, bloody oblivion of Babi Yar.

Bus loads of visitors approach the monument in silence. They walk quietly around the pits. Laying stones and flowers on the inscribed plaque, some fall to their knees. Some weep softly to themselves. Some gently intone the Mourner's Kaddish, the daily prayer to be prayed at the death of a loved one.

There is no record of the names of all who were slain here. In the first five days, more than 55,000 died. Soldiers were told to conserve bullets by shooting two or three at a time. They were ordered to throw children in alive. Witnesses tell us these soldiers grew weary of the bloodletting but were encouraged to be strong. "Let your will over-rule your heart," they were told. "Do not be swayed by children, old people or women. Kill them all. After the war a new world will dawn for you and your families. You will settle new lands. You will be cleansed and purified of these horrible deeds."

The soldiers were implementing the Nazi's *Ost* (East) Plan, a plan that had been carefully and rationally developed long before any shooting began. They were to eliminate 100% of the Jews, and 85% of the Ukrainians, Russians, Poles, and Byelorussians. The remaining 15% were to become slaves of the Reich.

This slaughter really happened. This really happened in our time. Intelligent human beings, lovers of Beethoven, Bach and Mozart, rationally decided to exterminate and proceeded to enslave races and nations of peoples. Against all objections about the gross inhumanity of such a project, they counseled, "Let your will overrule your heart."

Memorials such as Babi Yar are proliferating the world over. No longer tributes to heroic victories, our monuments increasingly offer poignant witness to immense tragedy. Each gives testimony to the violence and suffering that continues to engulf the world. Each represents the heart's response to the will's assertion. Each protests, for all to hear, "Never again! We will not forget! Never again!"

It would be less disturbing if this calculated and loathsome brutality were confined to one era, ideology or circumstances. Then we could isolate and analyze it as a grievous aberration. But sadly the holocaust did not end. Shoah continues. Other names and nations now offer other rationales but killing fields multiply. From Siberian river camps to Rwandan farmlands, Bosnian highways to Kampuchean forests, urban centers to remote tribal regions, human beings have savaged each other and destroyed all pretense to innocence. We have done it for many different "reasons" and we have done it unto the least of our own.

Is there another way?

In a small village in Kenya, an African woman was carving a sculpture outside her thatched house. She was wearing a dress so colorful that the rainbow would be jealous. A visitor, Sue Monk Kidd, engaged her in conversation:

'What are you making?"

'This is Ujamaa," came the reply.

"What is 'Ujamaa'?"

'"Ujamaa means family."

"Your family?"

"No. God's family."

Would you like to know what God's family looks like? It is not unlike the monument at Babi Yar, yet there is a profound and life affirming difference. Imagine an ebony totem. Sitting at the base are five human figures.

Sitting on their heads are five more, and on their heads are five more. It could go on indefinitely.

If you saw it, you would be struck by how inextricably all these figures are intertwined. They grow out of one another. Their heads join, their faces blend. One person's foot flows from another's hand. All their arms wrap around one another like vines encircling a great tree. This is God's Ujamaa. This interconnected human mass is not sliding into a pit, but rising toward the sun, not collapsing from despair but energized by fellow feeling. Where is God in this Ujamaa? Not presiding in some distant realm but within and between all the figures of the sculpture.

Ujamaa and Babi Yar are two striking images of the human race, and both are true. Both evoke the most profound emotions. Through memorials and monuments we remind ourselves of our capacity to inflict or suffer great harm. Through finely worked art we recognize deep and sacred ties that bind us together. Which image controls the future?

If we were not ujama, would we weep at Babi Yar?

Said Ms. Kidd upon seeing the Kenyan Ujamaa, "This image shattered my illusions of my separateness. It pried open my heart. How can I not help but twine my arms around this vast family?"

Can we stop the violence and halt the bloodshed? I don't have mega-answers to the mega-suffering of our time. I do know it is time to allow our hearts to overrule our wills.

Easter

All Things Intermingle

The Church has gone to great lengths to affirm that Jesus Christ was fully human. Flesh, blood, hopes, sorrows, fears, aspirations, loves, laughter, loneliness, disappointments, convictions, questions — all that we are, he was. The Church affirms that he suffered. The nails were real. The whip, the thorns and the spear were real. The blood and water that flowed from his side were real. The pain in his joints was real. His cries of anguish were real. His burning tears were real. His betrayal was real; his sense of abandonment was real. His loss of mobility, his loss of strength, his loss speech, his loss of consciousness — all of this was exceedingly real. It was not deserved. It was neither cleansing nor instructive for him. It served no rational purpose. From almost any point of view, his suffering was absurd. Absurd, but it was real.

Unlike many faith traditions, this view reflects and validates our own experience. We know that pain is real. To deny it is foolish, and to justify it is scandalous.

But the Church does not stop there. It also has gone to great lengths to affirm that Christ's resurrection was real. The disciples' experience of the empty tomb was real. The messenger's announcement of Christ's new life was real. His presence on the road to Emmaus was real, in the upper room was real, in the breaking of bread was real, and by the Sea of Galilee was real. Not an invention of the human mind, not a myth, not merely a memory, he came to them and knew them. They knew him, and he was real.

In his "Easter reality" he gathered all their bewilderment and concern, all their longings and questions, all the hopes they dared not express. In his realness he affirmed to them that Life is strong and love is stronger than death. In his reality they came to know beyond any doubt that Life rules life. Even in the valley of deep darkness, where fears control and pain prevails, the light of Life extends itself. Ultimately Life overcomes all that stands against it.

Our celebration of the resurrection is so much more than the annual springtime revival of a fertility god, or an acknowledgement of the endless succession of the seasons. The Christian gospel proclaims that there is much more to life than grim submission to universal principles, or accommodation to impersonal forces.

Easter shouts a new word altogether: Emmanuel, God-With-Us. God is in Christ, healing the world and bringing us back to innocence. The Holy One is found not above the world nor outside our experience, but in the midst of the life we live, the flesh we are, the love we share, and the joy and suffering that are uniquely ours. God is not a stranger to us, not a distant and alien Force, not remote and inaccessible. God expects no obsequious petitions or magical incantations. God already is with us. In all that we do, wherever we are, God is present. God embraces us, loves and cherishes us, dwells in our hearts and minds, in our questions and our dreams. The meaning of our life lies in the life we live. The meaning of all suffering and all joy already is present within them.

In the eighth chapter of Romans, Paul struggles to articulate this mystery: He came to an astonishing conclusion: "All things — the good and the bad, the lovely and the ugly, the sweet and the bitter — all things work together for good for those who love God, who are called according to God's purposes."

The original Greek is most suggestive. Susan Howatch writes in *Absolute Truths* another way to express Paul's thought. All things intermingle for good. They form patterns of light and darkness across a life and across the world. The best and the worst, the pain and the joy, the silence and the shouts, the denials and the affirmations, the cross and the empty tomb — in the end all these intermingle within a larger divine reality. Our lives contain patterns in which God is active. These patterns radiate outwardly into the world. They create the kaleidoscopic reality we have come to know as life.

To believe in Easter is to stand bravely before the twin mysteries of the cross and the empty tomb, and to turn away from neither. Even the hardest life contains an intrinsic goodness. Within the most searing pain there is a redemptive presence. Among the broken fragments of our shattered dreams lies everything we need to start again. This is to believe in Easter. To know that nothing is wasted, nothing is without significance, and nothing ever ceases to be precious — this is to believe in Easter. To love life with a desperate love, to suffer with it, and always — always — to slave against all odds to make everything come right — this is to live the Easter faith.

An Easter Mob

"Easter Mob" may sound like an oxymoron, but there is no other way to describe the mass of humanity compressed within and around the walls of The Russian Orthodox Cathedral of the Ascension in Novosibirsk, Siberia, on Easter Eve. This was the first time in more than 70 that they were permitted to ring the bells, and bells are a huge part of any Russian liturgy. From my vantage point high in the cathedral, I looked out over a vast crowd processing joyfully around the perimeter of the church. They carried torches, bells, crosses, banners and - of course — holy icons.

It was a curious experience for an American. All night long, people pushed, shoved and practically trampled me under foot. I couldn't get to places I needed to be. Yet I was receiving their warmest welcome, sharing their most sacred moment, made to sit while others stood, and invited to vantage points reserved for only a few.

From the balcony, I watched the sea of humanity beneath me — babies and babushkas, young military officers and sturdy nuns, the elegantly dressed and the impoverished. The sea moved in waves throughout the main hall. It swirled around circular candle stands. Its chanting sounded like the cresting and crashing of waves. All through the night, the sweetest aromas of incense and melting paraffin competed with the pungent odor of human hair singed by burning candles. No one was alarmed.

Three choirs, a dozen clergy and the whole congregation moved, sang, prayed, wept and laughed in a sacred choreography. As the evening progressed, the complexity and grandeur of the liturgy gave way to brief moments of stunning simplicity. Rococo basses and baritones dominated the night, but eventually they yielded to the stark clarity of a single soprano. She sang from the dome high above the crowd. The music was by Rachmaninoff, but the sentiment was ancient and primordial.

Although I do not understand Slavonic, there could be no doubt: she was the herald of the dawn. She announced resurrection and life, and the rebirth of all that refines and refreshes the human spirit. Her song was an exclamation of hope in the midst of a collapsing empire.

I was told later that this extraordinary vigil was not extraordinary; it has been celebrated similarly every year for more than a millennia. Certainly I was not to attribute the crowds to glasnost. This mob-like phenomenon was being repeated in twenty congregations — Baptist, Adventist, Lutheran, etc. — all around our sister city, and in countless settings across the former Soviet Union.

At the core of the Judeo-Christian experience is the imperative to choose life. Even in the midst of their present crisis, believers who inhabit the remnants of the Soviet Union are doing this. I will think of my friends in those Siberian churches as we celebrate Easter this year. I give thanks for the faith that unites us and gives us hope.

Easter Ever After

Many people have a Disneyesque understanding of Easter: death does its worse. Jesus rises triumphantly. Everybody lives happily ever after. But there is a problem with this view. In real life, even after Easter death continues to hack its way through our world. It fells the just and the unjust with a callous disregard to station or situation. It takes away a child at the threshold of his life while it leaves a lonely, paralyzed old woman to languish in her sorrow. The power of the citadel of negativity extends from first century Jerusalem to twentieth century Hebron, from a Samaritan hostel to a modern hospital room, and from Simon Peter's living room to your living room and mine.

I suggest that Easter is not about happy endings. Religion is not about painless living. Faith is not about getting what we want. Rather, Easter provides the basis for us to make a bold assertion of hope when there is no reason to hope. Religion provides us with the purpose for living when living itself is painful. Faith enables us to give up what we desire most desperately, trusting that God already knows and provides for our deepest and truest needs.

Easter presents us with an invitation. Do we hold fast to our familiar griefs and fears, our dreams for how things should be? Or, even in the midst of much suffering and tragedy, can we let go of them? Can we abandon our hope for a cure in order to know real healing? Can we stop trying to hold together the fragments of our lives so that we might come to know the real wholeness of our personalities?

Easter testifies to our experience that into our private anguish there comes a Presence capable of transforming our minds, hearts and spirits. Into our social despair comes One who can transform our communities and our world. Even in the depths of hell itself, the Christ ceaselessly is striving to set us free from the heavy chains of negativity that pull us toward non-being. Even when we have no energy for Life, Life summons us anew. We can believe with Nikolai Berdyaev that, "The power of hell has been vanquished by Christ, and the final word belongs to God." This faith has the power to change the world.

Eastertide

Choose Life

When it's over, I want to say: all my life
I was a bride married to amazement.
I was the bridegroom, taking the world into my arms."

Mary Oliver, from "When Death Comes," *Collected Poems*

In the heart of every religion lies its distinguishing affirmation: the Shema in Judaism, the incarnation/resurrection in Christian teaching. Buddhism's fourfold noble truth, the circle in Native American spirituality. Beneath these affirmations lies a deeper and more fundamental insight: to be human is to live constantly in the presence of choice. Choices are intellectual, ethical, and relational. Our choices open us to deeper life, or rob us of vitality. They expand our minds and hearts, or constrict our spirits. Every wisdom tradition offers its own hard won experience to guide our choices, but the choices remain uniquely ours to make.

Religion is obsessed with Life — life that is full, fecund and abundant, life that is alive and forever escapes definition. "I have set before you life and death, blessing and curse. Therefore choose life… ," thunders God to the people of Israel. Judaism's railing against idols is its way of distinguishing Life from all that imitates or diminishes it. Buddhists perceive the vitality within or beyond the illusions that clamor for our attention. "Why do you seek the living among the dead?" Jesus asks, and instructs us to, "let the dead bury the dead," — forcing a reconsideration of our most elementary notions.

This world bears an ambivalent character. On the one hand, this world continually disappoints us. It produces tawdry substitutes for authentic life. It offers cheap grace when sacrifice is required. It presents idols of attractiveness that promise more than they deliver. On the other hand the world carries within it the "original blessing" of God's creation; it is the chosen medium of divine life and self-expression. Only in this world do we know grace, loveliness and awe. Only in this world can we experience a love that casts out fear and a hope greater than death itself.

Something Gained and Something Lost

Vocatus atque non vocatus, Deus aderit.
(Summoned or not summoned, God will be there.)
                                        Erasmus, from an ancient Greek oracle

In Turkey one can take a journey of less than 1,000 miles — a few days at
most — and see in the most dramatic fashion how the Christian church
transformed itself from a humble but radical fellowship into an imperial religion. I made this trip a few years ago and I was caught off guard
by what it revealed about the church. I was more surprised by what it
revealed about me.

On a bright October morning I entered a simple cave-church in Antakya
(Antioch) not far from the Turkish-Syrian border. Its interior was dark
and nearly barren. I faced a simple stone altar. The rock that formed the
sides of this cave jutted starkly upward from the stone floor. The walls
were covered with the black soot of centuries of earnest devotion. The
sun cast kaleidoscopic patterns into the interior through a small window
high in the wall behind me.

Today the church is known as Peter's Grotto. According to tradition,
Peter, Paul and Barnabas stood where I was standing. Thecla too, and
Priscilla and Aquila. This was the first Christian church on European
soil. Those who worshipped here were the first to be called "Christian"
— not a compliment when the term was invented. They definitely were
not the movers or shakers of this third largest city of the Roman Empire.
Greeks and Jews together, they were living into a newly discovered unity
while trying to honor the practices of their separate backgrounds. They
probably earned their livings in commerce and the trades.

Tradition says that Peter came here in 34 CE and served this congregation for seven years before moving on to become Bishop of Rome. We
do not know how he came to lead this embryonic church in Antioch. He
was a blustering fisherman more at ease with ropes and nets than the
subtle philosophies of an empire. But he left behind the familiar village life where kinship was everywhere and family meant everything,
liturgies and customs seemed never to change, and a person's place was
fixed immutably within a complex web of relationships. He left it all,
never to return. I stood in silence as I pondered the radical quality of his

commitment. I tried to imagine the men and women who gathered here with him, people similar in some ways to us but who soon would face an enormous tribulation because of their newfound faith.

Many days later I had the opportunity to visit *Aya Sofya* (Hagia Sophia, "Holy Wisdom") in Istanbul. The Emperor Justinian commissioned today's magnificent cathedral in the early Sixth Century CE — the third to be built on this site. The epitome of Byzantine architecture, for nearly 1,000 years it was the largest cathedral in the world. It was the imperial church at the heart of Constantine's empire.

The original building was consecrated in the year 360 CE. It had been dedicated to "The Holy Wisdom of God" a mere 20 years before Christianity became the state religion. The creed, the Biblical canon, the day for worship and the hierarchy all were settled matters when the first cathedral was constructed. This new religion had become the unifying ideology of Constantine's Empire.

Less than 300 years separated Constantine from Peter. In those years the Christian faithful underwent fierce persecutions to defend their faith, and they fought bitterly among themselves to define it. Their endurance would eventually transform the very empire that oppressed them, but they would be transformed as they assumed the mantle of power.

I was awed and overwhelmed when I entered *Aya Sofya* for the first time. Separating myself from my group, I sat down on the stone pavement beneath its soaring arches; I remained in meditation for what seemed a very long time. The cathedral was dedicated to Jesus Christ as the "logos" or holy wisdom of God. Its grandeur and antiquity weighed heavily upon me.

That Jesus had challenged the "kingdoms of this world" energized the congregations in Antioch and elsewhere in those early years. But by 350 CE the rising incense of political power had obscured the clarity of his vision. The seduction of wealth had dulled the sharpness of his critique. The accoutrements of privilege had complicated his message and corrupted his followers. Alfred North Whitehead observed, "When the Western world accepted Christianity, Caesar conquered; the received text of Western theology was edited by his lawyers."

In 50 CE Jesus was the Lord against the powerful of this world. By 350 CE he had become the Heavenly Lord who ordained the emperors to their throne. In 50 CE women shared responsibility with men for teaching and governing the churches. By 350 CE their voices had been silenced. In 50 CE diverse theologies and practices were respected as Christian. By 350 CE there was a much stronger emphasis on authority and conformity; hostility toward "heretics" was hardening.

The requirements of an expanding empire had gutted Jesus' ethic of radical love — love even for one's enemies. It would never be entirely forgotten, but henceforth it would thrive at the margins rather than at the center of the faith. It had become possible both to exalt and ignore Jesus at the same time.

Gradually it came to me how much the church had gained and how much it had lost in its short journey from Antioch to Constantinople. Yet I also came to understand that, though the church is a flawed instrument deeply compromised by its conceits, God makes of it a channel for healing. "We have this treasure in clay jars," wrote St. Paul, "that the excellence of the power may be of God and not of us." (2 Corinthians 4:7)

My thoughts turned to my own ecclesiastical journey. From a small rural congregation in Capon Springs, WV, I had "progressed" through a succession of pulpits — rural to urban, small to large, and "solo" to "associate" to "senior". This "ascendancy" offered increasing perks and recognition. "A hand always above my shoulder" (Browning, Conn) had guided me from position to position, or so I thought. But did it? Or was my personal journey a replica of the early church's "cave to cathedral" mentality? Had I been listening to God or my ego? I too had gained much, but what had I lost along the way? Simplicity? Open heartedness? Joy? Calmness of spirit? Friendships?

Without intending it, I found myself engaging in a serious internal assessment. Under the vaulted dome of Holy Wisdom I looked closely into my life and motivations. I saw how ambition had masked itself as faithfulness, insecurity as arrogance, and greed as common sense. I saw how each of these — unobserved — had led me away from my true path. I realized that my desire to please had muted the voice of my conscience. But I also recognized that in spite of my mixed motivations, God had not abandoned me. God still was kneading the clay of my being and shaping it for ministry.

The time had come to push the reset button, and to return to Jesus Christ as the touchstone of my life and ministry. I rose to rejoin my group. We exited the cathedral and allowed it to disappear amid the lengthening shadows behind us. The warm October sun beckoned us toward the lively streets of Istanbul. The living Christ awaited us.

Do You Believe In Signs?

To the east of Mayflower, a church put up a sign. It reads, "Truth Revealed Here on Sundays." I know members of that church. I applaud the congregation's forthright declaration, but a host of questions comes to my mind: Whose truth? What truth? How revealed? How delivered? I hope people experience some measure of an ever deepening truth at Mayflower, too, but I am reluctant to make such claims.

Perhaps too often I am guided by the words of Lao-Tzu: "Those who know don't say. Those who say don't know." Here we approach truth more cautiously. There is factual truth and truth of the heart. There is knowledge and wisdom, information and transformation. At our best, we invite, suggest, elicit. The truth we encounter comes to us as we engage in what Robert Hutchins once called the "Great Conversation". We believe deeply in truth, and we have criteria to examine it. But few of us feel very comfortable declaring it for all.

To the west of us is another church, with words carved deeply into stone: "This is the House of God and the Gate to Heaven." When I first saw those words, I thought my pilgrimage had come to an end. All my life I have searched for the living God, One who proves to be both present and elusive on my journey. Finally I had found God's base of operations and the very portals of heavenly life. I needed to look no further.

Again, I contrast that with Mayflower Church, whose modest symbol is a small pilgrim ship sailing into a world unknown, seeking God in places unfamiliar.

I am reminded of one of my father's favorite stories. There are three donut shops on the same block. One advertises, "Best Donuts in the World!" The second has a sign, "Best Donuts in the Universe!" The third had just a little sign in the window: "Best Donuts on This Block."

Akpe

My son and I and other members of our congregation were privileged to travel to the Volta Region of Ghana, to the large Ewe city of Ho. Throughout our visit we were the recipients of a wondrous generosity — all the more awesome when we saw the lack of so many things that we take for granted. Every evening a different church group brought drums, dancing, songs and laughter to share with us. On Sundays we worshipped (again with dance, drums and song) in energetic services that lasted at least four hours each. But we really had come to climb ladders, straddle roof trusses and help construct a fellowship hall. We really had come to lug buckets of sand and cement and to dig (by hand) foundations for a new church building.

During our visit Gabe and I were befriended by one of the congregation's leading families. They welcomed us into their home, took us on tours of the community, told us stories and introduced us to many local people. They had one daughter, 13, named her "Akpe" (pronounced Ak-Pay). We asked about the meaning of her name.

> "When she was born," her father answered, "we just wanted to say 'Thank you.' We were so grateful. So we called her 'Akpe.' That is how we say 'thank you' in Ewe — Akpe!"

> "Now," her mother added, "every time we say our daughter's name, we also are saying 'thank you' for this blessing. And every time we say 'thank you' for any kindness done for us, we also think of our daughter."

If only each of us could incorporate such gratitude into our everyday lives. We have many reasons to be thankful — and most of them — like Akpe — have faces. Imagine that every person's name in the whole world secretly means "thank you". Imagine that, when we greet our neighbors or associates, instead of staying "Hi, how are you?" we are really saying, "Thank You". Think how that would change our view of everything.

To Serve the Song

From times immemorial, people have sung. Before the first caves were painted, the first totems carved, the first fires kindled against encroaching darkness, human voices rose together in song. They rose in celebration of sun, rain and stars. They rose in imitation of bird, wind and four-legged relatives. They rose in fear before unknown and sinister forces. They rose in lament over personal and collective tragedies. They rose in ecstasies sexual and transcendent. They sang silly songs and sorrow songs, planting songs and reaping songs, healing songs and building songs, songs of journey and songs of place. They sang in conquest and in slavery, when they worked hard and when they rested from their work. They sang to recognize accomplishment, and to embolden in the face of disaster. They sang at birth and at puberty, in old age and at death. They sang in chant and in plainsong, with wailing and with tenderness. They made love through song, and they used their songs in war.

Even now blending voices are joining an endless global song, a song emerging from the recesses of the centuries, a song sung in every imaginable tongue and in every imaginable place. In the heat of the desert they are singing it. In the rain forests they are singing it. In the icy barrens of the Arctic pole, they sing it. They sing it over rivers, bayous and lakes, on mountains and plains. They sing it in storefronts and stadia, in sweat lodges and grand cathedrals, in cabarets and opera houses. They sing it in solitude and they sing it in mass: in songs plain and songs passionate, in red hot and bluesy tunes, austere chants and embellished polyphonies. It is a song connecting the spiritual centers of every organism with the great Source of all being. It is our song. Within it our wills and intellects take their rightful places.

It is not surprising that music is of surpassing importance in nearly all communities of real faith and spirit. Talent, training, competence, comprehension, discipline, technique — all these serve a higher, integrative, unitive purpose. All serve the song. The Spirit's song cannot be performed; it can only be presented. It never is the vehicle to showcase ability; ability humbly offers up the song. The song carries a message from the heart of being into our hearts. Always it is a message of unreasonable hopefulness. The Spirit's song — in whatever mood or key — wants to lead us from the "no longer" to the "not yet". It wants to open for us "a way out of no way". The song calls us to "a still more excellent way".

Church choirs know this intuitively. Week after week the song visits us and we caress it with our voices. You — our choirs (of all ages), our soloists, instrumentalists and composers and certainly our music staff — you lead us and serve us as you sing and serve the song. You sing through the voices of Johann and Jonathan, Brahms and Blanck, Mendelssohn and Peterson, Gretchaninoff and Grundahl, Handel and Haugen, Vaughan Williams and Dorothy Williams. One Sunday a delicate Korean melody may waft through the sanctuary, while on another, hypnotic native rhythms will stir our hearts. The robust exuberance of South African freedom songs rouse us from our complacency, while the sublime cadences of medieval plainsong quiet our troubled spirits.

When we are yet the smallest children of wonder, your singing accompanies us. Your song embraces us as we pass through death's portal into the realm of light. You bring the loveliness of all the world into our prayer. You bless our whole community with an ever-expanding vocabulary of praise, and an ever-deepening sense of purpose. Because of you our souls grow bigger, our hearts more tender and our love more profound.

A number of years ago I was privileged to attend a dinner in honor of Sir Peter Pears. Sir Peter was perhaps the definitive interpreter of the vocal work of Benjamin Britten. He was a man whom Britten loved and for whom Britten wrote some of his most touching music. At the dinner Dominick Argento — who himself writes opera and teaches composition at the University of Minnesota — rose to speak. "Luciano Pavarotti is a master of the operatic repertoire," he said, "but Sir Peter is something more." He paused. Then he concluded: "Sir Peter is its servant."

We can say nothing better than this: you who lead our music are faithful servants of the song, the song that began at the beginning of creation, the song that will carry us unto the end of time.

Pentecost

The Holy Mobile

If you have ever visited the Philadelphia Museum of Art, you may have seen a great and colorful mobile by Alexander Calder, one of America's foremost modern sculptors. Calder's mobiles are huge, welded, metallic surfaces, delicately balanced and suspended so as to move constantly with the slightest currents of air. Calder himself was one of the great and colorful characters in American life. He was noted for his love of double entendres, his shocking bluntness, and his willingness to take great artistic and personal risks. He was not noted for spirituality, piety or for having even an inkling of religious sensibility. So the art world was puzzled when he named this Philadelphia mobile The Holy Ghost. Essays were written and theologians speculated. What could this possibly mean?

Then someone noticed that the beautiful fountain at Logan Square lay on a direct axis between the art museum and the Philadelphia City Hall. A grandiose statue of William Penn and four huge carved eagles all had been mounted on that building. They were the work of Calder's grandfather, Alexander Milne Calder, an immigrant from Scotland. The fountain itself had been carved by Calder's father, Alexander Stirling Calder, another prominent sculptor of the city. So naturally, when the modem "Sandy" Calder installed his work he thought of... Father, Son and... Holy Ghost!

For many people in today's world, even in the church, talk about the Holy Spirit carries just about this level of importance. If it is thought of at all, it is considered little more than an inside joke, and as little understood. It has been called the "poor relation" of the Trinity, a bit of an embarrassment to modem minds.

In the long history of the church, on the other hand, Pentecost was and is considered the third great festival of our faith. It brings to fruition and makes real the work silently begun at Christmas and declared to the world at Easter. It celebrates the gift of the Holy Spirit, the birth of the church on earth, and the gifts of the Spirit given to us for the transformation of the world. The Holy Spirit is God's way of being "present" now. It is "in" the Holy Spirit that we discover both our unique individuality and our deepest communion with others, our freedom and our most intimate love. The fruits of the Spirit, Paul writes to the Galatians, are love, joy, peace, patience, kindness, goodness, fidelity, gentleness, and self-control.

In the creeds the Holy Spirit is worshipped as "the Lord, the Giver of Life." The symbols of the Spirit are many; fire, dove and wind are among the most well known.

Calder's title for his Philadelphia mobile may have been more of a double entendre than he intended. For in 1951 he wrote, "The underlying sense of form in my work has been the system of the Universe, or a part thereof. This is a rather large model." And twenty years later he emphasized, "I work from a very large live model." Sounds like the Spirit to me!

A Beautiful Life

This is the Season of Pentecost, the Season of the Holy Spirit. The creeds call this Spirit "the Lord and Giver of Life" whose symbol is fire and who brings both freedom and community. Some theologians call the Holy Spirit the "Spirit of Beauty" who reveals to us not only the beauty of the presence of God but our own truest beauty as well.

Fydor Dostoevsky wrote that, "beauty will save the world." Dostoevsky meant that beauty must be our very principle of life — not a perception, not something found outside ourselves, but the guiding principle by which we choose to live. Everything we do must be done in beauty, with grace. Everything. Digging a ditch, writing a book, cleaning the pool, scrubbing the floor - all must be done in beauty. This doesn't mean we must become beautiful ditch diggers, or that we make a ballet of our floor scrubbing. It has to do with how we execute the task, how we live every minute, how we attend to the activity at hand.

Nancy Forest-Flier recently wrote (*Beauty Will Save the World*): "As I was cleaning the bathroom today, I was suddenly overcome with this sense that I must do this work as a beautiful gesture. This is the only free action available to me. If I act out of a sense of resentment (because others are not doing what I am doing), or anger (because the bathroom has a way of getting messy very often), or self-pity, then I am a slave to myself and my work will be exhausting. Even if I work out of a sense of pride (to make this place shine) or some simple ethic of good behavior, I am still a slave to my self. The only way to go about it with joy, as a free person, is to work in the presence of God, in prayer." And this, I think, is how beauty will save the world. "The paradigm for living this way is the Liturgy," she observed, where every action is a beautiful gesture, where we learn to live in the moment, within the climate of continual prayer, where we learn to be "grace-full people". As we move through the seasons of sacred time, let's live each day in beauty.

Playing with Fire

My parents were right about fire. They cautioned me not to play with it. Not to play with matches, or kerosene, or the gas burners in the kitchen. My mother was a nurse. She had seen what fire can do. My father was a fireman. He had watched lives and properties destroyed by fire.

On the other hand, we cooked our food and heated our home with fire. We shoveled coal into the roaring giant of a stove in our cellar. We learned how to start campfires with flint, steel and tinder. We made them blaze for storytelling, body-warmth and entertainment, and we turned them into glowing coals to cook the most amazing meals. My father said that sometimes he set controlled fires to fight wildfires — a concept that is still tinged (if not singed) with mystery for me.

Later I learned that our sun is a seething ball of fire, and beneath the crust of our planet lie fiery volcanoes, simmering. Wires in our house carry a kind of controlled and pulsating fire; too many plugs in a socket once made that unforgettable. Under the hood of our car an engine harnesses a sequence of fiery explosions to bring us to the park. Even my body burns calories in a continuous metabolic fire.

Fire can be released from rocks (coal, uranium), water, wind, oil, wood, or even corn. Controlled fire propels bullets, planes and rockets through space at unimaginable speeds. With it we build canyoned cities, cruise ships, and congested highways. Without it, war as we know it would cease upon the earth. Without it, nights and all enclosed spaces would be invariably and impenetrably dark.

Fire has always been associated with the Sacred. There is little wonder that fire is one of the four (or five or seven) basic elements of antiquity. No fire, no life. We are a long way from the Beltane Fires of pagan practice, but we still light candles, use incense and announce a pope's election with smoke. Why did the writer of Acts describe the arrival of the Holy Spirit as manifested by "tongues of fire"? Why have we retained fire as the very symbol of Pentecost — the third of our three greatest Feasts?

Does the Holy Spirit reveal a dangerous side of God? Krister Stendahl, former Bishop of the Church of Sweden and Harvard Dean, once compared religion itself to nuclear energy — an immensely powerful kind of fire. Like nuclear energy, he said, religion can do an enormous amount of good when respected and properly channeled. But if misused or treated casually, it can be awesome in its destructiveness. He said this before 9/11 and the radical simpleminded extremism of today.

When affirming belief in the Holy Spirit, our ancient creed heralds "the Lord and Giver of Life". The Holy Spirit brings liberating transformation; She is the source of all hope. The Holy Spirit is "God-as-change-agent". Pentecost reminds us that God, like fire, is above us and beneath us, around us and within us. She is the One who brings warmth and possibility. She is the Source of life itself, and accessible to everyone one equally. She is the Holy Comforter.

But Pentecost also reveals the awesome, fiery, unpredictable and passionate side of God. Our invocation "Come Holy Spirit, Come!" may never be said easily, indifferently or with over-familiarity. For me, this prayer will always be tinged with fear and trembling. I learned long ago never to play with fire.

Kanyakumari

As I journeyed to this place, I have seen mountains and *ghats* descend to the sea. I have seen great dams and bridges, vast fields of tea, paddies of rice, trees producing many wonderful products. I have been warmly welcomed in homes and guest quarters. I have enjoyed drums and chants, and the flowing music of Tamil and Malayalam. I have seen small villages and large cities, small shops and huge factories, ancient places and the latest in technology.

This is the place where three seas meet. Here the Bay of Bengal, the Indian Ocean and the Sea of Oman flow together, undulate to a single rhythm, respond as one to the winds above them and the trembling of the earth below. Hundreds of people gather on the shore before each dawn to watch the sun rise upon the sea, and the fisherman return with their catch. At dusk they gather again to watch the sun slip silently beneath the horizon. These are precious moments.

As day flows into night, and night flows into day, opposing realities approach and touch. They dance slowly together. They flow into one another. Meenakshi comes to Shiva, and Shiva to Meenakshi. In this cosmic conjugal embrace the world is recreated. These are the "between" moments — between sea and sky, between day and night. Though they are fleeting and unrecoverable, the gods are present in these times.

This life is our dwelling between the great portals of birth and death. We live between the "no longer" and the "not yet". The healthy ordering of our existence lies somewhere between riotous chaos on the one hand and stifling triviality on the other. We seek our way between the poles of unity and diversity, between innovation and conservation, between having and being, between personal fulfillment and the common good, between living for self and living for others, between creation and destruction, between justice and mercy, between male and female, between intimacy and objectivity, between risk and security, between the visible and the invisible. To the Benedictine, Paul Philbert, we live between two worlds, one of space and time and the other of promise and expectation. Between all of these, each of us must find our way.

Letter to a Young Friend on Her Confirmation

You have been given questions to which you cannot be given answers.
You will have to live them out — perhaps a little at a time.
And how long is that going to take?
I don't know. As long as you live, perhaps.
That could be a long time.
I will tell you a further mystery, he said. It may take longer.
(Wendell Berry, Jayber Crow)

I salute you on this important day. It wasn't so long ago that your parents stood where you are standing now. Your mother held you in her arms on that snowy December morning, until it was time for your baptism. You gurgled and burped as the minister took you and held you high for the congregation to see. You screamed as the cold water poured over your head, face and onto your shoulders. And then you smiled and cooed contentedly and slept through a sermon that was well worth sleeping through.

We have enjoyed your friendship through these fourteen years. When we thought we were your teachers, we learned from you. When we thought we were your healers, we were comforted by you. Your imagination and intellect outreached ours at an early age. You are gifted and caring. If you nurture that true self within you, the world will surely be blessed.

I am glad that you have chosen to confirm the promises made by your parents on your behalf, and by friends like me, on that December morning. I hope you are not merely completing your last religious obligation but truly embrace the possibilities of faith in your life. While we say that young people are "confirmed into the universal faith," it often appears that they are "confirmed out of the church," for we see so little of so many after Confirmation.

"What universal faith?" you ask. It is true that your religious instruction has been more free-form than that of your friends in more traditional congregations. Faith is more ambiguously espoused here. We believe that you should listen to the voices of the community of faith as they are articulated in creeds and manifestos, but we believe even more strongly that you must attend to that voice within you that already is calling out your destiny.

170

The rabbis used to ask, "Why does scripture say that "I am the God of Abraham, the God of Isaac, the God of Jacob" instead of "I am the God of Abraham, Isaac and Jacob"? They answered that this syntax encodes a profound insight. Each of us has a unique understanding of God and an individual relationship with God. Each one of us has our own Higher Power. Our church will suggest but we will not dictate the nature of your faith or your God. God will come to you as God came to Samuel. God will speak to you, comfort you and make demands of you in ways that only you will fully understand. Your faith is a part of your identity. Your life will always be, to some degree, a quest to understand that God-entangled identity. Keep God alive in your mind and in your heart. As Keith Ward says, "To believe in God is to believe that at the heart of all reality... is spirit, consciousness, value, reason and purpose."

Having said that, it is equally important to assure you that you are not alone and you will never be alone. At your baptism someone said words like these: "May she ever appreciate the goodness outside of herself, that she may cherish the goodness within." Look around you as well as within you for the truth by which to live. You are enfolded within the Community of Life and all that sustains Life. You are surrounded by friends, mentors, guides and companions. Learn from the experience of others; listen to the lessons they will have teach you. Take from them the truth that resonates with your own experience. Become wise in the arts of life.

I need to say a word of warning. You have been so honest in your seeking. Sometimes seeking is wonderful, but sometimes it is excruciating. I too have experienced the wrenching confusion of aims, of not knowing which way to go, of not knowing to whom to turn. I too have felt the rejection by others as a burning pain. I too have known how to hide my true self and do what is necessary to be liked or made to feel worthwhile. I too have sacrificed my inner voice to outside demands for conformity, success or even survival. Being true to one's self requires courage. Courage requires a centeredness and certainty that my self is worthwhile. This we affirm today.

There will be traps along your way that can ensnare and capture you and frustrate the journey of your soul. I'm not talking about obvious ones like drugs or alcohol. I'm not talking even about popularity and performance. I'm talking about necessities that are valuable in and of themselves. I'm talking about things you need to build your life, things through which you will make a contribution to our world. Philosophers would say that they are necessary, but not sufficient, for a meaningful life.

You will need money to live but if money becomes your measure, you will end your journey in bitterness. You will want to achieve success but success alone, in any field, is a demanding god who will sap your energy and return to you only temporary highs. You may pursue power and influence. These too are important gifts. They are necessary for the realization of worthwhile purposes but they also can bind you to an endless treadmill. Even building families and nurturing family ties can become a justification for ignoring the voice within.

Remember that whole industries are dedicated to corrupting you. Some of the best minds and most creative intellects in the world are paid big bucks to convince you to buy what you don't need, and to pursue what in the end will disappoint and may destroy you. I wish for you the gift of discernment, that you may see through such schemes and false promises.

And what about your doubts? All year you have studied various aspects of faith and you have indicated certain doubts. What about them? Do doubts keep you from God? Do doubts make you unworthy? Must you be doubt-free to affirm faith? My answer is an emphatic "No!" Of course, doubt can also be a trap on your spiritual pilgrimage. But more often your deepest doubts will contain keys for your deepest growth. In the prayer book of Reform Judaism you will find these words: "Cherish your doubts, for doubt is the hand-maiden of truth... It is the servant of discovery... It is to the wise as a staff is to the blind."

The poet, Ranier Maria Rilke, once wrote to a young friend:

> "Be patient toward all that is unsolved in your heart, and try to love the questions themselves... Live with the questions now... Perhaps you will then, gradually, without noticing it, live along some distant day into the answer. Take whatever comes with great trust, and, if it comes out of your inmost being, take it upon yourself."

Here will be your truth.

You assume obligations to us when you make your Confirmation vows. These obligations are life-long. You oblige yourself to live as openly and honestly as possible. To develop your own soul through whatever talents and interests you possess. To pursue beauty, truth, justice and peace in all spheres of your life. To affirm faith when you can do so in good faith.

To care for others and help create community through the church and in other broader circles of your life. To share in the advancement of a humanity at peace with itself and creation.

Remember, there are ample resources at your disposal. We live in a universe that is sympathetic to the highest of human purposes. Although it may not be apparent at any given moment, a moral order guides you and a spiritual reality sustains you through the best and worst of times.

As you are surrounded today by family, friends and well-wishers in the congregation, so too the church will be an ever present resource to you. Though it sometimes may be unimaginative or boring, yet it also offers community to the lonely, direction to the aimless, a critique to the comfortable and hope for the despairing. Who is the church? I am the church. You are the church. We are the church together.

Well, I've gone on much too long, and so I'll close for now. I give God thanks for all that you are and for the promise you contain. Blessings and congratulations!

Ordinary Time

Patriots

This is a solemn weekend for our families who will visit the graves of their fathers and sons, their mothers and daughters — those who died in the service to their country. The dead will be honored with ceremonies, speeches, volleys of gunfire and the laying of wreathes. But the only possible way to honor their sacrifices is through the deepest soul-searching on the part of the living. The only possible way to affirm the meaning of their deaths is to rededicate and reconsecrate ourselves to the highest values of our land.

It has been said by the poet and political philosopher Peter Viereck that ours is a "polity based on conversation" that requires a "vigorous moderation". True patriots are those who join vigorously in this public conversation, listening as deeply as they can to others and sharing the best of their reflections.

True patriots would never say "my country, right or wrong". If my country is going in a fundamentally wrong direction, it cannot endure and will not succeed. True patriots will call out a warning. They will urge the country to build upon the rock, to align itself more closely with the fundamental principles that govern the world.

Who were the true patriots in fascist Germany? Those who spoke against its government's rapid descent into the hell. Where would you find the true patriot in Stalinist Russia — in the Gulag or in the Kremlin? True patriots in the United States are those who protested and resisted slavery and segregation, those who spoke against the government sanctioned destruction of Native American culture. True patriots are those who courageously probe corruption and the abuse of power in high places and low — in prisons, corporations, ecclesiastical hierarchies and government — not because they hate America, but because they love this country so much that they want us to live up to our true calling and full potential.

True patriots also would never say, "My way is the only way" — or worse, —"My way is God's way." These are "haughty" words; the Psalmist warns and cautions against them. Particularly in a country as diverse as ours is becoming, true patriots will listen to others and share with others with great humility.

Pastor John Robinson, in his farewell sermon to the Pilgrims who set sail for New England aboard the Mayflower, told them to be open to others because "God had more truth to break forth from God's Holy Word." And we in the United Church of Christ, Robinson's spiritual descendents, are inspired by Gracie Allen's similar sentiment: "Never put a period where God has placed comma." Nations are works in progress. True patriots both speak up and listen carefully for the new truth that is sure to follow the comma.

America has been guided by the calling to be a city set on a hill, a lighthouse of liberty, a blessing to humanity. We have set very high moral and ethical standards by which to judge ourselves and with which others may judge us. We did not come together from every nation and every people merely to become rich or comfortable. At our best we are dedicated to the elevation of the human spirit, the improvement of the human condition and the blessing of humanity.

We have not always lived up to our creed. We do not consistently live up to it today. Our history is deeply stained by the violence and harm we have perpetuated against Native Americans, African Americans, and Asian Americans on this continent. Today news media around the world seize on the gross manifestations of our "dark side" — prisoner abuse in Abu-Ghraib or in Georgia prisons, prisoner rendition to Uzbekistan, and the countless innocent victims of an ill-advised war.

We know that these scandalous reports are factual but we cannot believe they are true. They do not reflect the heart and soul of our republic. We are as appalled as the rest of the world and we are as eager for justice, peace and respect for others.

On this weekend, we pay tribute to the countless men and women who have given so much that we might enjoy the life we share. We honor their sacrifices, and the sacrifices of their families, friends and communities. Yet we know that our words alone are lifeless and thin. Only our own deep commitments can honor their sacrifice. Today we renew our dedication to the fundamental values that call forth the best within us.

We love and honor God. We love and serve our country. Today we join as partners with those who are living, those who are dead, and those who are yet to be born. We dedicate ourselves to build a better nation than we were yesterday, better than we are today, and to make of ourselves truly a blessing to humanity.

May Our Children's Children Praise

Great Spirit and our God, present eternally in this land of prairies and lakes, urban corridors and intimate neighborhoods, fertile fields and family farms, be Thou our guide.

Great Spirit and our God, rule this state and its citizens so that our deeds may be prompted by a love of justice and right and be fruitful in goodness and peace. Bless us with a love of righteousness.

Teach us to work for the welfare of all, to diminish the evils that beset us, and to strengthen the virtues of our citizens. Help us to discern in all our decisions the moral within the political, and the ethical within the economic. Bless us with civic courage.

Help us to make real the dream of a "Beloved Community" and to end the harm we inflict on one another and the earth. Bless us with a vision of a peaceable community.

Grant us wisdom and patience, respect and compassion, humor and grace. May the diversity of our life together be celebrated with dignity and joy. Bless us with wise and feeling hearts.

Great Spirit and our God, you have endowed us with noble powers. You have given us freedom to choose. You have made us stewards of our communities and all creation. You have placed the future in our hands. May we exercise power with humility and choice with wisdom. May our stewardship be faithful to your purpose. May our children inherit from us the blessings of dignity and freedom, prosperity and peace, in a beloved and affirming community. May our children's children praise You for decisions we make this day. Amen.

Dear Ivan

It was a great pleasure to meet the members of your delegation to the university two weeks ago. I was a bit defensive when our translator said something like, "Dr. Ivanovich wants to talk to you. He knows you have something to do with religion." There are certain unpleasant stereotypes attached to the role of pastor or priest, especially in academic circles, and I've become a little shy when introduced like that. But I confess that I carried my own stereotype of you that evening: a secular, Marxist sociologist from whom I expected mostly hostility and argument. In the brief time it took you to cross the room I prepared for the confrontation I was sure was coming.

Your courtesies were disarming. Your gift to me at our next meeting of the reproductions of recent Russian paintings of Orthodox cathedrals conveyed a sensitivity that I sincerely appreciate. You obviously are deeply interested in the resurgence of religion among young people in both our countries. I wish there had been more time to explore this and other questions. I am as eager to hear your views on this phenomenon, as you were to hear mine.

It is a fact that American faith traditions are experiencing growth and an influx of younger people. These new members tend to be highly educated, many with advanced degrees, and engaged in successful careers in engineering, the sciences and the professions.

My first attempts to explain the phenomenon may have appeared feeble to you. I tried to present reasons which I thought a sociologist would appreciate: (1) the important role of religious communities in our mobile society to help us establish relationships and overcome (at least partially) that universal loneliness which seems so endemic to our age; (2) the search for continuity and linkages with the generations before and after us; (3) the opportunities to participate in activities related to social service and social justice, and (4) the support needed by young families who are seeking to provide their children with an ethical framework or a moral orientation in a radically pluralistic world.

You said you understood all of these, but that they failed to answer the question. You pressed the point: "What does the individual get from religion?" You proceeded directly to dogma and ritual, and how we relate to these. But actually, for many young people, these are the real, true and sufficient reasons for being involved in religion. A number of studies show that young adults in the United States affiliate with a religious community in spite of its dogma or formal rituals. It is not uncommon for churches to sponsor softball teams to attract new members! Nor is it uncommon for individuals to join a church because of its music program or service to the community. At least in this country, the trend among young people is to seek religious communities where rituals are informal and where dogmas are open-ended and allow for change.

Americans historically have been ambivalent about organized religion and especially about authoritarian forms of it, and about most dogmatic formulations. We hold "freedom of conscience" among our highest values. We believe that religious life is more journey than arrival, more process than state of being, more discovery than accomplishment. My church is only more explicit than most in affirming itself as a non-creedal, open-ended community of faith in which there is the widest possible latitude for individual belief and expression. Still, since we care a great deal about intellectual integrity, we sometimes are uneasy when we sing hymns or engage in liturgies written in eras when assumptions about human life were radically other than our own.

Yet I think you have a point. Labor unions, ethnic groupings or even sports clubs could meet all of the needs I have listed so far. They are basic human needs. Even in churches like mine, which are explicitly non-dogmatic, there is an implicit core of dogma that distinguishes us from labor unions or sports clubs. We study, teach, quote, and appeal to the Hebrew and Christian scripture (although reserving the right to be critical). We pray (although reserving the right to analyze and interpret this radically non-secular behavior). We celebrate Christian festivals (although many of us prompt serious questions about the historicity of the events they are thought to commemorate). All of these behaviors imply a belief that reality is other than mundane or ordinary.

They suggest that we believe — most of us, anyway — in a reality that is fundamentally numinous, intrinsically worthwhile and laden with mystery. Most of us want to use the word "God" for all this. Some of us believe that even this exalted word now carries baggage too oppressive to redeem. They are more comfortable with phrases like "divine spirit," "divine presence" or "the Eternal." In any case, we are seeking a view of reality that preserves its integrity and wholeness.

We recognize that we live in a scientific age when every assertion may be subjected to scrutiny. We acknowledge that even our deeply felt convictions are hypotheses about which reasonable people differ. Yet we also are aware that science and religion no longer are locked in conflict for our souls. Contemporary science neither precludes nor compels religious faith, and some of the greatest scientific minds are also profoundly religious. Science may function as a healthy check on religious claims when they become immoderate. Both science and religion are sources of profound intellectual and spiritual humility, as well as optimism and hope.

For us, religion makes possible what science, economics, and the study of history do not. Through it, albeit imperfectly, we express our conviction that the living and non-living reality that we experience is embedded in a deeper purposeful reality. We think it is possible for us to garner glimpses into that reality through reason, scriptures, tradition and experience. We regard that reality as a sound foundation upon which to build moral and purposeful lives.

In addition, we claim that every individual is a "child of God" or an expression of the sacred dimension of reality. Each one is intrinsically sacred and infinitely valuable. In a century unrivalled for its bloodshed and assaults on human dignity, sound religion offers a way to recognize and safeguard the very basic human rights of all individuals, and to affirm basic human dignity even when these rights are grossly violated. Religion requires us to nurture the fullness of our human nature.

In our view, the religious commitment relativizes all others. In a religious framework, all institutions, whether they are governments or nation-states, political parties, service agencies, commercial enterprises, or even religious organizations — all institutions - serve a higher purpose. They are accountable for their stewardship. Most Christians would regard love, even self-denying love, as the goal toward which creation is moving and as the plumbline by which all actions are or shall be judged. Although I recognize how terribly sentimental this must sound to you, it is in acts of love and cherishing - and not in dogma or ritual - that we draw closest to our experience of God, and thus to the answer to your question.

There are some who say that faith offers easy answers to hard questions. Albert Camus put the question sharply in his book, *The Plague*. An innocent girl suffers a painful death. Religion's representative, although caring and sensitive, can only say that this is part of God's unfathomable will. Camus' spokesman responds, "If this be God's will, then I must be God's enemy."

In fact, since the Holocaust, Hiroshima and Nagasaki, and now Kampuchea, the whole question of the suffering of innocents has moved with urgency to the center of religious dialogue. God's responsibility, complicity, or guilt is a logical consequence of traditional formulations of divine nature as all-powerful and all knowing. More than a few have said that, after the Holocaust, they could not believe.

But it is noteworthy that among the victims of slavery and oppression, often a different note is sounded: not that God is responsible, but that God is "an ever-present help in time of trouble." There is no explanation, whether religious, existential or other, that makes the death of an innocent child acceptable. Yet there are some perspectives that do provide strength to live through overwhelming tragedy, to face and overcome it.

Even in the midst of a harsh and brutal slavery, Black slaves in America reversed the prophet Jeremiah's poignant question, "Is there a balm in Gilead?" into a striking affirmation: "There is a balm in Gilead!" One finds countless testimonials to the wellsprings of a reality that can sustain us in the spiritual wastelands of suffering and oppression. It was also Aleksandr Solzhenitsyn's experience in the Gulag. Perhaps faith begins in the crucible of suffering.

In light of the horrible evils of our time, many are discovering new meaning in the crucifixion. Immanuel ("God with us") comes not as the mighty conqueror but as one of the *anawim* — the forgotten, the outcasts and the lowly. Was this not the "scandal" encountered by Fyodor Dostoevsky's *Grand Inquisitor*? It still may be a scandal that the deepest realities are mediated to us in such a fashion.

You surely are aware that this is not the "opium of the masses" about which Karl Marx and Frederick Engel once wrote so persuasively. Indeed, all over the world, this kind of religion is becoming a dynamic and liberating force. This God is more motivation than explanation. This God shakes foundations and challenges the status quo. This God encourages the discouraged, and enables the downtrodden to stand up. In the words of Prophet Mary, this God pulls the mighty from their seats of power and exalts those of low degree.

DeRostand's Cyrano once exclaimed, "How Fate loves a jest!" Perhaps
Fate is jesting with us now. Who would have expected a Christian pastor
in capitalist America to be writing of liberation to a Marxist sociologist
in Moscow? And who would have expected the Moscovite professor
to give pictures of shrines, churches and holy places to the American
pastor? Marx might call this dialectical, and Calvin, providential. But
between us, maybe, we can smile and nod, for we know that Fate does
indeed love a jest.

Why Me?

She stood before a room full of people. "All my life," she said, "I have had everything I needed. Even today I have a wonderful family, a lovely home, and money in the bank. I have never experienced the catastrophes and crises that affect so many lives. Sometimes I ask myself, 'Why me?'"

I think of her often. My own life is pretty undramatic. The rush of adrenaline hits me only on Highway 285. Mystical encounters seem to seize me only after too much jumping on our trampoline. I envy the intense spirituality of my monastic colleagues. I covet the capacity for focused inquiry of my academic friends. I crave the informed zeal of my more prophetic associates. Too much of my life is devoted to sorting laundry and paying the bills on time.

Recently I read with gratitude these words in *The Atlanta Journal Constitution*: "Normal life is the most difficult thing of all." At last, I thought, a kindred soul! Here's someone who understands.

This "someone" turned out to be the Irish playwright, Sebastian Barry. Never mind that he himself is famous and acclaimed. Never mind that he grew up in Dublin and has lived through the protracted carnage of recent Irish history. He understands. And this is what he wishes for the Irish people: a normal life.

War is "a kind of bizarre distraction from real life," he said at Emory University. "Normal life is probably the hardest thing on God's earth to deal with… the thing we struggle most with, like bringing the kids to school, paying the mortgage and all this, the terrifying things you have to struggle with yourself in a healthy way."

He is right. We are addicted to distraction, and crises provide the drama that we crave. We need problems to solve, fears to face, purposes to achieve, directions to follow, hopes and goals to guide us. They call forth our creativity and imagination. They keep us from getting stuck in the rut of mindless routine.

But as both Barry and my friend suggest, "normal" life itself can be a kind of protracted spiritual crisis. Lacking external distractions, we fill up our calendars and "to do" lists with necessities and preoccupations. Occasionally we wonder if we are missing something more important, a grander scheme unfolding elsewhere. And sometimes, rarely, the demons of boredom, longing or meaninglessness invade our well-ordered premises. As we unload the groceries for the umpteenth time we ask ourselves, "Why me?"

What are the spiritual challenges of such a life? "Before I was enlightened I would eat my breakfast and wash my bowl," goes the Zen proverb. "After I was enlightened, I would eat my breakfast and wash my bowl." To not be busy, but mindful; not active, but aware; not distracted, but discerning — this is the hard work of a normal life.

Pain or Spain?

I told my friends I was staying at *Chez DeKalb* but, truth be told, it wasn't a luxury condo. It was a hospital. The room's appointments were sterile and its decorations downright depressing.

Jutting into the room, a television descended from on high. Below it hung a large white poster. In blue letters across the top the poster screamed, "Are you in pain?" Beneath this sympathetic question was a scale from 0 to 10 — from no pain to excruciating agony. (The poster itself was guaranteed to drive the answers up a notch or two.) Every time my eyes drifted down from the TV screen I saw this question. Are you in pain? Was this the medical version of the Nilsson ratings: "zero" for numb to "ten" for unbearable?

Are you in pain? Whenever I opened my eyes I was greeted with this solicitous inquiry. Absolutely, I thought, otherwise I wouldn't be here. Grrrrr...

One afternoon Farah came waltzing through the door. She changed everything. A young Islamic woman, she had traveled to Spain and Morocco with me during last year's pilgrimage. She brought with her a large bunch of sunflowers to remind me of happier days when we were riding through golden acres in Andalusia. Farah took one look at this poster. With that audacity I have come to cherish in her, she picked up a marker and added a large "S" to the question. Now it read, "Are you in **S**pain?"

With a single stroke she had transported me from pain to Spain! Immediately I felt better. A lot better. During the remainder of my stay at *Chez DeKalb* I pondered this question — Am I in Spain? Is the *Plaza Mayor* just beyond my window? Is the *Plaza de Toros* just down North Decatur Road? Will they bring paella for dinner? Are those castanets I hear in the hall late at night?

No one else noticed this slight but momentous change in signage. Everyone else just looked at my vital signs — but not at signs of my vitality. I doubt if they ever heard the castanets.

That "S" was still there a week after I checked out of the hospital. I hope that future patients will be able to appreciate Farah's singular contribution to their mental health and recovery. If the health care police don't spot this avenue of escape, the staff one day will be confronted by cardiac patients dancing flamenco, and geriatric patients morphing into caballeros.

To this day when I feel glum or discontented, I say to myself: "Do I see only dull routines or endless tasks ahead of me, or am I looking for the sunflowers? Am I in pain? Or in Spain?" The choice is up to me.

Beauty

I listened intently. An Orthodox nun was responding to a question about which I care deeply: how to nurture spirituality in children. As parent and pastor, I often ponder this question but Mother Rafaela's answer took me by surprise. "The question really is," she said, "how to put beauty into a child's life."

Both beauty and ugliness have the power to shape and transform our lives and our communities. Mother Rafaela's point seems as relevant to stopping violence and curbing teen-age pregnancy as to spiritual formation. How can we put beauty into a child's life? Or, as Plato observed about the purpose of education, "How can we teach our children to take pleasure in the right things?"

Beauty occurs as readily in unadorned nature as in our most elegant gardens. It is not always "pretty.' It is not merely decorative. It may be — should be — cultivated, but beauty must not be confused with art. It is both less and more than art. The artistic function in our culture encompasses all manner of expressions, only some of which are beautiful.

When we experience beauty, we enter a dimension of life too deep for words, a dimension that transcends much of the ugliness, pain and fear that is our daily bread. We are touched by a gracious order. We are enabled to reach a new level of spiritual integration. We encounter a "lightness of being" (Tolstoy) that frees our spirit. Perspective, balance and catharsis are among the gifts that beauty bestows. The divine in us resonates with the divine in all creation.

The beauty I am able to perceive or create intimately shapes the meaning of my life. "Consider the lilies of the field," said Jesus. The so-called "amenities" of our community (both natural and cultural) feed my spirit and shape my soul. The pursuit of beauty in worship, conversation and a life lived well is among my most important motivations. Why should it be otherwise for children?

The composer Ottorino Respighi surely was one of the great joy bearers of the modern world. According to critic Geoffrey Crankshaw, "Beauty of expression was his perpetual aim. He hated ugliness, and eschewed any tendency toward the brutal." One could do worse than leave such a legacy to the world.

It is said that, when Adonis arrived in the underworld after his death, only one question was put to him by the shades: "What was the most beautiful thing you left behind?" If this were the standard to which all of us are held, I wonder how our children's world would change.

Kermit's Lament

It's a silly thing, really, to be standing in the kitchen with your wife, and both crying real tears because a man died whom you never met. Not only had you not met him, but you knew him only through a frog, and even the frog wasn't 'real'. That happened to us. The announcer told us that Jim Henson died. He went on, unheeded, to chronicle the impact of this untimely death on the various programs Henson had created, and on the Disney-Muppets merger.

If you know me well, you probably are aware that one of my favorite songs is the frog's song, *Green*: "It's not easy being green... Green is the color of so many ordinary things." Kermit laments his own lack of panache and elegance. I identify with this song (and with Kermit). I cried that his voice had been stilled.

Is it accidental that green is the liturgical color for the long season after Pentecost? In the church calendar, this is called "Ordinary Time." There are major festivals, and there is "ordinary time." One might hope that "ordinary time" would at least have a positive definition, derived perhaps from "ordained" or something similar. Alas, most books merely describe what it is not. "There are two kinds of Sundays," says a standard reference, "those which form our theological centers, and those which do not." The latter Sundays are, of course, "ordinary time."

As we work our way through the lectionary texts of ordinary time, we are discovering how ordinary faith is formed. Kermit is right: it's not easy. No major revelations guide us. No break-through dreams. No ah-ha! experiences. Rather we encounter only reflection, introspection, action and prayer - the small disciplines that slowly nurture spiritual maturity.

Most of us want more. Or less. We want the seventy-six trombones, but not the practice; the big parades, but not the marching drills. We want a faith that changes the world, but not ourselves, that moves mountains but leaves us unmoved. We are more Kermit than Henson. We face ordinary opportunities and ordinary challenges, live ordinary lives, do ordinary work, and are sustained by an ordinary faith. This truly is our season. It's not easy, being green.

The Last Guy

Arlo Guthrie, Woody's son, once wrote a little song about the "last guy."
While all of us have troubles, he said, we take comfort by knowing that
some people are "a lot worse off" than we are.

As a child, when I complained about anything, my father reminded
me how much worse life was for the little kids in Italy. Substitute Iraq
or Afghanistan and the argument still holds. Even today, when things
don't go my way, I often find myself saying, "Well, yes, Budd, but this is
a very high level problem to have. Think of the people whose lives are so
wretched that they cannot even imagine having a problem like this. Want
to switch places with them?"

If all of us feel better because we compare ourselves to "those less
fortunate," then somewhere there has to be a "last guy" who is the least
fortunate of all. Nobody has a worse situation. "The last guy," said Arlo,
"doesn't even have a street to lie down in for a truck to run him over."

A kind of inverted pyramid emerges. At the top are the myriads of com-
plainers who put up with minor annoyances. They get by because just
below them are people with more serious problems. They in turn survive
because below them are people with more severe situations. Each group
gets smaller as the misery intensifies. Each group takes comfort that
their situations are not as desperate as those of the people below them
who suffer even more. At the very bottom, of course, upon which the
entire structure depends, is "the last guy".

Of course the logic here is as wobbly as the pyramid. Does it really make
me feel better to know that homeless orphans in Africa are rummag-
ing through garbage cans for dinner? Of course not. Yet it does put my
grievances into a salutary perspective. As a white Protestant male I have
experienced discrimination, but it is nothing compared to the prejudice,
segregation, pogroms, abuse and lynchings that others have endured.
I have my share of health issues, and frustrations with our health care
system, but I also have access to some of the best health care in the world.
I may hate the traffic on I-90, but because of our freeways I can go places
and do things that were unimaginable just a few generations back. My
complaints reveal a privileged existence indeed.

The "problem" with spirituality is that it opens my heart to others. When they suffer, I suffer. When they rejoice, I rejoice. Examining my complaints, I find that my own deep gladness is deeply linked to — and dependent upon — the happiness of others.

Not just happiness is at stake. So is our security. Never has the reality of our interdependence been so apparent. An Icelandic volcano shuts down air traffic in Europe and strands millions. A single computer-generated error causes panic on Wall Street. Angry Pashtuns in the tribal lands of Pakistan create havoc in Times Square. Our demand for bargains creates sweatshops in Asia. And who can tell what horizons will be impacted by the collapse of the Deepwater Horizon drilling platform off the coast of Louisiana? In today's world, our survival requires us to attend to the misery and seek the happiness of each other. To be happy and safe, we must engage in *tikkun olam*, the healing of the world. To find paradise we must be concerned with the happiness and security of "the least of these."

Nicholas Berdyaev once wrote that none of us will be saved until all of us are saved. I can't be truly happy until the last guy is safely home.

The Silent Woman

When (Bathsheba) the wife of Uriah heard that her husband was dead, she made lamentation for him. When the mourning was over, David sent and brought her to his house, and she became his wife, and bore him a son.

(II Samuel 11:26)

Our story begins in the late Bronze Age city of Jerusalem. It had been captured by David who was turning it into a royal city. Had we used names other than David, Bathsheba and Uriah today — say, Eric, Megan and Jason — this story from the Hebrew Bible might easily be mistaken for a late night soap opera. David is the handsome young man whose life is a rags-to-riches fairy tale. Once a shepherd, he is intelligent, literate and musical. It turns out he also is something of a military genius. David is married to the daughter of the first and former king upon whose throne he now sits. He is the father of many children and already has made Jerusalem his own.

Harold Bloom in *The Book of J* describes David as one who transformed his people from an obscure clan into a dominant culture, from an inward-looking community into an international power, and from a preliterate society into one whose standards continue to guide our judgments. David is a paradigm and a new image of human existence. "What Abram, Jacob and Tamar strive toward becoming, he is."

About Bathsheba we know much less for reasons that will soon become apparent. We know that she is, in David's eyes, very beautiful. Her husband Uriah is a soldier, brave in battle and conservative in values. He is fearless. His loyalty to his king and his military oath will cost him his life.

The people of Judah and Israel have gone to war against a Syrian alliance. David is commander-in-chief as well as ruler of his people. This year he remains in his palace while his troops fight on the battle lines. His roof overlooks the entire city. From this vantage point he can look into the private interior courtyards characteristic of homes of that era. One evening he does just that. He sees beautiful Bathsheba bathing. He wants her. He discovers that she is the wife of one of his officers now on duty at the front. He sends henchmen to fetch her to his quarters. He has sex with her. He sends her home. She sends him word that she is pregnant. There is no question but that the child is his.

To cover his adultery, David brings her husband home from the front and sends him to his wife to lie with her. He sends over a feast with wines and rich gifts. But Uriah refuses to feast and vows to remain celibate until all the troops are safely home. (During the recent war in the Persian Gulf, I remember how inappropriate *I* felt at an elegant luncheon knowing that troops were fighting and dying. How much more so a dedicated soldier home on temporary leave.) David makes him drunk, but still he will not sleep with his wife. Nothing David does works, so he resorts to more drastic measures.

David drafts a message for Uriah to carry to General Joab, the Schwartzkoff at the battle of Kabbah. He instructs Joab to place Uriah in the front of the battle and then to withdraw support and allow him to die. Not knowing its contents, Uriah delivers the note. Joab complies, and Uriah dies in battle. Messengers bring this news to Jerusalem. Bathsheba is grieved; David is relieved. After a short but appropriate interval, David marries Bathsheba. She becomes his favorite wife.

Everything about this passage reeks of what we might call androcentrism. It was written by men for men. Commentaries, for the most part, also have been androcentric. As far as we know here, Bathsheba is just another pretty face, a Barbie doll, a centerfold to be collected by the king. Bathsheba is portrayed as silent. Where is her story told? Did she resist? Could she resist? David was at the center of a vast and powerful network of informers and emissaries who were able and willing to assist him in love and war alike. He sends his agents for her. What was she to do? What were Bathsheba's feelings in this matter? Was she protecting anyone? Were there other children involved? What were her values? How did she understand what was happening to her? How do we understand it?

But Bathsheba is silent in our text. Silent and compliant. She is silent except when she mourns for her murdered husband. Hers is the silence of the *anawim*, the "little people", the powerless and exploited people of the world. Hers is the shame of the victim, the pain of the victim, the silence of the victim. Hers is the silence of Melissa Johnson, of Mary Foley, of Jacob Wetterling, of an Iraqi Kurdish woman, of a "disappeared" in El Salvador, of a Chinese student unknown to us.

Even later, after David marries Bathsheba, the Bible continues to refer to her as "Uriah's wife." She is not consulted. She is not allowed to speak with her own voice about all that has happened to her or around her. The author is more concerned with David's sin against another man's property than his violation of Bathsheba's personhood.

This aspect of our story was ignored in every commentary I read. Almost unanimously, commentators used this passage and David's repentance that soon follows to glorify David and to demonstrate his "humanity". David lusted for Bathsheba — and not just in his heart. See, the commentators proclaim, how really human the Bible's characters are. David lusted, acted on that lust, felt panic, deceived and finally murdered Uriah, and then experienced profound remorse and repented. David was real!

Some commentators believe that the great penitential Psalm 51 was written by David at this very time. It is a moving and deeply felt lament. Yet if this be David's, even here he reveals a blindness to the suffering he inflicted on those around him. "Against God only have I sinned!" God only? Did he forget Uriah, Bathsheba, the soldiers, his family, his people?

While commentators praise David for his "manly" repentance, they ignore or even blame Bathsheba. Susan Brownmiller (*Against Our Will*) describes "the myth of the beautiful victim". I have not seen her insight applied to Bathsheba, but it should be. Indeed, in one recently published textbook, *The Hebrew Bible: A Socio-Literary Introduction*, by Norman Gottwald, there is only a single reference in over 600 pages to Bathsheba, the eventual mother of David's dynastic line. In that one reference she is "the woman who brings death to two men… her husband and her newborn son." How's that for blaming the victim!

Let us be clear. The crime was David's, not Bathsheba's. This is not a soap opera; it is real. It not just a story about rape and murder; it's about power and its abuse. How ironical that David, the Giant-Slayer, has become a new Goliath!

Let us continue the story. David and Bathsheba are married. She gives birth to David's child who is sickly and fails to thrive. David prays desperately because he fears that the child's impending death is really a judgment on him. The child does die. David repents and his repentance is searching and profound. God hears his prayer, but there appears to be limits to what even God can or will do.

Only one writer that I could find is critical, deeply critical. Perhaps significantly, that writer is not a theologian but a literary critic at Yale. Gabriel Josipovici, in his *The Book of God*, observes that although God's blessing has not been withdrawn from David, it has been corrupted. Like Adam after the fall, David henceforth must live with the consequences of the evil he has caused. David's favorite son almost immediately rapes one of his daughters, setting off a massive civil war. David is driven from Jerusalem by another son, Absalom, who appears to have the moral high ground. Absalom in turn is murdered in battle. David is not permitted by God to build the Temple, which is his singular lifelong ambition. His final words of blessing and advice, as a dying old man to another son and his successor, are filled with the bitterness of one who wants to settle old scores. David the young hero became David the voyeur, the rapist, and the murderer. But a repentant David emerges chastened, vulnerable, tarnished and real.

There is a way in which David was right in that penitential psalm. If all creation is loved and cherished by God, and expresses something of divine nature, then his grievous sin against Uriah, Bathsheba, the innocent young Israelite soldiers, his family and his people really is (also) a sin against God.

This story is about more than one man's abuse of power. "Here is a mingling of the moral and the political, (for) the social structure of the nation participates in the crime," according to Joel Rosenberg in *The Literary Guide To The Bible*: This is a story about the devastation that follows when we cease to be stewards of the power entrusted to us, and rather turn it to our own ends. Wherever or when ever selfishness and greed come to dominate private lives or public policy, this story needs to be retold.

Thirty-four Years to Go, But Who's Counting?

Thirty-four years. That's approximately how long I may have left, according to a friend. Thirty-four. The "average" man who lives to be my age can expect thirty-four years more. Since I am neither more nor less than average in most categories, why should I be different in this?

Thirty-four. Depending on your situation that may sound like a lot, or a little. To me, it's not much. Less than a "watch in the night" according to scripture. A "little day" according to a Jewish prayer. A raindrop falling ever more swiftly toward the sea.

It doesn't help to be reminded of what other people have done in less than thirty years. Mozart, for example. Or the young Einstein. Or Jesus. I know what I haven't done with more. I have more questions now than answers, more longing than satisfaction.

It's not that I want to be president or pope. I don't envy Bill Gates. I don't want to trade places with Donald Trump. Jimmy Carter has my attention, however. And Desmond Tutu. And the Dalai Lama.

I don't want to be the mayor of a major city, but I'd like to help a decent mayor create a humane community. I can't imagine being Billy Graham or Gardner Taylor, yet I'd like to speak a few original words that console or uplift. I do not aspire to the pulpit of a" tall steeple" church; I do hope that congregations I serve will come more closely to resemble the Beloved Community for which, I think, Christ lived and died.

As I face into what may be the last third of my life, this is what I know: Wisdom and wealth are not synonymous. Wisdom and poverty are not either. Power is neither evil nor good, but necessary for the realization of either. Silence contains more truth than many words. Sharing sorrow lessens it. Nice is not bad. Deep peace is possible in the midst of great suffering, yet a serene appearance may hide the deepest pain. Soul is real, but "real" itself is puzzling. Not one of us will be truly happy until all of us are truly happy. Grace is everywhere.

It isn't much, but it's a beginning. After all these years, it is a beginning.

Preach What?

Born Jewish, my best friend was raised in Paris during World War II. He remembers fleeing to Sweden to escape the Nazis. About eight years ago he said to me, "You should be preaching war."

"I beg your pardon?"

"War. Yugoslavia. It's genocide all over again. You should be preaching for us to go to war."

"War?" I exclaimed incredulously. "To a UCC congregation?" Although I was not comfortable with the absolutism of the various peace movements, our members were heavily involved with the nuclear freeze movement. At that time many even were advocating unilateral disarmament. I could imagine their astonishment.

"War," he repeated adamantly. If we don't go to war now, history will repeat itself. Genocide. Mass graves. Ethnic cleansing. It's happening all over again."

His prescient remarks haunt me as I survey the destruction of Kosovo and much of Yugoslavia. I didn't preach war. Or reconciliation. With all its ancient hatreds, Yugoslavia was too complicated. I preached relief for the victims of ethnic cleansing. Relief. Not war.

In this, I failed. It's not that I should have preached us off to war. But I should have paid closer attention. Since my congregation was choosing the way of pacifism, we had an opportunity and an obligation to engage this situation from a proactive, generous, non-violent perspective. It was wrong to turn away.

The nations of NATO have just spent billions to conduct an air war. The land we "saved" now lies in ruin. Another fortune will be required to rebuild it. If the economic and technical muscle behind this war effort had been deployed earlier, and with more imagination, would there be less carnage today? Could those same resources have been used differently? What would have made peaceful conflict resolution more attractive?

As we move into a new era of radical interdependence, these questions will intensify. What positive contribution can Christian faith offer to a violent world? What positive difference can we make when power is wielded arbitrarily? How can we encourage the brightest among us to devote themselves to a more humane world order? How can we strengthen the rule of law in international affairs? How can we protect human rights when they are threatened or violated? When is the use of force justified? How much "force" is justified?

True compassion always will be costly. To engage the world constructively requires all the wisdom and courage we can muster. Wisdom is born of faith and courage arises from our deepest convictions. If not war, then what? If not us, who? If not now, when?

Pomp and Circumstance

Jim and I were fellow seminarians. Neither of us is very tall, and I always admired the way he conducted himself. He was something of a prince — urbane, articulate, and even a bit haughty. His beard was precisely trimmed; his clothing was exquisitely appropriate to every occasion. I never saw Jim in a situation in which he was not in complete control.

Once he was asked to conduct worship for one of the more stately Presbyterian churches in Princeton. Jim was a master at ceremonies. What would seem hopelessly pompous in anyone else was merely dignified when performed by Jim; he was a good choice to direct the staid and proper rites of these eminent folks.

On this occasion, while he was leading a responsive litany, Jim felt a peculiarly insistent call of nature — one he could not ignore. Alone in the pulpit, he also could not depart to relieve himself. He glanced hurriedly through the order of service and devised a strategy. While the offering was being collected, he would sneak out behind the choir and return unnoticed before the doxology and prayer. Much depended on timing.

The first part of his plan went well. Enthralled by a typically magnificent anthem, the attentive congregation did not know that they were temporarily without a leader. But as the anthem neared its conclusion and Jim started back to his place, he found that the door separating him from the sanctuary had locked when he passed through. He was alone and trapped in an upper hallway. With the choir singing gustily away, no one heard him scratching behind the door.

But Jim is smart, as I say, and he never loses control. He found an open window and, with nary a pause to consider the consequences, he leaped through it — black robes, academic hood and all. Landing on his feet, he ran around the church as the organist hit the chords for the doxology.

The congregation performed its conditioned response of standing, and joined in the song, "Praise God from Whom all blessings flow... ." The ushers began their ritual walk down the center aisle with offerings great and bountiful. And marching right behind them, with head held high and singing as loudly as anyone present, was the Reverend Mr. Jim. He waltzed around the ushers in time to collect the plates, and gave a most deeply felt prayer of thanksgiving. Then he continued with his sermon.

To this day he swears that ninety-nine percent of the congregation never noticed anything unusual about that service.

The Fighting Answerers

Thank God for Charles Ives! Without him I couldn't have gotten through seminary. To be more precise, without his *The Unanswered Question*, I might have lost my sanity altogether. I discovered this short piece of music as I was plowing through the writings of the Early Church Fathers. (Yes, they were only Fathers in those days.) Mystics and theologians battled — literally — with one another over words and even over the spelling of those words. They argued with a vitriol I had not heard since I stopped listening to radio preachers years before.

One evening in Bound Brook, NJ, as I poured over these ancient texts, unable to fathom the light within them that had animated and agitated so many, the local public radio station broadcast Ives' piece into my study: *The Unanswered Question*. Fittingly, it is subtitled "A Contemplation of Something Serious." The music struck a chord with me, if you'll pardon the expression. It is hauntingly plaintive and inconclusive, and it has stayed with me ever since. It is a deeply humane composition.

Ives wrote *The Unanswered Question* in 1906 along with its companion, *Central Park in the Dark in the Good Old Summer Time* (subtitled "A Contemplation of Nothing Serious"). Within its simple structure there are three distinct kinds of music layered upon one another: a string chorale, an unchanging trumpet phrase and a chattering woodwind response. Ives wrote,

> "The strings play pianissimos (very softly) throughout with no change in tempo. They are to represent the 'Silence of the Druids — Who Know, See and Hear Nothing.' The trumpet intones 'The Perennial Question of Existence,' and states it in the same tone of voice each time. But the hunt for 'The Invisible Answer' undertaken by the flutes and other human beings becomes gradually more active, faster and louder… . 'The Fighting Answerers,' as the time goes on and after a 'secret conference,' seem to realize a futility, and begin to mock 'The Question' — the strife is over for the moment. After they disappear, 'The Question' is asked for the last time, and 'The Silences' are heard beyond in 'Undisturbed Solitude.' "

The contrast between the words on the page and the music in my ears was startling. The apodictic certainty of the theologians paled before the "Perennial Question" put by the trumpet's voice. I had great empathy with the Questioner, and a deep yearning for The Silences, but I felt the theologians were merely "Fighting Answerers" whose many words lead nowhere. In that moment I gave up forever the search for all-explaining dogmatic formulations. I turned whole heartedly toward ambiguity and embraced it. Henceforth The Question, not the Answerers, would be my guide.

Left to my own devices, I would choose to dwell within the Silence of the Druids. This is the "tacit dimension" about which the Hungarian physicist Michael Polanyi wrote so perceptively. It is the "imaginal world" of the 12th Century mystic, Ibn Arabi; it yields real knowledge though it can be accessed only through the creative imagination. It is the Tao of Lao Tzu, the Logos of St. John and the Wheel of American Indian spirituality. "We know much more than we can tell," wrote Polanyi. And we love much more than we can know.

In later years, I came to understand that theologians also are "Questioners" first, whose certainties grow out of their struggles with all that is unresolved in their own hearts and in our world. I accept their words as their hypotheses, their attempts to cross the chasm.

Charles Ives was a church-going New England organist, and a Transcendentalist, but he was more. He was willing to let words fail and answers dissipate. "Vagueness," he said, "is at times an indication of nearness to a perfect truth." Today, when too many are too certain about too much, a little vagueness would be salutary, and the Silences most welcomed.

Strange Steps in Jumpy Rhythms

Let the dead bury the dead.

(Luke 9:60)

Most of us are so embedded in our culture that it lives its life through us — its life, not ours. We never hear the inner voice; if we hear it, we ignore it. We let others tell us what is important, what books are essential, what jobs we should seek. We let them tell us what we must believe, how we should vote, what we should think. We let others tell us what is fashionable, how our homes should look, what music we should enjoy. Jean Paul Sartre described this as the "dance of respectability". There is a certain wrapped-in-cotton numbness about this kind of life, and a deadness at its core. It is possible to spend my entire life as the hero or villain in someone else's fairy tale, as a character in someone else's script.

It takes courage to live the singular life that has been given uniquely to each of us. Bill Holm, in his collection of poems called *The Dead Get by with Everything*, once wrote:

> *Someone dancing inside us*
> *has learned only a few steps:*
> *the 'Do-Your-Work' in 4/4 time,*
> *and the 'What-Do-You-Expect' waltz.*
> *He doesn't notice yet the woman*
> *standing away from the lamp,*
> *the one with the black eyes*
> *who knows the rumba*
> *and strange steps in jumpy*
> *rhythms from the mountains of Bulgaria.*
> *If they dance together,*
> *something unexpected will happen.*
> *If they don't, the next world*
> *will be a lot like this one.*

"Strange steps in jumpy rhythms" may be as gritty as remaining seated in the front of the bus when the world tells us to move to the back, or as radical as renouncing all personal ambition to tend the indigent dying in Calcutta. They may lead me to become an executive when I thought I was poet or a poet when I thought I was an engineer. They could involve years of preparation for a profession or career of great importance or service, or abandoning a profession or career to serve God and others sacrificially.

Life is forever alive. It cannot be pinned down. It cannot be defined or controlled. To be alive means to say "yes" when the dark-eyed God invites us to dance, without knowing for sure where our response will lead. To be alive means to go beyond anything our parents or teachers have dreamed for us, beyond even our own most carefully crafted plans, and sometimes even beyond our dreams.

Thoughts on My Obituary

At some point in the not too distant future, someone else may have cause to write something about me. It won't be called a bio; it will be called an obituary. It may reference my place of birth (West Virginia) as well as the place of my disappearance; it may describe my educational pedigree (Frostburg State University, Princeton Theological Seminary, Howard University). It may say something about my career (ordained minister within the United Church of Christ) and the communities I have served (Bound Brook, NJ; South Paris, ME; Minneapolis, MN; Reston, VA; Atlanta, GA, and now, Crystal Lake, IL). Perhaps the writer will be kind enough to mention the causes which consumed me: working to overcome racism and homophobia, striving to broaden interreligious cooperation and interfaith friendships, and searching for common ground. If there is enough space, the editor might mention the few skills entrusted to me: preaching, writing, networking, spiritual direction and congregational leadership.

Certainly the obit will tell the public that Gretchen and I were life partners and fellow travelers since 1968, and that I was the proud father of Gabe and Gaia, two amazing individuals who were, in fact, my teachers. And the proud father-in-law of Johnny, whose questions kept me forever on my toes. And the proud grandfather of Maia Marion, who is completely reshaping my understanding of incarnation. It surely will name my sister, Bonnie, a spiritual master with a great heart, and it will tell of my lifelong reverence for my parents. The article may say that my hobbies included the enjoyment of many forms of music, the acquisition of rudimentary Spanish, the appreciation of dance and art, and cross country skiing. If the writer is perceptive, she even may acknowledge that I devoted my life to becoming — with less success rather than more — a citizen of the earth. She might say something about my sense of playfulness and humor.

There will be many things left unsaid. My love of belly dancing, for example, will not make the final cut. Nor will my loyalty to — pick one — the Twins, Braves or Cubs. My intense interest in dreams will go unmentioned, and the many deficits that have hobbled and inhibited me at every step: my vanity, my needy ego, my lack of deep humility and my inability to listen. I never learned to dance. I think too much. I am too cautious. Sometimes, although you may think you see and hear me, I am not present. I both crave and fear intimate encounter. I lack the courage of my convictions. I have too many foci and too little discipline. Too much patience and too little indignation. Too much ambition and too little discernment. I am more adept at herding cats than at recognizing the lion that roars.

There is one thing more the obituarist will miss because it cannot be captured in words. There is one thing more that I want you to know about me, but it cannot be expressed on paper: all that has been written is not I.

It is the mere husk of the longing that I am. It is a collection of words that describe the roles I have chosen to play. It is the evidence left behind by someone or something who once bore my name and lived in this vicinity. My bio describes the clay of a bowl, but I am its emptiness waiting to be filled. These words are the notes written on a staff, but I am the space between them that makes possible my song. These facts comprise my wardrobe, but I am the yearning upon which this clothing hangs.

The part of me I most want to share with you I am least able to describe. I am elusive even to myself, known tacitly if at all, and apprehended mostly through indirection. I am not finished. What you see today may be the sum of all that has been written, but the writer has moved on.

The Trampoline

Our insurance company was so unhappy with us that its agents threatened to terminate our policy. They discovered that we owned a trampoline. Unless we dismantled it immediately, they wrote, and swore in blood never to reassemble it, they would cancel our coverage immediately.

So on a crisp morning in late October, with sledge hammer in hand, I marched into our backyard. There sat the offending platform, no longer in use, covered with the debris of early autumn. One by one I carefully detached the coils, allowing the net to go limp; soon it fell to the ground completely. Next I lifted the large metal ring from the stanchions we had so carefully erected nine years before. Finally I removed the posts themselves. I piled everything into a heap to be carried away the next time the garbage truck rolled through our neighborhood.

My children were nine years younger when we installed it — and so was I. They have long since outgrown this trampoline. But me? Well, not quite. We spent many hours happily jumping together. (The family that leaps together keeps together?) We punctuated schoolwork, picnics, bad news and good with bouncing. Our kids developed unique and wonderful routines that they were eager to show our visitors. Visitors themselves loved to spin, jump and drop with us. Together, we were corn in a popper. Alone, I would steal outside for a few seat drops before returning to my supposedly more mature pursuits.

Our trampoline served other purposes too. On mosquito-free nights we rolled out the sleeping bags. Looking down on us through the finger-like branches of a huge and ancient oak, the round moon illumined the round bed on which we lay. We drifted to sleep under the blinking lights of silent airplanes gliding far above.

Even Denny, our fearless hairless Crested, loved the trampoline. He jumped with us when he could, but he also had his own agenda. He loved to lie on top of it on sultry afternoons, and beneath it he found shelter from pouring rain and scorching sun.

Denny watched accusingly as my blows transformed our jumping platform into a heap of rubble for the recycler to haul away. Dismantling the entire structure was unexpectedly easy; it took less than two hours to do the deed. It required some hard pounding with the hammer, some tugging here and some pulling there. I wanted the trampoline to put up more of a fight. "Do not go gentle into that good night… ," I implored, but the trampoline offered little resistance to its own demise.

A door was closing forever, and my hand was on the doorknob. I came away from my work that day with a deep disgust for the violence I had so willingly perpetrated, and the sacrilege I had so easily performed. I asked forgiveness from everything that remained of the trampoline. But crumpled and cast off, it refused me absolution. I turned aside feeling the palpable loss of innocence. I grieved possibilities that would remain unrealized. I learned that a few hammer blows at the right place — like a few harsh words at a critical time — can destroy forever something more precious than we know.

Singing

In my mind, I am a convinced rationalist. I honor God with words. Although precise verbal formulations never capture reality, words and phrases can evoke and reveal what might otherwise remain obscure. Words are our hypotheses, thrown before us into the abyss of the unknown. They are our bridges, linking soul to soul. They reassure us with their compelling logic. They comfort us with their illusory ability to name the un namable.

But in my heart, something more is going on. Why is the worship of many African American congregations so moving? Why do I come away from the liturgy of a Russian Orthodox Church physically exhausted but spiritually soaring? From whence comes the thrill in my breast as bright Brandenburg cadences dance through the hall? From what well flow the tears in my eyes as the plaintive wail of Louis Armstrong's trumpet engulfs me?

I am incapable of making what all others, save John Cage, might recognize as a legitimate musical sound, yet music has a strange power over me. I am not one who can discourse learnedly on technique and interpretation; I am naive almost completely. I am defenseless and completely at the mercy of the sonorous possibilities that await me at every concert. More than once I have been ambushed by clever composers or performers who set up decoys to occupy my mind, and then go straight for my heart. Most recently it has been Sergei Rachmaninoff, but in years past Johann Bach and Clifford Brown have alternately teased, taunted and finally taught me a great deal more about life than my mind was willing to grasp. "What we are is so much more than what we know, and what we know is so much more than what we understand… ."

Words may be our bridges but music is the rising dew, the meandering stream, the roaring cataract beneath — now gentle, now ominous, now elfish, now raging, now sorrowful, now luminous, now full of dread, now full of mystery. Where words circle or suggest our reality, music draws us deeply into it. Where words are our hypotheses, music is our affirmation.

Singing, especially. Singing is to humans as roaring is to lions, as neighing is to horses, as chirping is to birds. The breath of creation flows through us as it blows through tree branches and tumbleweed. When we stop singing, the breath of life is blocked in us, and life itself begins to wane.

From times immemorial, we have sung at the hearth, in public arenas, around campfires, in the market place. We have sung old songs and new. We have sung at birth and at war, in joy and in fear. Our songs have linked generations. What will become of our world when that last real songs pass from our memory, if no new songs take their place and if we are left only with iPods to fill the void?

Singing knows neither tomorrow nor yesterday, yet it links us to those who have gone before and those who will follow us. It gives energy, yields meaning and invites commitment. It originates in the mysterious depths of life itself and calls us into the Community of Life. It may be that my breath and your breath together produce the sound. But is that sound not waiting already on the lips of God, waiting for our breath to bring it to life in this world? When we truly sing together, do we not open ourselves to the breath of all life, the breath of all being, and let it sing its song through us?

Singing together — in concert, as it were — is one of the great pleasures in life. Whether the music divides us into parts or pulls us along from the beginning in some irenic unison, it fashions a community from the separate selves that we bring. As we give ourselves to song, does not the song give back to us? Although it depends upon our individual gifts, does not our singing transcend our individuality? It brings — at least for the moment — minds, hearts and bodies together with a common passion. My singing involves my commitment to life. Our singing together involves our commitment to share our lives in community.

We welcome the lilt and loveliness of our music. As its chords and cadences come to life among us, we honor the songs we sing.

It Was Bad Enough, Being Short

Blessed are you when people hate you, and when they exclude you, revile you, and defame you on account of the Son of Man. Rejoice in that day and leap for joy, for surely your reward is great in heaven; for that is what their ancestors did to the prophets. But woe to you who are rich, for you have received your consolation. Woe to you who are full now, for you will be hungry. Woe to you who are laughing now, for you will mourn and weep. Woe to you when all speak well of you, for that is what their ancestors did to the false prophets.
(Luke 6)

It was bad enough, being short. But to be non-athletic and to have a pockmarked face that resembled the surface of the moon — that made the curse unbearable. My teeth were crooked and my unruly hair defied the buckets of Brylcreem and the mountains of hair wax I applied each day. But there was one thing even worse. Call it my existential dilemma. In my tender teenage years, I was caught between two huge and conflicting sets of expectations.

On the one hand were my parents and my church. They encouraged me to be the best I could be, to study hard, to make everybody proud and to make the world sit up and take notice of me. Every accomplishment was celebrated. I was told that Jesus wanted me to be an honor student, to be well liked by my peers and to be happy from the inside out, with a joy that gushed through me like a river. True Christians are never sad, never have crises, and never ever feel inadequate because God's love has overcome all.

On the other hand were my parents and my church. They taught me that to succeed in the world was to fail in the eyes of God. If I were a true follower of Jesus, others would despise me. The Christian life is filled with suffering and the way of the cross leads home. To be concerned about my appearance was to neglect my soul, which was all that really mattered. Righteousness, not success or popularity, was the only goal worth pursuing. Righteousness meant not swearing, smoking, drinking, dancing, playing cards or having any fun on Sundays. Righteousness meant turning the other cheek when mocked. Righteousness meant carrying my Bible to school every day on top of my books as I moved from class to class as a witness to my more iniquitous peers. Righteousness meant maintaining a constant censorious attitude toward all that I saw or heard, filtering and disapproving the lewd, the crude and the stupid. Righteousness was equated with ignorance about sex; knowledge about sexuality was clear evidence of a carnal spirit. Jesus wanted me to be constantly repentant, constantly engaged in a spiritual warfare with the world, constantly struggling with the temptations of the flesh which, however, I was not supposed to understand.

I grew up trying desperately to be popular and despised simultaneously, successful and repentant at the same time. I discovered that to be successful was to fail, and to fail was to fail.

In fairness, my church also gave me clear and uncomplicated messages about the presence of God in all creation — in the sunrise and sunset, in the thunderstorm, in the corn growing under the hot summer sun. My church taught me to measure my life not in terms of the next ten days or ten years or even ten decades, but in terms of eternity. It taught me the importance of being useful, of making my life count for something beside myself, of serving others. My father and I and others worked side by side doing chores for people too frail to do them for themselves. My church, to its credit, began to raise the questions of racial justice — we would have called it "fellowship" — before 1954, before Brown versus Board of Education, before the civil rights movement of our time. Best of all, my church was a place where sinners could repent and start over and we, who knew their waywardness firsthand, cheered them on, wishing them every success.

But the tension I felt as a teenager was a real one. It was an existential dilemma then and it is an existential dilemma now. Even today I feel caught between our culture's definition of success and my Christian conscience. Resolving this dilemma is a fundamental problem.

Praising God with Dandelions

She has a knack for creating lovely arrangements with flowers and greens from her yard and the woods near her home. When she brings her work to grace our Sunday worship, we are reminded that all of nature joins with us in our joyful praise of God.

On one such Sunday, as she approached our meeting place, her daughter ran from behind and thrust a handful of dandelions into the middle of her carefully crafted arrangement. At first she was perturbed because she hardly had time to repair the damage. Then she decided to leave the arrangement exactly as it was, dandelions and all. Dandelions are everywhere, she thought, yet they are never included in anybody's arrangement. "Sometimes I feel like a dandelion," she explained during the coffee hour.

The dandelion, of course, is well known to all who would perfect their lawns. It is sturdy, tenacious, aggressive, prolific and capable of growing under the most adverse of circumstances. It is a survivor. It intrudes where it is not appreciated. It brashly disturbs the otherwise quiet elegance of a cultivated lawn. Powerful poisons have been designed to destroy it, but it returns.

Its greatest offense may be that it is so common. It takes no skill to grow a dandelion; having a crack in one's concrete step may be sufficient. I have never heard anyone brag, even in the most indirect manner, about the dandelions in their gardens.

To an impartial observer this may seem curious. The dandelion has all the requisites of a lovely and useful flower. It had an exotic name derived from the French *dent de lion*, or "lion's tooth", because of the toothlike outline of its leaves. Its soft yellow blossoms, when massed, create carpets of brilliant color over sunlit meadows and fields. Its puffballs possess a fragile beauty whose design has been copied by sculptors. Generations of earth's children have enjoyed blowing into these puffballs, watching them disintegrate and vanish in the breeze.

In ancient times the dandelion was considered a useful herb. Even today people add tender dandelion greens to their spring salads. The delicacy of the color, bouquet and taste of a well-made dandelion wine defies verbal description. This lowly flower may simply be the victim of a very bad press.

Someone once said that a weed is merely a flower misplaced. I quite agree. I am grateful to my young friend who saw the beauty and dignity of this common plant and who gave it the place of honor on a Sunday morning. She has not yet learned to see it as a weed. I suspect that she sees beauty in a great many other places that I overlook. Is it any wonder that so many of our spiritual leaders have insisted that children have the clearest vision of us all?

Economics of the Spirit

For where your treasure is, there will your heart be also.

(Matthew 6:21)

Jesus was a teacher, healer, mystic, or even a social revolutionary. Did you know that he also was an economist — perhaps one of the greatest of all times?

You may think that it is inappropriate, and perhaps even irreverent, to use the vocabulary of economics when referring to spiritual matters. How can economic terms begin to describe the pathos, passions and poetry of human longing? But when Jesus described "real life," he frequently sounded more like an economist than a shaman or a poet.

Jesus spoke of profit, gain, debt, loss, forfeiture, coins, livestock, inheritances, wise and foolish investments, shrewd purchases, the careful management of resources, bribes, the forgiveness of financial obligations, profligate spending, wages, bargaining, negotiation, water resources, farm crops, fruit trees, indulgent spending, the costs of health care, planting and harvesting, transportation, assets, reserves, the relative security of various forms of savings, poverty, employment, robbery, taxes and extortion. (This is the gospel truth!)

Economic activity is, of course, a universally human activity. Where two or more are gathered, economic arrangements must be made. By using the language of the market, Jesus appealed to a broadly based and deeply rooted human experience.

Could it be possible that our economic practices actually are measures of our spiritual maturity? Even more profoundly: Is our spiritual growth an expression of our economic commitments? Can such traditional spiritual activities as prayer, gratitude and even love itself be measured by their economic consequences? If we are uncomfortable talking about money in church, does this shows how far we have deviated from one of Jesus' most central and pressing concerns?

I would like to suggest some principles of "spiritual economics" for us to ponder.

(1) The spiritual realm is driven by an economics of abundance and

216

not by an economics of scarcity. In the grand scheme of things, the physical resources available for spiritual purposes are expandable and renewable far beyond our ability to imagine. Value is determined not by scarcity but by intrinsic loveliness and usefulness. Consider the lilies of the field. Whether it is "manna" from heaven or common loaves and fish, the material world is capable of reflecting the inexhaustible beauty and all-sufficient grace of its Creator.

(2) In the spiritual realm, as in any other, there are trade-offs to be considered and choices to be made. This is not because of a scarcity of resources, however, and most decisions need not be driven by grim necessities. Rather, it is because, in this economy of abundance, freedom characterizes all activity. We are free to choose this or that, to give or to hoard, to forgive or to keep accounts, to love or to hate, to cherish or to ignore, to be receptive or defensive, to serve or to dominate, to take up a cross or to nail another to it. We can gain the whole world, materially speaking, and forfeit our souls. We can amass great wealth into barns, warehouses and bank accounts and yet lose our true identities. "We become what we love," said Saint Augustine. "Where our treasure is, there will our hearts be also," taught Jesus.

(3) Capital formation, in the spiritual realm, occurs through the sacrifice of self and through the care and empowerment of others. "Sacrifice" means to make holy by offering to God. "Greater love has no one than this — that she lay down her life for a friend." In the spiritual realm, such sacrifice is not tragic but rather the epitome of fulfillment. To love God, self, neighbor and earth are the most important economic as well as spiritual commitments we can make.

Conversely, as the rich young ruler discovered, hoarding and accumulating assets can be stifling and counterproductive. To the degree that our neighbors (broadly defined) suffer physical, emotional or spiritual deprivation, and to the degree that we stand idly by, we also suffer the erosion of our souls.

(4) The formation of spiritual capital follows the law of increasing supply. The more I love, the more love I have to offer. The more I give of myself, the more of me there is to share. If I hide my light under a basket, if I bury the coins entrusted to my care, if I hoard my talents in a secret place, if I seek only my own happiness, I become less of a person and I have less to give and less to enjoy.

(5) The economy of the spirit is oriented primarily to the present because the spiritual realm exists only in the present. "Give us today our daily bread," we pray. Manna collected yesterday is worthless this morning. "Take no thought for tomorrow," Jesus taught, but take lessons from the foxes, birds and flowers. There can be neither a balance of God's grace carried forward from the past nor a rollover of that grace into the future. God's grace, which is sufficient for all purposes, must be claimed in the present moment if it is to be received at all.

(6) Paradoxically, today is the guardian of both yesterday and tomorrow. An economics of abundance neither encourages nor sanctions wasteful indulgence. The Bible instructs us in the preservation and prudent management of assets entrusted to our care. Pharaoh was counseled in a dream to gather the harvest while it was plentiful against the day when there would be famine in the land. The prodigal son who wasted his inheritance was not a role model to emulate.

The present encompasses the past and the future. Decisions and actions in the present will shape both the future we anticipate and the past we remember. We seek to conserve and transmit the collective inheritance we have received from the generations who came before us. We want to enrich the legacy we will bequeath to future generations. God's grace in the present moment can transform the evils and misfortunes of the past into stepping stones for growth. God grace today can create "a way out of no way" into an unimaginable excellence for us all.

(7) To be a steward is the defining characteristic of being human. God entrusts to each of us a share of the resources of creation. These are our assets. We are given time, money, skills, energy and aptitudes. They are not provided to us forever, or for our own benefit alone. They are given to us for the well being of creation, the improvement of our communities, and the healing of our world.

(8) It is better to forgive than to keep accounts of wrongs and rights. Keeping accounts for selfish reasons makes no sense in a realm of abundant resources where giving is the primary economic activity. Keeping accounts tempts us to selfishness and self-righteousness and thus restricts our access to spiritual resources. Keeping accounts ties up spiritual energies that can better be used for the formation of spiritual capital. Forgiving debts, trespasses and injuries, on the other hand, liberates both our debtors and us from the necessity of keeping accounts.

Forgiveness frees us to live energetically (rather than grudgingly) in the present. It allows us to love without regard to past behavior or future consequences. Our forgiveness of others demonstrates our knowledge that we ourselves live in a constant state of being forgiven for our own debts, trespasses and sins. Yet we experience this forgiveness only as we are able to truly forgive.

(9) It is better to be humble than to be great. It is better to give than to receive. It is better to serve than to rule. Our proper posture in the universe may be with basin and towel, kneeling to wash the feet of others, rather than with sword and scepter, seeking to conquer or rule over them. It is better to seek out the place of lowest rank, rather than to seek to sit at the head of the table. The place of highest honor is the place where the greatest service is performed.

Earth's Sacraments, Too

Some truths are universally valid for all people at all times. Perhaps this is the stuff of theology. Yet our circumstances inevitably shape our perceptions of these truths. Different people have different theologies. A theology that satisfies a New York City cab driver might not satisfy a long time resident of our area — not that his is true and ours is false, but simply that our life-experiences are quite different.

I embrace a natural theology which is rooted in life lived on this planet, organic life, communal life, and the solitary existence of us all. I believe in growth and decay, generation and dissolution, ebbing and flowing, surging and quietude. To me, the indigenous points to the transcend.

We are earth's children. What we make, we make from its substance. We participate in its rhythms. It feeds us, clothes us, shelters us, teaches us and receives us when we die. We celebrate its bounties and suffer its deficiencies. It speaks to us of ages when we were not; it calls out to unimaginable extensions when we shall not be. But when we are attentive, it tells more. It speaks of a primordial unity from which we have arisen and in which we yet participate. Through us, earth becomes conscious and hopeful; in us she transcends herself.

The ancients of the east called this unity *Tao*. In the west, we deemed it *Logos* (Word). Our ancestors taught us to look for God in the loving heart. Jesus said that the reign of God is already with us, if we can accept it like a child.

In the sacrament of baptism we accept from earth her natural gift of water — that lifeblood of the planet. In the ancient oceans of earth, and the watery wombs of our mothers, we recognize our origins. We come from water, are water and without it we die. Water, unadorned, is sacred and fit for our most solemn rituals.

But earth produces more. To grapes and wheat we add imagination and labor. These too are holy. In the Eucharist we offer for consecration not only earth's bounty but work done by farmers, wine makers and bakers, transporters, store owners and retail clerks.

In addition to the traditional meanings carried by these sacraments, they testify to our vital dependence on earth. As we experience this, we become aware of the immense significance of all things. New vistas break through our limited horizons and fill us with a sense of the uniqueness of each moment within the Eternity of Being. An ethic of reverence and agape for all things becomes the guiding force in our lives. We are "born again" to the earth and we see it with new eyes. "Truly God is here," we say.

In Us the Journey Is

Tony Kushner began his rambunctious chronicle of contemporary life, *Angels in America*, with an ending. But like the funerals of most admirable people, it carried a challenge as well — a challenge to persist, a challenge to continue and a challenge to keep faith.

Rabbi Isidor Chemelwitz — played by Meryl Streep in the HBO version — is conducting the last rites for a modern day Sarah — a woman who had left home, country and everything familiar to begin a new life in a foreign land. But Sarah Ironson had not so much left the villages of Russia and Lithuania as she had brought them with her to America. He told the assembled congregation that they are who they are today because of her tireless efforts and sacrifice. She had, he said,

> "... carried the world on her back across the ocean, in a boat, and she put it down on Grand Concourse Avenue, or in Flatbush, and she worked that earth into your bones, and you pass it to your children, this ancient, ancient culture, and home. You can never make that crossing that she made, for such Great Voyages in this world do not any more exist. But everyday (in) your lives the miles (of) that voyage between that place and this one you cross. Every day. You understand me? In you that journey is."

We don't have to be Jewish to appreciate this story. I once attended a retreat conducted by a woman of Lakota descent. She asked us each to bring a photo or emblem of what she called an "ancestor". When we arrived, she seated us in a circle. Each of us told the name and gave details about our particular ancestor, and why that person was important to us. Then she asked us to place these photos and emblems behind us. Though they never were mentioned again in the course of the retreat, they were there. Far too earthy to be called a "company of saints", or even a "great cloud of witnesses", nevertheless they were more than silent bystanders to our conversations. Their presence contributed to our dialogue and the room was filled with their presences.

Think of your ancestors. Take a moment right now and remember people who have shaped your faith (and your doubts) and contributed to your journey. See their faces. Imagine them sitting in front of you or behind you or beside you. See them for who they really are — flesh-and-blood fallible human beings, yet also human beings on a journey. How would your life be different if they had not lived or had not struggled with their own deepest questions?

Perhaps Mr. Kushner is right that, "Great Voyages in this world do not any more exist... ." Yet we know very well that now, "in us the journey is."

We have not chosen an easy journey. Like Abraham, Sarah and Hagar, we are called to step out into an adventurous journey, leaving behind the so-called certainties of the past. Like Noah, we are called to a radical vision that embraces the salvation of all creation, in spite of our neighbors' envy or disdain. Like the prophets we are called to speak for those who have no voice, often against those who want to hear only their own voices. Like Peter and Paul, Junia and Thecla, we are called to push the boundaries until our faith becomes truly diverse and global, and to serve the unknown God who is known in many faith traditions.

Great Voyages in this world (may) not any more exist... (yet) in us the journey is.

Sanctified

I spent nearly every Wednesday evening of my childhood in the social hall at St. Luke's Church. Wednesday evening was Prayer Meeting night. The faithful gathered at 7:30 to drone through a few great and familiar gospel hymns and then listen to Rev. Fulk elucidate, verse by verse and phrase by phrase, a chapter or two or three of the Bible book of the month. We shared our prayer concerns and then we entered into our "Season of Prayer".

To the eight year old I was, or the teenager I became, these were the most tedious moments of my life. We sat on hard metal folding chairs; my feet dangled above the dark green tile floor. I stared through rows and rows of attentive elders and out through the open windows into the backyards of my neighbors and friends. I heard the occasional crack of a bat against a ball accompanied by screams and cheers. I heard dogs barking, bicycles skidding, crickets chirping. I heard adults engaging in languid, lazy conversations on their front porches.

The voluptuous odors of honeysuckle, the heavenly aromas of baking bread, the ionized purity of storm-washed air would waft through the hall on the summer's breeze. I squirmed on my seat. I poked my sister's ribs. I fanned myself or the woman in front of me with one of the cardboard fans donated by Brown's Funeral Home. On some, Jesus stood forlornly at an ancient door, knocking and knocking, week after week after week. On others he sat gloomily with his hands folded piously in prayer, his face raised devoutly toward a distant light, his feet tucked snugly under a boulder.

The Bible study was difficult to sit through but the Season of Prayer was impossible. It could last for thirty minutes, thirty of the longest minutes on earth. Prayer time was never over until Rev. Fulk said, "Amen," and he would never say Amen until everybody had had their chance to pray. Over the years I observed that there were different kinds of pray-ers. There were the timid, lifting up their concerns in quiet, inaudible voices that only God could hear. There were the topical, who regurgitated what they had read in the daily paper. There were the sincere, who offered heartfelt prayers from within their various states of pain or gratitude.

And then there were the heavy hitters. This was their moment to shine. I learned to recognize the same phrases, the same cadences, and the same passions week after week. They jockeyed with one another for position, waiting interminably to be closest to the last "Amen". They sparred with one another in their prayers. Tears often streamed from their eyes. They quoted scriptures, taught theology and voiced their politics in their prayers.

Sometimes I tried to find the gumption to pray something, too. (I once prayed for the immediate end of the world. I guess I really wanted out.) More often than not, as I started to speak someone else intoned a "Dear Jesus" more loudly and more quickly than I, and I lost both my nerve and opportunity. I managed a few vocal prayers over the years, but my un-vocalized prayers were every bit as earnest. I prayed for my mother, father and grandmother, of course, but most of all (silently) I prayed that the Season of Prayer would be over before the last inning of the game.

Yet I have come to recognize that some of the most important directions of my life were laid down in those prayer meetings. I came to know and even to love God because of them. My deepest faith and my heart's vocation were established during those "Seasons of Prayer."

Over the years I discovered that I am something of a "contemplative". Silence has never felt empty to me. To the contrary, much of the noisiness of modern life oppresses me and quiet time can be restorative. (Gretchen says that she is going to have "Alone At Last" carved upon my tombstone!) Silence can be full, fertile and refreshing; it can be intimate and embracing. It has the capacity to enfold, soothe and heal.

As a child, I sometimes rose before dawn to hear the first bird sing; it is still one of my greatest pleasures. As teenagers, several of us — Jewish, Orthodox, and Protestant — rode bicycles to the park, hunkered down in a circle, read a few verses from our scriptures, and then we just sat. Silently. It was glorious. We discovered that we could be together — really together — in silence and prayer, when we could not be together in the public worship services of our respective faiths.

To quietly paddle across a lake, to noiselessly hike a mountain trail, to rest on a porch swing as thunder roars and rain falls, to walk hand in hand with the love of my life, to watch a candle flicker, a star twinkle, a dragonfly flit lightly across the surface of a river — these experiences contain more constructive significance for me than more glamorous or costly pursuits.

But back to Wednesday nights. During those prayer meetings there were long — very long — pauses between the prayers. These were the silences. In these quiet moments, in that room stilled by reverent expectations, in that holy hush, when the sound of my own breathing encountered only an occasional cough or creaking chair, when the sound of my own heartbeat was so near and the sounds of playing children so very far, it was then I encountered God and God entangled me.

It took many years to discover this simple fact. Unfortunately, I had identified "religion," "truth," "God" and "faith" with the words that others said about them. Because I had trouble with so many of those words, I was left with a kind of spiritual schizophrenia. I was unable to affirm the words required of me and unwilling to deny the innate awareness of God in my life.

Another aspect of those prayer meetings stands out after all those years. It was the absolutely ordinary quality of our concerns and our prayers. Week after week, year after year, we established a communal discipline of regularly bringing the substance of our lives to God in prayer. Rev. Fulk wasn't a guru from India. We weren't high rollers or high-wire artists, but common people with common concerns: a new home, a baby's illness, a daughter's graduation. We expected "no sudden rending of the veil of clay". The quietly transforming presence of Christ's Spirit in the midst of our routine and average lives was quite enough.

Finally, there was a real communion among us. Of course we annoyed each other. Can you tell? But we also cared deeply for one another, prayed for each other and shared the substance of our lives. In the same room where we gathered for prayer on Wednesdays, we gathered for food, fun and fellowship on other evenings. We were encouraged to pray for those we most resented and to examine our own behavior in the light of Christ's claim on us.

The whole intent of our congregational life might be summed up in a single word: "sanctification." Sanctification involves the gradual but deep transformation of our very being. Our sincere desire to yield to the sovereignty of Christ meets with God's exceeding graciousness toward us. It is a lifelong journey toward wholeness and a return to our original nature. It is Christ residing in us, love growing in us, the divine presence overshadowing us.

As we become increasingly aware of the magnitude of our frailty and sin, and our stubborn resistance to grace, we are driven toward remorse and humility. As we become increasingly mindful of the trustworthiness of God, and of our deep unity with God's creation, we are given an ecstatic appreciation for the radiant beauty that dwells within creation.

Sanctification involves aligning our will with God's will and our energy with the life-giving energy of God that permeates and percolates through the world. I suspect that this is close to what Orthodox Christians mean when they speak of deification, and what Benedictines mean by our "continual conversion to Christ".

Oblation

Snow fell quietly all night outside the windows of the small octagonal oratory. The single candle illuminating the room cast an uncertain light on the bare wooden walls. I had come to Saint John's Abbey, about two hours west of Minneapolis, for a solitary retreat. Earlier in the day the Director of the Episcopal House of Prayer, David Keller, had welcomed me to this retreat house. Now I was alone. Enfolded within the warmth and loveliness of this space, deep within the stillness of a Minnesota winter night, I began to cry. Two icons of the Theotokos emerged from the flickering shadows to become, in a very real sense, companions in my solitude. Tears of relief, tears of an immense sadness, tears I cannot begin to explain trickled down my cheeks. I knew I was where I needed most to be.

I had been born on my mother's birthday, and given my father's name. My mother died in a Utah nursing home on April 19, 1995 — the same day that Timothy McVeigh drove his truck up to the federal building in Oklahoma City. My father, felled by a stroke some years before, remained a patient in the same nursing facility. I remember nothing about the bombing. I remember every detail of the phone call from my sister.

This was my fiftieth birthday, the first without my mother. In the morning I walked over to the Abbey Church for Morning Prayer. The Guest Master welcomed me to sit in the choir stalls; other guests guided me through the several books of prayer, scripture and song. During the day I found myself drawn to a small alcove where a Twelfth Century Burgundian carving of Mary solemnly but gently held her Child, the King. In that dimly lit room she was not just the mother of Jesus, but the Great Mother, not just a nurturing parent but the substance from which the Christ emerges. She was not just the vessel of divinity but its throne, and not just its bearer, but its expression. My hand trembled as I placed a votive candle before this ancient sculpture. Though my Methodist mother never would have understood, this candle was for her, and for us, and for all that had passed between us down all the years.

During the next few months I returned frequently to participate in the prayers of this community. I began to learn more about the Abbey and the Order of Saint Benedict. I became acquainted with various monks*, and with the veritable beehive of activities fostered by this contemplative community. I became an "oblate candidate" of the Abbey. I — a Protestant minister, married and the father of two children — began to explore a deeper connection and a committed relationship with this Roman Catholic Benedictine monastery.

Oblates are men and women who do not live in the monastery but who choose to associate with a particular monastery to deepen their Christian spirituality. Although they live "in the world" they make promises to seek God more intensely through the principles of the *Rule of St. Benedict* and in partnership with the monks of the Benedictine community with which they are affiliated. Saint John's has over 700 oblates worldwide. They are male and female, single and married, gay and straight, lay and clergy, Protestant and Catholic, liberal and conservative. I learned that one becomes an oblate of a particular monastery and not with the Order in general. However, through my commitment to Saint John's I would be connected to a venerable spiritual tradition and a global spiritual community.

Under the tutelage of Father Allen Tarlton, OSB, the Abbey's Oblate Director, I began to study the *Rule of Saint Benedict* and the history of the Order and this Abbey. I began to read Benedictine authors. I began to fashion a daily "rule" for my own spiritual life, something that had been missing before this time.

Becoming an oblate implies a kind of mutuality of care and concern. I would be assuming a responsibility for the well being of the monks and they would be assuming a responsibility for mine. I would be expected to carry the Benedictine witness into in my setting, even as the monks care for the world in theirs. My appreciation for both the wisdom and practicality of the Benedictine ethos grew as I learned more about my own need for a balanced life of prayer, study and work. I began to understand my journey as a process of continual conversion to Christ. I found that Benedictine virtues such as attentiveness and careful listening, stability, hospitality, community and even obedience have the capacity to enrich the ministry I bring to others.

---

* At Saint John's Abbey the monks obviously are men. I use "monks" as the gender-inclusive term it originally was. Many women monastics prefer "monks" and "monasteries" to the more common designations of "nuns", "sisters" and "convents".

The following summer, I accepted a call to serve a congregation in Atlanta, Georgia. The move from Minnesota was profoundly disorienting for me and my family. For reasons I am only beginning to understand, my relationship to Saint John's became more important even as I was more distant from it. I communicated with Father Allen and others mostly by e-mail while I continued with preparations for my oblation.

Then on December 18, 1997 my father died. He had been my Boy Scoutmaster, my teacher and the best man at our wedding. For over four years he lay in a nursing home, a continent away from our hometown in West Virginia. He was paralyzed, couldn't speak, walk or even feed himself. We don't know how much he understood. His death released him from what had become the pain and burden of his flesh but it left me a "stranger in a strange land."

We returned to Martinsburg for his funeral, but most of my friends had moved away. The vast extended family of my upbringing was, for the most part, gone. One night I dreamed that I was adrift in a small boat on a dark sea with no oars, no anchor nor any guiding light.

My vivid memories of these monks and their occasional communications with me deeply refreshed my spirit and contributed to my healing. There is something transparent — "thin" as the Irish say — about Saint John's for me. Of course the Abbey is a temporal community, subject to the foibles and corruptions of any human project. But unlike any other community of which I am aware, it points beyond itself to the domain of the Eternal. Though I live far from these monks, I carry within me a daily remembrance of them. In my mind's eye I see the tailors, bakers and university professors. I see them in Birkenstocks with cell phones tucked beneath their scapulars, and in jeans and heavy parkas. I see men in black spiraling day by day and year by year through the turnstiles of the daily office.

I couldn't return to the Abbey until the following summer, when I happily made my "final oblation". I felt then, and I feel each time I return, a profound sense of coming home.

Between Cloister and Congregation

On Friday I will travel to Saint John's Abbey, a monastic community of the Order of Saint Benedict in Collegeville, Minnesota. On the Feast Day of Saint Benedict, I intend to make what is called my "Final Oblation." I will be entering into a deeper relationship with that particular monastic community, with a worldwide fellowship of Benedictines as diverse as anything we in the UCC can imagine, and with a tradition of spiritual formation that reaches back 1500 years to Nursia, Subiaco and Monte Cassino, and to Saints Benedict and Scholastica, his sister.

To make an "Oblation" is to become a lay associate of a particular monastery. Oblation comes from the Greek term for offering; I offer myself to Christ through this attachment. I will be committing to a *Rule* as well as to a community, to a practice as well as to an ethos. To make a Final Oblation is to take the last step of a two year process of prayer, study and mutual discernment. It thrills me to join with other candidates on the very day that the monks make their solemn vows to live according to *The Rule of Saint Benedict*.

By making this Oblation, I am beginning to honor the contemplative side of my life, the part that had nowhere to go when I abandoned the fundamentalism that provided the formative framework of my early years. Benedictines understand and welcome the fullness within the silences.

But though a contemplative, Benedict was an immensely practical man. He located the Sacred within ordinary acts of daily living. For example, he instructed us to treat the undistinguished implements of pedestrian life as sacred vessels. He was a brilliant a psychologist and a perceptive spiritual director. He paid enormous attention to the nuances of our living in community. He recognized the differing needs of differing personalities.

I find in him a kindred voice. To seek and find the Holy within the commonplace, to honor the vast diversity of individuals in a community, to know that even the most petty of our squabbles contains opportunities for the most profound spiritual learning, all of this I also have come to believe with heart and soul.

Benedictines place high values on listening, hospitality, humility, balance, rootedness (stability), work, leisure, community, simplicity, and prayer. These are marks of spiritual restfulness in a world that is suffocating from greed, selfishness and consumption. Benedictines often speak of our spiritual life as a "continual conversion to Christ." By making this Oblation, I am beginning anew to examine my own life in terms of Christ's truth, to turn toward Christ and to seek the health and wholeness God desires for me.

Does my Oblation have significance for us as a community of faith? We have our own traditions, disciplines and continuous history. Yet I go to St. John's not simply as an individual, but also as an ordained minister within the United Church of Christ and as your pastor. We are Protestant; Benedictines are Catholic. We are congregational; they are monastic. Is this an appropriate decision?

It is noteworthy that the Order of Saint Benedict has its roots in an era of our common history that predates the divisions and schisms of later times. Before there were Protestants, Catholics and Orthodox there were Benedictines. The Order of Saint Benedict is honored in both East and West. It is one of the most open and ecumenical of all Catholic orders. There are Benedictine communities within the Catholic, Orthodox, Anglican, Methodist and ecumenical communions.

The United Church of Christ has always embraced its own great ecumenical dream: "That they may all be one." This vision appears on our logo; it is actually Christ's prayer recorded in John's gospel. It is a Benedictine prayer as well. Anyone who carries this prayer in his or her heart will receive a congenial and generous affirmation from the Benedictines.

Local congregations of any persuasion have much to learn from the monastic experience. For over 1500 years the Rule of Saint Benedict has guided and formed the life of voluntary spiritual communities. People are people, whether vowed monastics or covenanted church members. Need is need. Prayer is prayer. St. Benedict's advice to abbots and monks can be instructive for local pastors and their congregations.

The great modern religious pilgrim, Thomas Merton, once said that we will never overcome the divisions of this world until we are able to take them into ourselves. The most appropriate place for this meeting of separate traditions is within the hearts, prayers and practices of all who seek wholeness for our world. It is with this spirit of seeking unity that I will travel to Collegeville on Friday. I ask that you hold me in your prayers.

Start Seeing Motorcycles

"Start Seeing Motorcycles!" the bumper sticker screams from the car in front. No doubt an enthusiast for the open road, I think, or an anxious mom. These words assume (rightly) that most of us don't see motorcycles. They imply (also rightly) that road running cyclists (and not the rest of us) are most at risk when drivers fail to see them. They remind us of the obvious: bikers are especially vulnerable in accidents. The conclusion surely follows that all of us on the road share a particular responsibility for the safety and well being of motorcyclists. To see them means to respect them, to treat them with common courtesy, to yield rights-of-way and, sometimes, to give them the benefit of a doubt. Not to see them means to violate their space, cut them off and marginalize them as citizens of the highway.

Some people don't like cyclists. If you are one of these, already you are conjuring rear view images of leather clad, motor-gunning, chain laden, grungy, frowning, freeway marauders who interrupt the serenity of your Sunday drive, who rapidly bear down on you with God knows what intent, who arrogantly weave, pass, and lean recklessly into the ground. You see helmet-less hair trailing in the wind. And you are thinking, "Who do they think they are, anyway? Why should I be responsible for them?"

But you are. And the bumper sticker is right. Whether our vehicles have two wheels or ten, highway travel is a great equalizer. We have responsibility for each other. It behooves us to see everyone on the road we share.

To start "seeing" motorcycles is to discover something important. Bikers are as diverse as shoppers. For every "Hell's Angel" there is a college student on a Harley. More than 500,000 bikers will converge in Sturgis, South Dakota, for the 70th Annual Road Rally in August. There may be violent types among them, but there also will be attorneys, doctors, dancers and housewives. There will be potheads and teetotalers, carnivores and vegetarians. There will be weekend riders and those colorful free spirits who meander the continent like medieval vagabonds. Some may be living out their wildest machismo fantasies, but most will be plain and friendly folks. They are part and parcel of the multicultural stew of contemporary America. Not to see them not only endangers them; it impoverishes our own cultural self-understanding. I wonder how many other people I see, but fail to see, because of my fears, prejudices and stereotypes?

I wonder also how many people fail to see me even when I stand directly in front of them. Do they see only my suit and tie, my white skin and balding pate, but fail to see me? Do our jobs, gender, race, age, physique, accent, religion, or neighborhood get in the way? Do our tattoos and piercings or lack thereof make us invisible to one another? I'm ready for another bumper sticker: "START SEEING EACH OTHER!" Do you think it will sell?

Defender Of Frogs

I know that we just finished a sumptuous meal. My remarks may seem in-delicate for such a solemn occasion. If you are squeamish and this speech makes you a little uncomfortable, for that I apologize in advance. How-ever, I see no other way to make my point. While I will do everything I can to spare you discomfort, I will understand if some of you need to retreat from the hall from time to time. Such is the price a speaker must pay if he is to say the full salientian truth in times like these.

Those of you who have been in the Parish for a long time know that Doug's office is full of frogs. Although no more real than the velveteen rabbit, they are everywhere, all shapes and sizes. There are ceramic, cloth, wooden and other varieties of frogs. There are frog cards, frog clothing, and frog pictures everywhere. Not since the Israelites escaped from Egypt has the world seen such an anuran concentration.

In today's world, of course, we are psychologically sophisticated. We know these fixations do not arise randomly. They symbolize deep subconscious truths about us. It occurred to me that if we could but penetrate the mystery of frogness, we would have a truer understanding of Doug, and the meaning of his ministry with us. He has been, dare I say, the embodiment of this myth in the Parish, and also of the Hunters Woods Congregation that is widely and probably irrevocably known as the "frog kissing congregation".

The Encyclopaedia describes the frog as "a small, tailless animal with bulging eyes." Frogs are amphibians, of the orders Salientia and Anura. "True frogs" are a class apart, and classy. Scientists carefully distinguish them from toads and other imposters. The Encyclopaedia Britannica notes that the name "frog" is often used to distinguish typically smooth skinned, leaping amphibians from the squat, warty, hopping ones often called "toads".

A recent Norwegian immigrant tried to define the frog with precision. In *The Houston Chronicle*, he wrote: "What a wonderful bird the frog are. When he stand, he sit almost. When he hop, he fly almost. He ain't got no sense hardly. He ain't got no tail hardly, either. When he sit he sit on what he ain't got, almost." (Really, does this not also sound like a splendid definition for an ecumenical Parish like ours?)

Frogs live on every continent, except Antarctica. Like the Parish, they are relatively new on the planet; the first frog appeared only 180 million years ago, a mere watch in the night in God's time. And like the Parish, they are relatively rare; only 2700 species are known ever to have existed. (Compare this to the 800,000 kinds of snails, for example.)

Frog sizes vary from the foot long "Goliath frogs" to those of less than half an inch. They have many colors and body configurations. There are tree frogs, flying frogs, hairy frogs, climbing frogs, land frogs, water frogs, even 'dagger' frogs whose thumbs have become sharp spines.

Frogs are known for good eyesight, but did you know that their eardrums are located in their eye sockets? Did you know they have an abundance of taste buds in their tongue and mouth? Did you know they have a very delicate sense of touch? This is because they, unlike the warty toads, have a smooth, thin skin. Did you know that, in most species, only the males have a voice?

Frogs have appeared in human literature from ancient times. One of the great satires of all times, written when that genre was still in its infancy, was a play by Aristophanes called *The Frogs*. In it the poet lashed out with prophetic vehemence against contemporary evils and attacked the war policies of contemporary policy makers.

In scripture, frogs are the second plague inflicted by God upon the Egyptians in a liberation struggle. If you remember, they invaded even the kneading troughs of cooks and bakers and the bedroom of the king.

Around the world frogs appear in fairy tales with double or hidden identities: they are princes, princesses, queens and kings, but also brides, witches, sons, daughters, wives, and travelers. Frogs are paired with a variety of God's creatures: oxen, antelopes, crabs, crows, hens, leopards, snakes, hogs, horses, weasels, and bulls, to name a few.

Frogs found their way not only into Pharaoh's bedroom, but into classical and modern literature as well. Frogs are the subject of much prose and poetry: not just Aristophanes, the Bible and fairy tales, but also many ancient Greek poets (one of whom actually wrote a poem that begins: "Oh, to be a frog!") as well as Keats, Goethe, Shakespeare, Dickens, Emily Dickinson, Mark Twain, even Dylan Thomas. There have been famous frogs and frog celebrities, like the prince who needed kissing, the celebrated jumping frog, the frog king, and now my son's favorite, Kermit the Frog.

John Bunyan described the frog rather unfavorably: "... by nature damp, cold, mouth large, belly much will hold." Conrad Aiken describes the frog as "ancient and omniscient" who chuckles a "gross, venereal hymn". Charles Lamb was most unflattering when he described a poor relation as (among other embarrassments) "a frog in your chamber". Of course, we all know what little boys are made of in addition to snails and puppy dog tails.

Virgil described the frog's sound as an "old lament". Another writer, more down to earth, thought the frog an apt symbol for religion and especially for those who believe in eternal life. He said that the frog is the only living thing that has more lives than a cat. It croaks every night.

Izaak Walton, writing in 1653, in his book *The Compleat Angler*, wrote: "Thus use your frog... Put your hook through his mouth, and out at the gills, and then, with a fine needle and silk, sew the upper part of his leg, and with only one stitch, to the arming wire of your hook... and in so doing you will use him as you love him." If this be love... .

Most poignantly, the Roman Plutarch: "Though boys throw stones at frogs in sport, the frogs do not die in sport, but in earnest."

Like frogs, many people in today's world appear to be unsightly, un-seemly, unpleasant, and an embarrassment to most. They may be homeless, poor or otherwise disenfranchised, in Washington D.C., on the pathways of Reston, in South Africa — indeed, on all the continents except Antarctica. Many of the holders of power and wealth love the little people like Izaak Walton loved the frogs; their embrace conceals a very hard edge indeed. Many of us in more affluent circumstances may treat the poor as the Roman boys did the frogs — as objects of sport. But they, like the frogs, are not dying in sport; they are dying in earnest.

Your ministry Doug, where it has succeeded most, has been as a De-fender of the Frogs, as one who reminds us in many ways of the conse-quences of our actions and our decisions. You call us to kiss the frogs, and to liberate the royalty imprisoned therein. Your ministry deserves the greatest respect and appreciation, and for that we all say, humbly and with gratitude, a profound Thank You!

Homily or Sermon?

In recent months I have found myself wanting to substitute the word "homily" for "sermon" in our Sunday orders of worship. "This is curious," I said to myself. "What is this about?"

At first I suspected my desire to appear more southern than I have a right to claim to be. Homily. Hominy. Homily. Hominy. Homily. Hominy. This word association evokes all things truly southern. The very sound of it suggests a languid, non-pretentious, warm morning, southern repast. Perhaps I will even develop a drawl.

"Hominy" derives from the Algonquin term for grain; it never occurs alone. What is its partner? "Grits." True grits. Real Southerners spot us interlopers a mile away:

"What would you like for breakfast, sir?"

"I'll have a grit."

"A grit? I'm sorry, sir. They never come alone."

I think a good sermon ought to be a little "gritty", don't you? Grits on your plate keep you humble. The best upscale sermons ever savored still have some down home common sense about them.

But I don't think this is it. My Catholic friends point out that they "do" homilies while Protestants "do" sermons. So maybe there's a wannabe priest lurking in my robe. But while I confess to being an ecu-maniac, and believe with every fiber of my being that we should work that "all may be one", I have no desire to exchange the riotous freedoms of our tradition for the particular restrictions of another.

I asked my erudite colleagues to tell me the difference between a homily and a sermon. No one seems to know. I asked you who sit through them. "Homilies are shorter," you say. With all due respect, I think you beg the question. Certainly my homilies are not shorter. ("Pastor," pleaded one member, "your words don't have to be eternal in order for them to be immortal.")

Finally I looked in the dictionary. Homily is rooted in the Greek *homiletikos*, meaning "conversation." Sermon comes directly from medieval

Latin for "speech", and that probably derives from *serere*, "to link together or string together" like beads on a necklace. While both words carry the meaning of "a religious discourse before a congregation," the nuance of homily is "an informal exposition usually of Scripture." Sermon carries the additional shade of "an annoying harangue".

I am allergic, by temperament, to harangues. I cherish dialogue. I like the thought that what I say from the pulpit is one piece of a much longer conversation that has been going on for centuries.

So as I prepare for our worship, perhaps I am asking myself this question: "What shall it be this Sunday? An informal exposition, or an annoying harangue? A speech, or a searching conversation?"

A Calm and Anxious Presence

I want to tell you a story. Certainly I did not tell it to any search committee that interviewed me. But before I tell you this story, I have to tell you another one to help you grasp the full significance of what I am about to say.

In 1971 my car caught on fire. We were visiting friends in the country, farmers who lived just north of the Shenandoah Valley. The ink had not dried on the auto loan documents when this, shall we say, "vintage" diesel burning Peugeot caught fire in a country lane. Far from any fire station (or even telephone), we watched it burn.

After it cooled, I had it towed. An insurance adjustor made a visit. Walking around the charred remnant of our pride-and-joy, and my only means of transportation, he simply shook his head. He kept clicking his tongue. "Totaled," he said. "Where should I send the check?"

We were between seminary and my first church that summer, between Princeton and South Paris, so I asked him to mail it to my parents' home in West Virginia. "Done," he said, and he left. A few days later, a check for $1,500 arrived in the mail.

Since we were in transition, we had closed our bank account in New Jersey and had not opened one in Maine. My parents agreed for us to deposit the check in their account until we got settled. Then we would transfer the money, pay off the loan, and go from there.

My father and I went into the local bank. This was the same bank our family had used for 25 years. My father knew everyone in the bank and they knew him. Nevertheless, he was nervous. Very nervous. As we approached the teller to deposit the money, I noticed that he dispensed with his usual pleasantries. A simple transaction in those days could take up to twenty minutes as people exchanged information about their children, their church, the weather or a host of other matters.

Not this time. Rather than just depositing the check, my father obviously felt the need to explain why he would be putting such an extraordinary amount of money in his bank account. He actually was apologizing, or so it felt to me. He explained the fire, the insurance settlement, and our plan to transfer the funds. To the teller!

As worldly and sophisticated as I had become at the age of 25, I was annoyed with my father's embarrassment. Why should he, Gilbert Jones, my father, have to explain a $1500 check to anybody? "Let them wonder," was my attitude.

But in that moment I had a sudden revelation: Money made my family nervous. Large sums of money made us especially uneasy. A $20 bill was a scary thing to us. It was rarely seen, used or handled. If one happened to make its way into our house, we would pass it around the dinner table and marvel at it; it was more precious than gold, frankincense and myrrh. We were accustomed to nickels and dimes, not to $1500 checks. Our biggest investments, other than our modest home on Virginia Avenue, were our Christmas Club accounts, a few savings bonds, and my father's coin collection.

It was with this deeply internalized history of money jitters that I will now tell what I have told no congregation before. I had just arrived as the new senior minister. I was still moving into my office, unpacking my books and setting up my desk. The staff and the members were still taking my measure. I fantasized that they needed to see an experienced and confident leader. In fact, the buzzword for successful leadership in those days was "non-anxious." I was trying to display my cool, non-anxious presence for all to see.

The Conference staff had told me that this church especially needed non-anxious leadership. It was coming through an enormous upheaval. In the previous two years it had lost half of its pledge base to other churches. Attendance was plummeting; many of the people who remained were unhappy with each other. I had to hit the ground running. I would have to be skilled at conflict resolution and at convincing the church that its future was viable.

So I was in my office unpacking my books in a non-anxious way, having confidence-inspiring coffee with the staff, and getting to know the office volunteers. The mail arrived. Included in the mail was a small envelope. It was addressed by hand to "The Pastor". It bore one of those "Love" stamps in the corner, and the sender's name and address in the other.

When I opened it, a check dropped out. No letter, no explanation, except in the "Memo" on the check itself: "From the estate of ... " and it gave the name of a deceased member. The check was exactly like those checks we write at the grocery store. It had been written by hand, and it was for $235,417.35. This was more than the entire endowment of that congregation.

If ever one needed proof that "the acorn never falls far from the tree" this was it. I sat at my desk with this check in my hand, and I was paralyzed. My mind went numb. I did not know what to do. I wasn't sure whom to call, or what procedure to follow. I didn't know whether this church handled these matters confidentially, or if I should share the good news with everyone.

Well, I thought, I've got to do something. So I decided to photocopy the check. I don't know why I decided to do that but it seemed like a good, non-anxious action to take.

I carried the check into the workroom, past a table around which volunteers were collating the newsletter. We enjoyed some polite small talk between us while this secret check grew hotter and heavier in my hand. I went over to the copier, placed the check face down on the glass and hit the button. Once, twice, five times. I collected the copies of the check and nonchalantly made my way around the volunteers back to my office. I looked at the copies and wondered what I should do next.

But something was not quite right. The copies were there, but not the original. With horror it dawned on me that the check itself was missing. I investigated every pocket at least a dozen times. I looked around my chair, under my desk, in my chair. My heart sank. I retraced my steps. Now pale and obviously anxious, I tried to engage in more small talk with the volunteers while I also furtively scoured the floor. I looked on the copier, under it and tried to be inconspicuous while looking under their chairs and everywhere I could imagine. "What are you looking for?" they asked. "Oh, nothing important," I responded, "just a piece of paper I was copying."

But it was nowhere to be found. It had vanished. Gone. I slunk back to my big executive desk and pondered my fate. My first administrative act as an experienced and confident leader was to lose a check for $235,000. It took me less than half an hour to sabotage a promising career. I was sure that only the guillotine itself could right so grievous a wrong.

I was composing my letter of resignation when Helen, the Associate Minister, popped her head in the door of my office. She waved the check at me. "Let's see," said with huge grin on her face, "Hmmm. $235,417.35.

Is this the little piece of paper you were looking for?" She was laughing. "I found it behind the copier."

My life had been restored to me. By this I mean not just a check for $235,000.

If I may digress: in that moment she also punctured my haughty pretension to confident leadership. She made leadership by posturing — even non-anxious posturing — impossible. In its place came the important realization that a calm, non-anxious presence is not a posture that can be learned. It flows from a true vision of the strengths and weaknesses of the church. It derives from a genuine faith in God's power to transform any situation and in people's abilities to respond in new ways to changing circumstances. The church required not a calm non-anxious leader but a pastor who loved them, listened to them and cared.

But I do also mean the check. I don't mean to be crass but at that point in time I had been reunited with something of extraordinary importance. I nearly jumped over the desk. I still remember — I still feel — the enormous relief of that moment. I was elated. I was euphoric. I didn't know her well enough to hug her but at that moment I would have climbed the highest mountain for her if she had but asked.

¡Ojalá!

Ojalá is one of the most beautiful words in any language. It is Spanish, and pronounced Oh-ha-LAH. It expresses a strong desire for something to come to pass. Ojalá I will get the job! Ojalá she will sell the house to us! Ojalá he will win the tournament! Modern Spaniards say it means "may it be so" or "I hope that" or "I wish that" something will happen.

But like many of other words (goodbye, for example) its meaning is much richer than this. It expresses a nearly universal sentiment that is religious to its core.

For historical reasons, many Spanish words are rooted in Arabic. Ojalá is one. Its predecessor in Arabic is *Insha'Allah!* — "if God wills." To this day when pious Arabic speakers plan for the future, or make promises, resolutions or pledges, they begin or end with Insha'Allah — if God wills. A friend recently announced her wedding plans by saying, Insha'Allah, Hud and I will be married this summer."

Ojalá and Insha'Allah both introduce a note of deep uncertainty about life. We will marry — if God wills. In the face of circumstances beyond our control, ojalá expresses an attitude of profound humility and acceptance. We declare our strong desire or intention, but the success of our endeavor does not depend upon a particular outcome. In West Virginia we say it this way: "Lord willin' and the creek don't rise."

Unless I am a saint, however, God's will and my wishes often clash. If I haven't given my life into God's hands, then ojalá takes its thinner, more modern meaning: "I wish" or "I hope". "I hope the Braves win." God becomes the servant of my self-indulgence: "I want God to make it possible for me to have this house!"

But the recognition of uncertainty concerning everything I cherish also may reveal a greater certainty — the certainty of a fundamental commitment. If I have committed my life to God, then ojalá ("if God wills") is what I most truly want. I may yearn to own this house, to marry or to get that job but I crave even more to fulfill God's purpose for my life. Jesus ended his famous prayer with its Aramaic equivalent: "I want to avoid this suffering," he said, "but — ojalá — your will be done."

Medieval Spaniards, contemporary Arabs and traditional West Virginians share this basic piety. In the proper ordering of a life lies the intrinsic beauty of this word.

The Intimate Crucible

My mother valued achievement highly, and the outward recognition that comes from it. But my father never trusted public adulation and would often quote the text where Jesus says "Blessed are you when people revile and persecute you for my name sake, for great is your reward in heaven." My mother worried constantly about the future, while father exuded a Zen-like enjoyment of living in the present. My mother tried to budget the family's meager resources; my father couldn't resist yard sales, flea markets and bargains at the local store.

My father's family was vaguely nomadic, living variously in the rural areas and small towns nestled around the Alleghany Mountains; my mother's family was rooted in "civilized" communities along the Potomac. My father's family were manual laborers all, while my mother's family included preachers, governors and senators from Virginia. In her mind and heart my mother was what many would call a fundamentalist. Though he also was a devout believer, my father could not resist questioning every assumption and challenging every text. My father never understood the racism of the Klansmen (and women) on my mother's side of the family.

These differences felt irreconcilable to me. Both of my parents made heroic efforts to create and sustain a common ground. Both were on lifelong journeys to reconcile the differences that their parents had bequeathed to them. Each was appreciative and deeply loving toward the other, and toward us. But the intense proximity of their different orientations engendered the questions of a lifetime for the next generation. Long after my mother and father have gone from us, my sister and I still wrestle daily with these matters.

"Achieve. Accomplish. Make us proud."/"Be humble. Be careful. Serve others."

 "Stay close to home."/"Explore the world."

"Be disciplined. Work hard."/"Relax. Enjoy the moment."

"Seize the day."/"Be patient."

"Fight for what you believe."/"Don't be violent or cause harm."

"Be assertive."/"Don't be pushy."

I have careened on my path from *Crazy* by Patsy Cline to *The Passion According to St. Matthew* by Johann Sebastian Bach, from country ham to escargot, from earthy humor to a longing for refinement and distinction.

It is not too much to say that all families are in some ways like this. In today's mobile global village it is even more likely as we form unions across religions, nationalities, languages and other differences. But even if we meet and marry someone within our own economic and social strata, we are uniting differing cultures. I have known people who grew up on the same block and went to the same schools only to discover in their marriages the vast distance between their psychic "beginning places".

All families contain imperatives and contradictions, and often contradictory imperatives. To the child who inherits them, their reconciliation is never easy. It is, in fact, the work of their lifetime. It involves a search for deep integrity. It will carry them far beyond where they began.

Such familial conundrums summon us into uncharted territory. They cannot be resolved by the capitulation of one to the other in an either/or sort of way. But they can generate enough energy to carry us into new awareness and discovery.

For integrity's sake, we must reckon with our starting places, and suffer the questions we inherit. As we do, some of us will develop new vocabularies, see new visions and hope new hopes. When we do, the world will be better for it.

Pies, Mugs and Votive Candles

But Jesus said to him, "Friend, who set me to be a judge or arbitrator over you?"

(Luke 12:14)

The Friday evening blowout for Ray and Birgitta Banner was being planned. There were — as you might expect — many meetings to make decisions: the tent, the food, the entertainment, the costs, the beverages. The volume of e-mails increased dramatically as the date approached. Among the last questions to be raised — repeatedly — were these: Would we have enough pies? Enough beer mugs? Enough votive candles? (The mugs, I hasten to add, were for floral arrangements.)

It occurred to me that more was at stake here than supplies for a celebration. The tent and tables, the ribs and hotdogs, the skits and music, a fire truck, even the "Jesus Loves You" hand stamp — all these assured that the party would be a success. Why were we so preoccupied with pies, mugs and votive candles?

Well, how do you symbolize a ministry? A bishop has her miter, a queen her scepter, a welder her blowtorch, and a schoolteacher his chalk. But what are the deep symbols of your ministry among us, Ray? The planners probed deeply into FCC's collective unconscious and three symbols emerged: pies, mugs and votive candles. These have been the symbols of your pastoral office.

Pies. Pies are America's prototypical comfort food. How many pies have you eaten at church functions in the course of your ministry? Usually sweet, almost always nourishing, pies invariably remind us of home and family. Their presence on church tables is a reminder that our faith began in homes; at its best, our congregation continues to function as an extended family. You, Ray, have fed us, nourished us, comforted us, and sweetened us. No matter how challenging the circumstances FCC has faced, you gently called us to be family to one another and to make this place our home.

Mugs. Maybe a cross, an icon or a box of tissues are suitable symbols for other clergy. In our collective discernment, however, the beer mug emerged as yours. There is more than a hint of irreverence in this symbol, intentionally. People think of the Spirit when they think of ministry, but we know there also are spirits, and never the twain shall meet. When we worship the Spirit, we put on our "go-to-church" demeanor; when we get out the mugs we let our hair down — such as it is! Mugs speak of conviviality, fellowship and good times. Mugs help us not to take ourselves so seriously. More than most pastors, Ray, you taught us that the sacred and the silly are never far apart. Like Jesus, you refused to bless the pompous, and no one will ever accuse you of holding to a "terminally serious" faith. Yours is a seamless spirituality that embraces the fullness of human experience. You inspired us to be ourselves – perhaps because you always knew that our true selves bear the image and likeness of divinity.

Votive Candles. Candles, of course, add a touch of elegance to every occasion. They did on Friday night. They offer light and warmth, but always in a quiet and gentle manner. Votive candles especially do not draw attention to themselves: they are designed to express reverence for the saints and prayers for the rest of us. Candles are symbols of self-giving generosity; only by burning do they fulfill their destinies. In a sense, they exist entirely for others. Their flames, partaking of ancient mysteries, have accompanied us down through the centuries. Scripture speaks of the column of Fire that led God's people in the darkness through the wilderness, the Fire that consumed the people's offerings, the tongues of Fire that empowered God's people at Pentecost. Your quiet and gentle presence, Ray, graced us with elegance, warmth and light. But even more, you invited us to live in the presence of mystery, of the Holy Fire that guides, consumes, empowers and transforms.

In today's scripture lesson, two people in the crowd wanted Jesus to settle a dispute for them. He responded that conducting negotiations and passing judgment was not why he had come. Too many of his would-be successors have been all too quick to do just that by issuing edicts and passing judgments on everyone. But not you, Ray. "Help us to understand… ," you said repeatedly. Instead of passing judgment Jesus tried to reframe their apparent dilemma. Their dispute over an inheritance that seemed huge to them disappears if they can but learn the true nature of the world in which they live — a world of infinite resources, a God of awesome generosity, the possibilities of joy beyond anything most of us imagine. It was to this world, this God and these possibilities that you led every day.

You have been a good disciple, Ray. You glimpsed the transformational quality of Jesus' message. Immersing yourself in that reality, you turned away from judgmental pronouncements, divisive politics and moralistic condemnations. By example, you helped us to turn away from all that denies and negates the joy of living. We thank you for all the pies, mugs and votive candles of these past eleven years.

World Communion

Christian Mission in the Global Village

*And the Holy One will wield authority over the nations, and will judge
between many peoples; and they will beat their swords into plowshares, and
their spears into pruning hooks. Nation will not lift up sword against nation;
neither will they learn war any more.*

(Isaiah 2:4)

For the first time in history, we are faced with the fundamental fact that
the survival unit is not the individual, not the family, not the community,
not even the nation-state. The survival unit of our time is the whole human race and its environment. In a keynote address to the World Food
Conference in Rome in 1974, then Secretary of State Henry Kissinger
stated:

> "As we move toward the next century, the nations assembled here
> must begin to fashion a global conception. For we are irreversibly
> linked to each other... Global community is no longer a sentimental
> ideal but a practical necessity... We are faced not just with the prob-
> lem of food, but also with the accelerating momentum of our inter-
> dependence. The world is midway between the Second World War
> and the twenty-first century. We are stranded between old concep-
> tions of political conduct and a wholly new environment, between
> the inadequacy of the nation-state and the emerging imperative of
> a global community. We must act now and we must act together to
> regain control over our shared destiny... ."

We are witnessing the birth of a planetary society. At the same time
and on a worldwide scale we are seeing the resurgence of nationalism,
tribalism and fundamentalism. Nations are throwing off the yoke of past
political and economic domination and seeking control over their own
destinies. So we find ourselves in a world already interdependent, while
we try desperately to hold on to customs, traditions and ways of life that
give us meaning. What does all of this imply for the Christian churches,
rooted as we are in the local communities?

First I think it means that the era of missionary expansionism, the
conversion mentality and religious imperialism must come to an end.
We need to see ourselves as a single world community of diverse faiths in
which all the parts have responsibility for one another as peers.

Secondly, I think we will see an increasing emphasis on the universalism implicit in the Christian faith. We have always taught that all human beings are God's children with an equal claim to human dignity. Today theologians are speaking of the "global humanism" of our faith.

Finally, I think we will see the erosion of influence of traditional European and American centers of theology, and the growing prominence of African, Asian and Latin American perspectives.

Traditionally, missionaries were seen as white, middle class Christians who went somewhere else to serve the world. Sometimes they were charged to "convert" the world but very often their aim was genuine service. When we aren't caricaturing them as people who sought to put moo-moos over lovely Polynesian bodies, we recognize the tremendous amount of good missionaries have done. Because of their tireless efforts, colleges and universities, hospitals and medical centers of the highest quality exist around the world.

At the same time, we admit that often our missionaries were but the first wave of an advancing western civilization that was insensitive to everything in its pathway. In the sixteenth century the captain of a Spanish ship boasted to Japanese rulers that the greatness of his empire was due, in part, to the missionaries who prepared the way for the armed forces of the Spanish king. Wittingly or unwittingly missionaries were often instruments of cultural subjugation. Though the message of Jesus Christ was carried to distant continents, it was a very Western Christ.

I heard anger and pathos in his voice when Burgess Carr, the Bishop of Liberia and General Secretary of the All-African Council of Churches, addressed a gathering of ministers in New York City last fall. He described the colonial experience as a cruel passage for Africans, leaving a harsh legacy of poverty and degradation. He spoke of the "Gothic Captivity" of the church: its buildings, forms of worship, prayers, organizations, and hymnody. All these were transplanted from the West while native forms were suppressed. "Even our names were lost," he said. North American Indians say the same thing.

Such traditional missionary activity is anachronistic in Africa, said Bishop Carr. The whole church now has a missionary function to the whole church. Daisy Gopal Ratnam, General Secretary of the Church of South India, echoed his thoughts: "The church has one mission in one world,"' she says. Preferring the term "international church service persons", she envisions them flowing in every direction of the compass. "All are receiving, and all are sending churches."

While American service persons are working in the Philippines, young Germans are working with low income families in Lancaster, PA. While US citizens may be teaching in Turkey, Latin American Christians conduct a viable outreach in the East Harlem Protestant Parish. These are but a few examples. We are rapidly becoming a global church in this global village as we begin to take responsibility for each other.

We are hearing more and more about the universal dimension of our faith. We are beginning to appreciate the fact that the love of God knows no bounds. The parenthood of God makes us all sisters and brothers together: one human family on one planet earth.

Last spring we celebrated confirmation. Our young people did an excellent job of conducting the worship and presented talks on subjects they had chosen. We all joined to welcome them into membership in the church. Visiting me on that occasion was a Welsh pastor named Vivian Jones. He had great praise for the young people and the quality of their participation. "But," he said, "when it was all over, I didn't have any sense that they were joining my church, the churches in Wales, or anywhere else in the world. They were joining Plymouth Church, but somehow I wanted to make them welcomed in the larger, universal fellowship."

Increasingly our congregations will come to see ourselves as many and diverse centers of the one great church of Christ linked together by a common mission. Harry Emerson Fosdick's observation will become increasingly true: "The glory of every local church is that it holds before members a map of the world."

Theologically, the simultaneous resurgence of nationalism and the growing recognition of our interdependence mean that all of us will be listening more closely to our brothers and sisters in the Third World countries as they try to articulate the meaning of Christian faith in their environments. Bishop Carr spoke of a growing "ethno-theology" in Africa that is reflecting theologically on the African experience of humiliation. He spoke of a God incarnate in Africa, of ethnicity linked to divinity, of a God who is rich but becomes poor in order to take His place beside the poor, of a Christ incarnate in the multitudes. "Third World people carry the weight of the cross of Christ," he claimed. "It is therefore they who know the liberation of the grace of Christ."

In Latin America the Pope confronts a church divided between traditionalists and a new theology known as "liberation theology" that weds institutional loyalty to radical social and political change. Already Father Camillo Torres (Colombia), Father Ernesto Barrera Moto (El Salvador), and Father Caspar Garcia (Nicaragua), have died in combat against what they regarded as oppressive regimes.

In China we know less about the Christian churches, except that it is possible for visiting Protestants and Catholics to find familiar worship experiences on Sunday mornings. Apparently Chinese Christianity is more philosophical and intellectual that our accustomed fare. Its adherents have a great deal to contribute to the growing dialogue of faith.

In Central Europe, denied all the perks and privileges of official recognition, Christians are discovering new dimensions in their faith. They are living in what they call the "post-Constantine" era, and they give thanks. In Native American communities more attention is being given to "creation theologies" and the relationship of Christian faith to the naturalism so integral to Indian life. In Japan, the whole notion of God is being reconsidered and Christian faith is being reinterpreted in light of traditional Japanese thinking. Palestinian Christians remind us that they have kept our faith unbroken in the land of the prophets and yet today have become strangers in their own land.

The examples are endless. Who hasn't been stirred by African translations of the mass in the well known recording *Missa Luba*? Who hasn't been moved by a Filipino crucifix, or a Madonna carved by an Alaskan Eskimo?

It is now abundantly clear that Christianity is not a solo with only one part. It is not even a Welsh chorus, with four. It is a symphony with textures and interpretations we are only beginning to explore. It is World Music.

What then is the role of the church in this global village? Granted all of the changes, my answer is as predictable as it is simple: the role of the church in this global village is the same as that of any church in any village: to become a meeting place for Christians for the celebration of God's presence in their lives and to become an agency for God's work of reconciliation in a broken world.

Traditionally we have described this mission in three ways: the pastoral, the prophetic and the priestly. It is our pastoral mission to reach out to all in need, wherever they are, whether friend or enemy, acquaintance or stranger, to stand with the powerless, give hope to the hopeless, and relief to those who suffer.

Yet we also know that every outpouring of charity may also be a signpost that points to injustice. We need to be concerned with the victims, yes, but we also must be concerned with systems and societies. Our contemporary world is marred with corruption and injustice. It is our prophetic mission to stand against systems that brutalize some while privileging others unfairly.

It is our priestly mission to proclaim God to the world and intercede for the world to God, to affirm that the realities of today are not fixed and that God calls us to an unknown future. It is our opportunity to learn anew that no theology, philosophy, ideology, scientific theory or economic dogma will ever be big enough to explain the mysteries of divine or human life.

Suggested Remarks at Bitburg Cemetery

A week from today our President will lay a wreath at a military cemetery in Bitburg, West Germany. This particular site was once a staging ground for the most ferocious battle ever fought between Germans and Americans. In six weeks, 19,000 American soldiers died and 50,000 were wounded; Germany suffered an estimated 100,000 casualties. President Reagan intends his visit to this quiet cemetery on the 40th anniversary of the end of the war to be a gesture of reconciliation between former enemies. What better location can there be to consign this painful memory to history or to proclaim the new era of cooperation and goodwill?

Opposition certainly could be expected from some veterans groups and survivors of that awful conflict and from family members and friends whose losses can never be assuaged or justified by the twists and ironies of history. But no one anticipated the storm that was to break when the trip was announced. We are told that the President's decision reopened old wounds within the German Republic and that it threatens a crisis in German-American relations. Across the American political spectrum, opposition has been voiced to the President's plans. Indeed, over 80 U.S. Senators and 257 Representatives have asked the President to cancel this visit.

Within this cemetery lie the graves of approximately 2,000 German soldiers. Most of them were conscripts; many were teenagers. They died in the Battle of the Bulge. Of those 2,000, 47 graves contain the remains of Nazi SS officers. The Waffen-SS was the elite corps who developed and ran the concentration camps and crematoria. It generally is considered to be responsible for the deliberate slaughter of ten million people, most of whom were Jews. This fact, this terrible Holocaust, makes World War II unlike all other wars. Any ceremony of reconciliation between these former enemies must take into account this stark and awesome reality.

In fact, Mr. Reagan inadvertently made matters more difficult for himself. Because of his penchant for keeping things upbeat, he originally vetoed the idea of also visiting one of the death camps. Later he suggested that German soldiers buried at Bitburg were also victims of Nazi terror, and in a way he was right, but the suggestion that conditions for conscripts and Holocaust victims were similar makes thoughtful ethicists cringe.

Under heavy pressure, he added a trip to the concentration camp at Bergen-Belsen to bring balance to his itinerary. He also will honor Germans who fought against Hitler. Reports have it that he is trying to recruit one or more surviving Jewish victims to accompany him on his visit.

Since President Reagan is determined to visit Bitburg. I have taken the liberty to write a speech for him to deliver. I offer it humbly. Perhaps it can help him redeem a very troubling situation.

The Speech

Forty years ago Allied and German forces met here in one of the bloodiest battles of our history. Those who fell then lie now beneath this sod. That battle and that war, like all battles and all wars through all the years, were neither grand nor glamorous. Many who lie here were mere teenagers when they died. Had there been no war some of them might be playing with their grandchildren today, concluding long and productive lives. Instead, they - like soldiers buried in cemeteries everywhere in the world — went to their deaths prematurely. Whether they died valiantly and with courage, or fearing the retribution of their own government, is beside the point. The contributions they might have made in science, literature, music, statecraft and the arts are now forever lost. Such is the unspeakable magnitude and tragedy of war.

Under conditions of war, many of the normal restraints that protect us from our more sinister impulses are loosened. This is true in our present state of "cold" war as much as it is during periods of violent conflict. We allow ourselves to think thoughts and do deeds that would be repugnant to us under other circumstances. We allow ourselves to project on to others all of the inadequacies and evil that lurks in our own hearts, and to claim the power of righteous judgment that belongs only to God. Thus did the Nazis and their SS agents to the Jews of Europe. The result was a Holocaust— a "burnt offering" — made on the altars of ethnicity and nationalism. This Holocaust brought unforgettable shame not only to the German people, and not only to European civilization, but to our whole human species.

This deliberate and systematic genocide was onerous; we can scarcely perceive what distorted passions motivated those who perpetrated it. We firmly believe that their cattle cars, concentration camps and gas chambers represent the nadir of human accomplishment. Future generations will recoil in horror at our era, and wonder how we could have been so brutally cruel and inhumane to one another.

Yet it would be too easy to look upon the Waffen-SS as some sort of bizarre mutation of our species: alien, remote and unrelated to our own minds and hearts. It would be ironic indeed if the Nazis, perfecters of the tactics of scapegoating, themselves became scapegoats for the rest of us, if because of their great evil we are spared the difficult task of exorcising the evils that reside in us.

Were the deliberate destruction of millions of human beings, each one of infinite value in the eyes of God and humanity, an isolated occurrence in our time, it would still forever damn us in the eyes of our posterity. Our saving grace is that there were many — Germans and non-Germans — who were willing to rise up against this demonic evil and pay a supreme price to destroy it.

Unfortunately this Holocaust, though extreme, has not been the only example of our inhumanity to each other. In this very decade we have witnessed the wholesale destruction of cities and towns in Kampuchea, and the willful slaughter of millions of Cambodian citizens. Genocidal policies are being employed in the conquest of Afghanistan. Terrorists think nothing of destroying whole villages of innocent people if it serves their purposes. Explicit theories of racial superiority still inspire oppression, apartheid and the passions of fear, rage and hate. A savage barbarism has been unleashed that haunts us all. As that Jewish rabbi Jesus once said, "If you sow the wind, you will reap the whirlwind."

Nor can I speak to you today with any inflated sense of the moral perfection of my own nation. The United States is a great democracy. We are committed to the ideals of the free world but we too know the shame of history. The land that we call our own once belonged to another people. Those who remain now languish on barren reservations and in urban ghettos, struggling to preserve the fragile remnants of their once proud ways of life. Much of our land was developed by the slave labor of our Black sisters and brothers. They were caught in a web of exploitation that viciously degraded human and personal dignity. Many of their children's children now struggle in our cities and countryside against the consequences of generations of segregation and unequal opportunity.

But I carry yet a more serious concern today. A far greater Holocaust threatens our world than those perpetrated by all the tyrants of history.

I am speaking of nuclear war. As we speak, giant missiles with lethal payloads stand poised in their silos. Bombers above us and submarines in the oceans' depths carry armed projectiles with awesome power. Huge armies face each other across vast boundaries around the world. The fate of the world hangs in a most precarious balance. Should even a limited nuclear exchange be initiated, the destruction of human life and culture will surpass any holocaust we have yet witnessed.

Too often, I am afraid, we disown the evil that is ours. Like the Nazis of a generation ago, we look for scapegoats who will carry away our sins. The "Jews" of that generation might be the "communists" or the "capitalists" of this. Depending on one's persuasion, "infidels", "radicals", "fundamentalists", and "counter revolutionaries" are some of the labels in common currency today. We protest our innocence and goodwill. We proclaim their malice and deceit. Thus we destroy any basis for affirming for one another our essential and God-given humanity. This is what we who are Christians mean when we confess that, "we have done those things we ought not to have done, and we have left undone those things we ought to have done."

As I lay this wreath today, I would like more than anything to lay to rest this inclination of ours to place all the blame for the world's troubles on the other guy. It is too easy and too simple minded to divide the world into the good and the evil, the just and the unjust, the oppressed and the oppressors, the forces of light and the forces of darkness. This spirit was so ignominiously exaggerated by the Waffen-SS, with fearful consequences to our world. But this tendency resides in every one of us, and in the institutions and structures we have created.

Let us allow both the victims and the perpetrators of those heinous crimes of forty years ago to find their proper places in our histories. Let us recognize that the capacity to exact a holocaust from our victims now lies within our hands. We acknowledge with deep humility that neither evil nor good is bounded by national borders, genetic inheritance, religious practice or political convictions. Let us proceed to lay foundations of mutual respect, trust and affirmation that will contain and control the beast within us all.

All Souls

When a Friend Dies

As I write these words, one of our beloved members stands before death's door. We are planning a memorial service for another. We are talking yet with others about the recent deaths of parents, friends and siblings. Families and friends, unknown to each other, gather in grief, gratitude and farewell. We mourn together our separate losses. We seek solace within the depths of our traditions, the sharing of our memories and the embraces of our community.

As I write these words, a group of members are proposing a memorial garden and columbarium for our church where the remains of loved ones may be scattered or interred. There is a growing recognition among us that the "gathered community of saints" (to used the language of our ancestors) includes all who have given and received nurture through this community.

As I write these words, the richly textured music of Duruflé's *Requiem* still resonates through the sanctuary. The choir and orchestra presented this challenging music so beautifully, offering through it the gifts of comfort, joy and serenity. "Give them eternal rest," intones the liturgy, and this is the fervent prayer of all who are left behind.

Yet as I write, these words collide in my consciousness. They are too solemn. Most of us also need respite, especially if we have endured much suffering. Even sufferers would become bored with "rest eternal." Given eternity, we must be more creative.

When a friend dies, I sometimes turn to a different piece of music — Mussorgsky's "Great Gates of Kiev" from his *Pictures at an Exhibition.* Far from the subdued world of a funeral chapel, it is extravagant, elegant, boisterous, lavish, embellished, loud and simply grand. As I listen I imagine the greatest of gates — ornate and elaborate beyond compare — flung open with wild abandon. I imagine my friend — erect now and whole — walking through them with vigor and panache like royalty into the welcoming crowd. Free at last from the burdens we know too well, my friend steps gaily through with eager anticipation. This is how I imagine the long awaited homecoming of the soul.

A Gentleman and A Scholar

"Just call me Maggie with the light brown," Howard often said. But more often we called him "Howard", "Howie" or even "Butch". Whether you were a General Mills executive or the checkout clerk at the local grocery store, Howard always had a story or a bright word of encouragement for you. He was, as the saying goes, a gentleman and a scholar.

Howard's life began in the small town of Marshall, MN. He came of age during the Great Depression. But because of economic circumstances he was not able to finish college. Denied a formal higher education, he determined to educate himself in a deliberate and lifelong manner. He immersed himself in fine arts and great literature. Learning was his passion; collecting and organizing information was for him a lifelong endeavor. In his younger years he meticulously created fourteen scrapbooks that were anything but scraps. In the carefully preserved pages of these carefully crafted books are poems, aphorisms, and reprints of great works of arts — all edifying to the spirit of the young Howard, all pointing to cultural fascinations that would inform his later years.

He read the New Yorker as faithfully as any saint reads the Bible. James Thurber, Ogden Nash, E. B. White and Eustace Tilley created the structure through which Howard learned to view the universe. Indeed, to hear the family describe it, a visit to the Algonquin Restaurant in New York City, and to its famous 'round table' where noted writers gathered, was something akin to a visit by jazz lovers to the Savoy, of sports enthusiasts to Cooperstown, or of pious believers to the Garden of Gethsemane.

"We thought that everyone grew up with a father who quoted Shakespeare," said one of his daughters. Long before E. D. Hirsch, the contemporary advocate of 'cultural literacy,' Howard was prescribing for his daughters the essentials of an adequate education. Allow me to quote at some length from a letter he wrote ten years ago, giving fatherly advice to a daughter:

> "Then there's Brahms to be acquired: *Symphony #2 in D*, of course, and probably the *Fourth in E Minor* too. Also, one would need more Tchaikovsky naturally: the *Pathétique Symphony* (#6 in B Minor) of

course (another must), and probably #4 and #5 too. And Beethoven's 3rd and 7th are also both in the must category.

"That's where my primary interest lies, but one would need some Debussy, such as *Claire de Lune, Nocturnes* and *L'apres-midi d'un faune* (the latter a must). And one would need some Richard Strauss ... and a barrel of Chopin as played by Rubenstein (conjuring up the Tchaikovsky *Piano Concerto # 1* which is also in the "must" category, as is Bach's *Toccata and Fugue* — in D Minor, I think — written for organ but better by far in an orchestral arrangement.) And there's the *Scheherazade* by Rimski-Korsakov; that's a double "must" in any listing.

"None of which touches on the operatic field, in which there is a huge quantity of "must" music. One needs excerpts of Puccini's operas: *Madame Butterfly*, certainly, and *La Bohème* and *Tosca*; Verdi's operas too: *Aida, La Traviata, Il Trovatore*, plus at least the overture to *I Vespri Siciliani*. And one can't leave out the Met's A, B, C — *Aida, Bohème* and *Carmen*. And one would need some light opera: particularly Gilbert and Sullivan, and, for me, some of the big band era: Wayne King, Guy Lombardo, Bon Bernie, Sheep Fields, et al. One could go on forever... ."

And Howard could! How many Saturday afternoons did he still the household and tune into the Metropolitan Opera? Yet one would never describe him as cerebral or stuffy. At a party in Stockbridge, Massachusetts, he was seen standing before the long haired rock musicians waving his finger in time with the thunderous beat and obviously enjoying himself.

Like the renaissance person he would be, Howard's interests were larger and more encompassing than just the arts. When his daughter moved to the woods, Howard measured the trees. He was interested in astronomy, observed the cycles of the moon, instructed his family about Halley's Comet, and noted with an attitude approaching awe that on March 7 the moon came as close to the earth as it had ever been. He was a good photographer. His numerous photographs are now indexed and organized into 25 separate albums, each page giving the exact day of each picture.

But always, the life of the mind was of paramount importance. He appreciated the "received tradition" in art, music and literature more than the avant-garde. The National Gallery, not Dupont Circle, was his venue. Herbert Von Karajan, not Herbie Hancock, was likely to draw his applause. Howard valued an ordered universe, and did everything in his power to create and maintain that order. His was an aesthetic appreciation for the order of the world. He appreciated its structure and composition. Timeless principles gave ephemeral personality its meaning. He communed as much with Beethoven as he did with you or me.

Yet there is more to life than order and more to the good life than duty or pleasantness. There is intimacy, tenderness and play. There is spiritual stretching and risk taking. Order is always a precarious balance between chaos on the one hand and triviality on the other. Order is our attempt to impose meaning and coherence on an ambiguous, fluctuating, dynamic, ever changing reality. Something in us praises folks like Howard who can will an ordered universe into being. But something in us also rebels.

Although he was rarely emotionally demonstrative, he was capable of exultation and even awe. Tenderness was not his forte but he was deeply caring in his very particular way. He attended every school event for his children. He stayed in touch, and fretted and worried when life threw a curve ball at any of his daughters. At the end of his life he was more worried about Evelyn than concerned for himself. There was so much ordering still left to do.

No one can in all things be perfect. So 56 years ago Howard had the great good sense to share a seat on the train from Chicago to Minneapolis with the woman who became his wife. Evelyn brought to his wit a matching sense of humor. To his tough-minded objectivity she brought tenderness. To his classical bent she brought a deep humanity. Evelyn loved him and he, her, for all these years.

When Howard died Evelyn summarized their years together in three words. I can think of no better way to describe his impact on all of us: She said simply, "He brightened me."

Clowning Around

We're going to miss Craig Babcock.

Remember that big, red clown's nose in that little, blue Volkswagen? That was Craig.

And the guy walking down Main Street of South Paris with an attractive girl on his arm and a brown bag over his head? That was Craig.

Or how about the softball player whose hair resembled your mother's dust mop with a bad case of static electricity? That was Craig.

He had the body of a college tackle yet could move with incredible grace and skill. Whether aping the ape on stage or mimicking the rest of us in town, he was a superb performer. He could engage us in conversation, tell us in all seriousness that the ground beneath him was slowly giving way, and we would extend a desperate helping hand as we watched him sink away — almost. That was Craig: whimsical, capricious, and unpretentious.

We had a sign in front of our church that read, "Come As You Are". Craig once asked me if we meant it. The sign was changed soon after that.

In the bank he once announced his intention to deposit two potatoes. He filled out a deposit slip for his potatoes and gave it — and them — to the teller. The teller showed wit of her own, however; she promptly recorded the transaction in his Record of Deposits.

Two weeks later he returned to the same teller with a check he wanted to cash. It was for one- half of a potato. She said the bank would be happy to honor his check but, seeing that it was for such an unusual amount, he would have to collect the next day, after it had "cleared".

That was reasonable he thought; he returned the following afternoon to claim what was rightfully his — and he was paid!

If having a jester makes one a prince, then Craig made royalty of us all. The town, and not the stage alone, was his court. Predictably, not everyone enjoyed his antics. Many of us were uncomfortable with the idea that we could be mimicked, could be rendered laughable in the sight of others.

266

Craig stood in line in a crowded bank lobby once, directly behind an officer of the law. He decided to put on his clown's nose, which he did, and then stood solemnly still. First one person and then another noticed him until everyone was looking. Some snickered while others were embarrassed and pretended not to see. The venerable gendarme became noticeably uneasy until he too turned around to see what was happening.

He stared at the nose as his face filled with rage. "You'd better be careful in here!" he exclaimed with all the prosaic authority of his office. He looked menacing as Tony (Montanaro — Craig's mentor and boss) rushed to intervene. "Clowns are harmless," Tony insisted to the officer. But the nose came off.

What a wasted opportunity! The trooper might have given that nose one heck of a squeeze and everyone would have laughed, but he muffed it. Most of us would have muffed it too, had we been in his place. By and large we are more like the trooper than the teller: more prosaic, more literal and more threatened.

But clowns don't hurt people. They make us laugh. They invite us to play along in the intriguing games of life. They reveal our pretenses for what they are, and help us to smile a little bit. And that's why we're going to miss Craig Babcock.

Paul on Paul

Paul Rice was one of the first members of Central I came to know after I arrived from Minnesota. Less than two weeks into my new ministry here, I was privileged to drive Paul and Elfriede to Charleston, where Paul would receive the Henry Weaver Peace Maker Award for his efforts to eradicate malaria. Paul could barely get in and out of the car, but he was most gracious in speech and demeanor. He told stories of his family and Elfriede's. He talked proudly of his children and grandchildren. His words were carefully chosen and precise; an understated eloquence thinly veiled his immense intellectual vitality. I often wish that my most carefully crafted manuscripts could begin to compare to what I heard that day.

In the weeks and years to follow, Paul became a good friend and a mentor to me. I still covet his gift of articulation and his graciousness of spirit. We shared communion together in his hospital room just two days before his death. I asked Paul if there were a favorite scripture he would like me to read. Without any hesitation he chose this 12th chapter from Saint Paul's *Letter to the Romans*. Indeed, it provides a fitting lens through which to glimpse something of the soul of this great and gentle man.

Present your bodies as a living sacrifice, the Apostle wrote. Our bodies exist within our souls. They are ours, these bodies — ours to give or withhold, ours to please or punish, ours to nurture or neglect. A body is more than flesh and bone. It is the center of physical, emotional and spiritual energies. It is vigor and weakness, health and infirmity, strength and fragility together. Our bodies are the medium of our presence.

Saint Paul asked that we share our bodies. "To sacrifice" means simply "to make holy". It is not holy to mortify our flesh, nor burn it upon an altar, nor engage in extreme forms of asceticism. Neither is it holy to live selfishly, indulgently and for our selves alone. Paul Rice understood this perfectly. He offered his presence in the service of the world. He gave it freely, even joyfully. He offered his intelligence, wit and stamina — a living sacrifice, a holy gift.

At the end of his life, he offered his growing disability with as much grace as previously he had offered his ability. In his frailty he allowed us to become his caregivers; he continued to teach us lessons of gratitude and graciousness.

Do not be conformed to this world. Paul loved this world, loved its color, loved its diversity, loved its apparent order and loved its complexity. He fathomed its mysteries with the passion of an inquiring scientist. He cared for it with the regard of a faithful steward. He respected it with the tenderness of one who understood both its stubborn resilience and its surprising fragility. He loved nature, and people, and communities. He appreciated that he himself and all that he cherished are embedded in its unfolding story.

Perhaps because he loved that story most of all, Paul did not conform to the mores of this age. He was not taken in by the excessive and aggressive compulsions of our era. Greed, wealth and status did not compel him. Modesty hung comfortably upon him like the Izod sweater that kept him warm.

But be transformed by the renewal of your mind. To the very end he engaged the world with intelligence and goodwill. His soul underwent its necessary transformation — indeed, he directed its transformation — by his unfailing and rigorous pursuit of knowledge and understanding. At the end of his life it was a different kind of understanding that he sought: not of the external world, but the world of relationships; not the reality of nature, but the nature of reality.

Hold fast to what is good. Paul Rice was always a man of faith: rational faith, thoughtful faith, faith that encouraged exploration and inquiry. Certainly his faith sustained him as he faced into the greatest uncertainty any of us will confront. His soul grew large as he recounted the good he had received, the good he had encountered, the good he had done and the good that awaited him.

Rejoice in your hope. What is hope? On what basis do we hope? Paul was a hopeful man all the days of his life. But there was realism in all his hopefulness. Paul and Elfriede traveled the world engaging the powers of disease, poverty, tyranny, ignorance and misfortune. As there was no false modesty in him, neither was there an easy optimism. Yet he believed in the possibility of the human spirit to overcome all that oppresses it and he dedicated his considerable abilities to freeing it from everything that weighs it down.

269

Be patient in tribulation. The Apostle counseled patience because he was persuaded of a greater good to follow. Paul's patience, which impressed us all so deeply, was of a different sort. It was based neither on a conviction of things to come, nor on a stoical resignation to things as they are. It was rather a kind of embrace of life as it is given, a delight in the simple pleasures of sunlight and bird song, of summer breezes and visits from friends. It was a patience sustained by the vast network of care that surrounded him — Elfriede, Steve, Glen, Dennis, all his family, his church, his colleagues, his professional caregivers and his many friends. It was a patience founded upon a scientist's perception of the rhythm and constancy of nature. It was a patience rooted in the virtues of his early family life. It was a patience firmly embedded in a stable and loving partnership with his wife of nearly 61 years.

Be constant in prayer. Paul Rice was never one to parade his piety before the rest of us. Yet he loved scripture and was a lifelong and devoted churchman. When Kristi last visited him at Wesley Woods, he offered a prayer for her ministry. Paul's prayer was conversational, always. He offered his thanksgivings and his concerns, his fears and his deepest hopes. I sensed that God and Paul were partners in a lifetime conversation.

But I think Paul's prayer life was bigger even than this. It included his contemplation of the vast and intricate designs he found in nature. It included the joy he found in children, family and friends. It included the long story of his long life and the longer story that enfolded his life to make him what he was. It included us, what we have been and what we might become.

As I early discovered, Paul Rice was one of the greatest conversationalists any of us will ever meet. He cared about articulation, nuance, precision, grammar and diction. One could hear the periods, semicolons and commas in his speech. His paragraphs were sensible and complete.

I think there were many commas and semicolons in Paul's life too, but few if any periods. There were certainly interruptions, and question marks along the way. But as he approached his final hour he wanted us to know that even death — with all its seeming finality — was to him a comma, a pause, a break, a moment to catch one's breath before beginning the next phrase.

All Creatures Great and Small

Our dog, Shiloh, a member of the Shih Tzu breed, developed his tendency to car sickness early in life. But it was what he saw out the car window, not the ride, that upset him one day as we passed Mayflower Congregational Church in south Minneapolis. In reaction, he sent (with a little help) the following letter to the Rev. Budd Friend-Jones, a pastor at Mayflower. Thus began an unusual correspondence.

(Jean Johansson, in *The Metro Lutheran*)

Dear Rev. Mr. Friend-Jones:

Just a note to let you know that it was quite disconcerting to see the sermon title, *No Comfort in Shiloh* that recently appeared on the signboard outside Mayflower Church. My owners have quite often told me that they derive great comfort from me, sometimes just by looking into my big, expressive, brown eyes.

My owners tried to smooth things over by saying I shouldn't take the sermon title personally, as the Shiloh in the title undoubtedly referred to an Old Testament temple location. Since my particular breed tends to be affiliated more closely with Buddhism (having supposedly originated in Buddhist temples in Tibet), Bible literacy is not one of my strong points. I defer, therefore, to the knowledge of my Lutheran owners, but thought you should be aware of how someone outside your congregation reacted to the signboard message.

Sincerely,

Shiloh, the Shih Tzu

Within a week an envelope from Mr. Friend-Jones arrived, addressed to Shiloh. Inside was this letter:

Dear Shiloh:

I must apologize for the disconcerting sermon title. Sometimes we in the church can be so negative! It especially troubles me, given your Buddhist origins — and, perhaps, consciousness — that unwittingly I may have damaged interfaith as well as inter species relationships in our community.

I must confess that even I was depressed by the title. (Things are really bad when the preacher is depressed by his sermon; pity the congregation!) By Thursday I had changed my title to "Where Yearning Meets with Yearning," and felt a little better for it.

I have, of course, only the vaguest notion of your yearnings, so I will not presume to send you the manuscript. (I'm sure you could think of many uses for it besides reading it.) Suffice it to say that yearning met yearning on Sunday morning in the vicinity of Shiloh; this was indeed an Old Testament temple location.

Please forgive my insensitivities. And thank you for taking the time to call them to my attention.

Sincerely,

Budd Friend-Jones, the Minister

Shiloh felt compelled out of courtesy to send a response:

Dear Mr. Friend-Jones:

Thank you for taking the time to address my concerns. I realize that most humans wouldn't think it worthy of their time to correspond with a member of the canine family. Some might even scoff at the idea. And yet, St. Francis of Assisi deemed animals worthy of his time and attention.

Keeping in mind that "Shih Tzu" is Chinese for "lion", I leave you with what, in an attempt to increase my familiarity with the Bible, has recently become my favorite Bible verse: "But whoever is joined with all the living has hope, for a living dog is better than a dead lion" (Eccl. 9:4).

Sincerely,

Shiloh, the Shih Tzu

Flirting Saints

One of the first hymns Donna remembered hearing was *My God and I*. Fifty years later, when her body was undergoing cancer's ferocious and deadly attack, she fondly recalled this hymn. It is a simple song, describing God in the loveliest way I can imagine: a friend, a companion, a confidante, even a lover. We walk together and share secret thoughts. God tells us how the "verdant" beauty of the world awaited our arrival. In God's presence, our voices ring with laughter. Is laughter a sign that God is with us? Donna laughed easily and often, and made us laugh as well.

Donna loved to dance. She would dance with us on the dance floor or for us on the tables! I can't help thinking that religion would be a lot more interesting if there were saints like Donna — classy, sassy, spunky, beautiful saints. We need saints who dance their way through heaven and flirt with us now and then. We want saints who land in our laps and make the angels laugh when things up there get a tad bit too serious.

Donna's illness lasted nine months, roughly the equivalent of a human pregnancy. "And the time came that she should be delivered." Although certainly it was a death, an ending, and a departure, it was something more.

Peter Marshall once said that birth must feel like death to the baby who experiences it. Inevitably the baby is pushed unwillingly from the womb, the only place she has ever known, the place of warmth and comfort where every need is met. She is pushed by forces beyond anyone's control, natural forces that must feel cosmic in nature. But when the baby finally is delivered, she is welcomed into loving arms, wrapped in the softest blankets and fed from her mother's breast. She arrives here to fulfill, as the hymn-writer said, "heavenly plans... to come to life, earth's verdant glory see."

We saw a birthing in Donna's dying: the birth of a wisdom that comes when our fondest hopes are denied, a strength of character that arrives when we are sorely tested, a clarity of focus that emerges when what we love most is most threatened, and a letting go of the hurts and frustrations of a lifetime when we can no longer hold on.

Something similar was being born in us as well. We learned that sometimes loving someone means letting go. We look at each other with new eyes, seeing how vulnerable we are. We are discovering that the most important moment in our life is the present one — for it is the only one we have.

As painful as it was for her — and for us — Donna was pushed and pulled by forces beyond anyone's power into the loving arms of her Creator. She is beginning the next stage of her journey — a journey into the big, big heart of Love.

Deacon Blashfield

Live such a life that if every person were such as you, and every life a life like yours, this earth would be God's Paradise.

(Phillip Brooks)

On his 100th birthday, Herb Blashfield and his (fourth) wife Marie invited us to dinner. On their dining room wall hung a landscape Herb had painted when he was 19. Natural crevices formed a cross on the side of a mountain. He casually mentioned that in real life the cross no longer is visible; time and nature eroded it away.

At 90, Herb was told to have his knees replaced. He had them both done at the same time. "Yes, it hurt," he recalled, "but I only went through it once." At 100 he was driving, shopping, reading, cooking and writing a book. He kept himself abreast of the latest developments in politics, science and the arts. Although he experienced many tragedies in his long life, he exuded optimism. He reveled in the marvels of creation. Herb was the perennial choice of confirmation classes to speak at their celebration dinners.

When he turned 100 the church elected him Deacon. He was very proud of this. In every generation back to New England colonial times there had been a "Deacon Blashfield" in his family. Now Herb continued that tradition.

During our dinner Gretchen asked about child rearing "back then." "I'm so busy with the future that I don't have time to think about the past," he said. What bothered him most about turning 100 was the diminishing time he had left: "There is so much to do, so much to learn. I'm ready to start another PhD at the University."

At 103 he was speaking up lucidly and passionately at congregational meetings. Always he argued that the church should support the young. "We have limited resources," he would say. "Let's not waste them on my generation. We have lived our lives. Let's support young families and everyone who is involved in raising children. In today's world, they need all the help we can give them!" To me he advised, "If you have to choose between visiting me and helping a teenager, go with the teenager."

At 104 Herb began to slow down. He gave up driving. Marie's dementia got worse and she was admitted to a medical facility. Herb sat with her for hours every day, but he tired more easily. Finally, he told us that he wanted to finish his book, have a party, and die.

Exactly one month before his 105th birthday, Marie passed away. On the day of his birthday his book was released. His friends organized a big party that he clearly enjoyed. That same night he was admitted to the hospital. Three days later he peacefully passed away.

All Saints

To Heal the Circle

We do not live to ourselves, and we do not die to ourselves. If we live, we live to the Lord, and if we die, we die to the Lord; so then, whether we live or whether we die, we are the Lord's. For to this end Christ died and lived again, that he might be Lord of both the dead and the living.

(Romans 14:7-9)

Winter is upon us. Cold descends. Snow swirls. Earth hardens. Darkness expands its domain. Our dead have gone from us, and we feel winter's icy fingers clutching at our hearts.

Winter is upon us. We have planted their memories deep in the soil of our being. They were our laughter and our hope, our shelter and our journey. They were our lovers and the children of our love, our companions and our guides. Life dwelled within them and kindled our affections. Our energies commingled, and our hearts were strangely warmed. Now the circle is broken. They have gone from us and we feel winter's icy fingers clutching at our hearts.

Cold descends. Snow swirls. Around this table we gather, bereft and wounded. Around this table we ponder the mystery of memory, and the memory of mystery. Around this table we remember with the ache of longing and the keenness of anticipation.

Earth hardens. Jesus Christ invited us to share at this table, to share this feast spread for all from the beginning of time. Jesus Christ invites us to sit at this table, to take our rightful places here among the vast multitudes who have gathered through the ages and will gather until the end of time. This is a feast without beginning or end, existing only now and yet always existing and never passing away.

Darkness expands its domain. But here we remember the goodness of God and the mystery of God, so intimately embracing our world and our flesh. In Christ, all suffering — even death itself — has been taken into God's own being. The hurts of our spirits have been received in the heart of God. Through Christ, an infinite compassion reaches us, touches us and unites us in love with each other and with all others.

Our memories become sacred memories. Powerful, dynamic, living memories. Memories that bring Life and transformation. Those who have gone from us return to dwell within us. They commune with us in thoughts and dreams; they become part of the great conversation we are having with the world. They shape our expectations. They invite us to enter a larger and mysterious, universe.

Winter is upon us. Cold descends. Snow swirls. Earth hardens. Darkness expands its domain. Our dead have gone from us. Yet they are present, and their presence comforts us. Around this table we gather today, remembering the mysteries of our faith, and marveling at the mysteries of our memories.

To Behold the Beauty of The Lord

One thing I asked of the Lord, that will I seek after: to live in the house of the Lord all the days of my life, to behold the beauty of the Lord, and to inquire in his temple.

"Come," my heart says, "seek his face!" Your face, O Lord, do I seek.

(Psalm 27: 4, 8)

Over the years I have collected icons, mostly from the Russian Orthodox tradition*. Recently we moved into new offices. For the first time, I hung my collection where it could be seen — above the couch on the only wall available facing my desk.

There is the famous Vladimir icon — the most treasured in all Russia. It also is called the "tenderness icon" of Mary and infant Jesus. Of course the adult Jesus is there in several of the icons. The famous "hospitality" icon by Andrei Rublev, the young 15th century iconographer, has a prominent place. Russians call it the "Old Testament Trinity" because it depicts the three holy visitors to Father Abraham and Mother Sarah at the oaks of Mamre. The meal they share looks very much like the Holy Eucharist. Bible scenes such as the wedding at Cana are represented, and flaxen-haired angels, and the creation of animals and stars.

One icon depicts a group of women collectively known as "the myrrh bearers." These were the women who supported Jesus throughout his life and ministry. Another icon is St. Xenia. In her later years she wandered the streets of St. Petersburg wearing her dead husband's military uniform. Elisabeta Feodorovna also is there. In contrast to Xenia, Elisabeta was the granddaughter of Queen Victoria and the sister-in-law of the last czar. Hers was a profoundly selfless ministry to Moscow's most disenfranchised until she was brutally executed by the Bolsheviks.

One of my favorite icons comes from Czestochowa in Poland. This image of a young, dark Mary carries the scars of repeated assaults by foreign invaders — slashes across the face and a gouge left by an arrow in her neck. When restoring this icon, the people wanted these visible scars to

---

* With two exceptions, mine are not genuine icons, but copies. Genuine icons are prayerfully hand painted ("written") according to strict guidelines by trained iconographers who are ordained to their work, and the icons themselves are blessed.

remain, and they have become an intrinsic part of her identity. Her scars contribute to her unique beauty and sanctity.

Icons in the Orthodox tradition are not considered artworks. They are not merely religious pictures. They are rather a "technology of spiritual contemplation". The veneration of an icon can lead a person into an awareness of the mystery of Life and the holiness of all Being.

To the Orthodox, the material world itself is but an expression of a divine and holy energy. "Saints" become saints in this tradition by their intense openness to this energy. Though they inhabit the material world just as you and I, the Divine Light shines more brightly through them. Such people appear in every generation, in all stations of life, in all circumstances and in every part of the world. And though their icons also are merely material objects made of wood and paint, nevertheless they are thought to retain something of the transparency of the saints they depict. Russians speak of them as "windows" through which we gain glimpses into another and sacred dimension of reality.

For many not brought up in this tradition, music, poetry, art, dance, photography, mathematics, or research may function in a similar fashion. While participating in this world of matter, time and space, they also encode messages that carry us quite beyond it. Our active attentiveness to the smallest insect or a common flower reveals such delicate beauty and exquisite complexity. We marvel at the sheer fact that things exist, and that there is so much beauty and life all around. We become aware of our intimate communion within this interconnected web of being.

One night after I had hung the collection, I sat alone at my desk. The building was empty. I looked straight ahead and I had the strange sensation that these icons were looking back at me.

I felt as though I were not alone. In fact, my office felt crowded. For the first time in my life I had a palpable sense of what St. Paul once called the "great cloud of witnesses". I felt as though a vast community of well wishers were supporting me on my journey. I felt that I was sitting in the company of teachers, forbearers and friends. This effect has not abated in the years that have intervened.

Of course I have meetings in my office. People stop to chat. Almost invariably they sit on the couch beneath the icons. Thet are teenagers and older people. People of substantial means and people struggling to survive. Gay, straight, married and single. People who travel the world on jet planes and people who travel to work on buses. People searching for answers and people excited by new discoveries. People from many different walks of life, with different skin colors, speaking differing native languages, worshipping God in different traditions. People who vote Republican and people who vote Democratic. People on a mission and people seeking one. Young couples with new babies, and grown children with dependent parents. People aware only of stress, and people rejoicing in their blessings. Some depressed and some elated.

As I sit across from them, their faces sometimes seem to merge with the faces on the wall. They too become icons for me. I catch glimpses of a divine light within them. I see the image and likeness of God in these faces that smile or scowl, laugh and cry. I feel the unbroken and interconnected holy community surrounding us as we converse. Whether they are perplexed or confident, skeptical or believing doesn't seem to matter.

Some of the people who sat with me in the midst of this company of Light have since passed on. Each was unique and special. Each had her or his own distinct energy and personality. Each left memories in my keeping that continue to influence the person I am becoming. Each revealed something I had not known before.

I have learned to carry this new awareness with me wherever I go: I am not alone. I am embedded in this mysterious sacred energy of Life. It flows around me but also through me and connects me to others who cross my path — and, indeed, to all others. And every person I meet carries within herself or himself something of the divine likeness and the image of God. However high-spirited or mean-spirited, however petty or destructive their words or behavior may be, God's sacred likeness resides in them. Though it may be hidden it can never be completely eradicated. We are all of us saints-in-training.

Shenandoah Blessing

It's a beautiful sight to behold. The white frame church sits perched by the side of that small country road where folks have been singing *Blessed Assurance* for more than a hundred years. Facing east, its sanctuary windows are open to capture the north-south breezes that blow down the muggy valley. Across the road lies the cemetery where the best and the worst of preceding generations — and all those in between — have been committed to await the final consummation. Beyond the cemetery fields of hay and corn, pastures and woods steeply rise; the Massanuttens climb sharply from the valley floor.

Old timers tell me that they see these mountains differently than the rest of us. "You city folks look at those hills and see fall colors and peaceful farms. We see Stonewall Jackson and his men riding along that ridge. You see real estate; we see stories. You look and pass by, but the land holds us here; it connects us to everything important."

The lazy moans of cattle and the languid clanging of their bells drift from distant fields over fence and headstone into the sanctuary. The chatter of squirrels closer by and the seamless chirping of crickets everywhere bathe the little church in the sounds and illusions of timelessness. Strong, pungent odors of freshly spread manure and the thick, sweet fragrance of southern honeysuckle form the devotional incense borne on hot and humid air.

The sun drifts far behind the church to the west, beyond old Route 11 and the new Interstate 81, beyond Lacey Springs and Timberville, beyond the turkey farms, the buffalo farms, and the farm where the Driver family is raising peacocks and peahens, on beyond the apple orchards and the processing plants. Beyond all these the sun gently descends into the waiting bosom of the Blue Ridge Mountains. The sliver of a moon and the first few stars appear in the still light sky to greet freshly scrubbed worshippers in their Sunday evening best. They carry flickering candles. Singing, they process from the sanctuary across the gravel parking lot into the fellowship hall. They smile and laugh; children run ahead and underfoot.

In the darkened fellowship hall tables have been set for a meal. Down the centers of the tables lie the implements of their daily labor: hoes, rakes, canning jars, chains, bailing twine, seeds, scythes and sickles to be sure, but also hypodermic needles, adding machines, math books, spark plugs, a pressure cooker, ledgers, files, a necktie and a steering wheel. Interspersed between these items are chalices, loaves of bread and holders for their candles. One by one the parishioners take their places, their faces illumined by the soft light of the candles they hold. They place their candles in the holders and are seated.

The entire room is now alive with the flickering light of so many candles; shadows dance on the walls behind them. They sit contentedly, contemplating the singular beauty of this moment. Even the children are captivated, their eyes glistening. Here are the sum and substance of their lives: Work. Bread. Drink. Friends. Community. Light and Darkness, Daily Life and Vast Eternity commingle.

In 1965, Jimmy Stewart starred in an antiwar film set in this very valley. He played the single father of a large family of adult children; they maintained a prosperous farm near Shenandoah Gap during the American Civil War. The father was irascible, defiant and stubbornly independent, but he loved his family deeply. He practiced certain religious rituals out of respect for his deceased wife, but it was clear he wasn't a believer. At dinner he gathered his grown children around the table and pronounced the following blessing: "Dear Lord. We cleared this land. We plowed it, sowed it and harvested it. We cooked the harvest. It wouldn't be here — we wouldn't be eating it — if we hadn't done it all ourselves. We worked dog hard for every crumb and morsel, but we thank you just the same. Amen."

Such is the attitude of many today: we work dog hard for every crumb and morsel, and we deserve everything we get, but we thank you just the same.

Not so the people in our story. They are experiencing an array of emotions that the cinematic father never knew: Gratitude. Wonder. Appreciation for the bigness of creation. The sense of being a small part in a vast chain of being that stretches forward and backward into the infinite recesses of time, and horizontally into every direction of earth.

They know the sense of being part of a community that embraces each of the people in this room: Linda and Bobbie, bashful newlyweds; Perry, Bernice and Yvonne, their severely handicapped daughter; Albert, the plasterer, half of whose jaw is missing because of cancer, and Katie, a fifteen-year-old who surely is sowing wild, wild oats. The faces of each one are wonderfully radiant and connected by the candles' glow.

There are other faces here too, here only in the minds and memories of these people. There are faces in the outer circle, in the shadows, in the world beyond this church, beyond this valley. There are other faces.

The light from the candles casts its ambient glow on tools that lie on the tables. Though they are bound to them, and earn their living with them, the people see these tools as if for the first time. A rugged dignity permeates these humble implements. Calloused hands that the years have fitted to the handles of carving knives and crosscut saws now rest quietly in laps, but they feel — the hands feel — the warmth, light and dignity as surely as they know these instruments to be extensions of themselves.

The tremulous light weaves together into a cosmic unity all that the tables hold: tools and workaday instruments, but also chalices filled to the brim and warm loaves of home-baked bread. Yes, they acknowledge, this simple sustenance is also one of life's great pleasures. It comes to the table now through the work of these tools, these hands, and these people. They have always known that the earth is sacred. All it produces is sacred. By the light of these candles the sacred character of their own labor also becomes apparent.

The minister stands before them, and tells them that — for good or for ill — their work transforms everything it touches. All work, whether it is the farmer's or the accountant's, the teacher's or the bureaucrat's, all work transforms. Work is evidence of life, and life depends on work. Work is not the opposite of grace; it is a means of grace. Surely work can be monotonous, tedious or even destructive; it also can be a way of participating in the positive transformation of our world. The value of our work lies not in how much we are paid but in the quality of our contribution. Our success lies not in the lifestyles we maintain but in the values we live and work by. We are invited through our work to become co-creators with a loving God.

The people pass the bread and cup. They serve each other in liturgy as they serve each other in life. They smile and nod. Here in the broken bread the earth is transformed into food for body and spirit. Here in the cup the earth becomes remembrance and anticipation. Here the earth's products and the human work of transformation are conjoined. In this sacrament, past and present, work and grace, memory and hope, and the all embracing community of life are celebrated.

The gifts of God for the people of God. Thanks be to God.

The Reign of Christ

Joe and the King

Each summer when I return to Saint John's Abbey, I visit the grave of a friend. His name was Joseph O'Connell. Garrison Keillor once said that Joe looked like a boxer and talked like a carpenter. He was a no frills lover of jazz and straight talk. You could usually find him in his studio at the College of Saint Benedict where he carved and chiseled extraordinary visions of humanity. He imbued stone with weeping and whimsy, wild impertinence and the deepest reverence.

Joe was two thirds into a monumental triptych called *Christ the King* when he received the diagnosis: cancer of the esophagus. His doctors recommended a course of treatment that would weaken him considerably but give him a 28% chance of survival. Without it, he had only months to live. With it he might not have strength to finish the triptych. Joe pondered, talked with his family and decided to forego the treatment. For the remaining six or so months of his life, he moved between home, hospital and studio, working against the clock to finish his creation. He literally held the chisel until death came.

If you ever visit Las Vegas, I hope you will go and see this triptych now installed at Christ the King Catholic Community. It is one of the most beautiful and gentle images of Jesus you will ever see, and one of the most inclusive visions of humanity ever assembled in stone. We are all there — children, nuns, prisoners, baseball players, prostitutes. He has bestowed upon each figure a soft dignity and innocent playfulness that reveal its innate loveliness. Yet he also has captured the haunting desperation and injustice of the human condition. Christ comes sitting on a donkey, arms outstretched and large hands ready to embrace. Joe's work is at once a celebration of life and a call to liberation. This triptych reveals just how well he knew the King. Joe carved into this work these words from Matthew:

> "I was hungry, you gave me food; thirsty, you gave me drink; a stranger, you welcomed me; naked, you clothed me; sick, you took care of me; in prison, you visited me. Just as you did for the least of my family, you did for me."

On The Eve of the Millennium

A huge granite stone dominates a modest Russian churchyard deep in the Siberian heartland. Although it is rough-hewn, the rock obviously has been chiseled to accommodate a commemorative plaque. The plaque itself is gone. Only the square indentation remains, now a very different sort of commemoration.

Siberians love to tell the story of this rock. A rapacious holder of vast estates was known far and wide for his cruelty. He exploited the land without regard; he abused his workers in ways worthy of a Dickens novel. He owned many villages and grew fat on the suffering of others. But as time passed and he grew older, he became increasingly troubled by his own mortality. The day came when he realized that even he must die.

Die perhaps, but he was determined not to be forgotten. He had his peasants drag a boulder to the churchyard. He had his metal workers fashion a bronze plaque with his name and likeness. He had his masons attach the plaque to the stone. He was sure that at least here the ravages of time could be kept at bay. At least here his memory would live on.

Soon after he died, Russia entered one of its innumerable wars. The country needed every scrap of metal to make vehicles and weapons. The Czar ordered that "superfluous" metal be confiscated and dedicated to the national cause. The plaque was pried from the stone, melted and recycled.

As the years passed, the name and identity of this magnate have been lost. Only the stone and its story remain. The baron's singular memorial became (briefly) a few cubic inches of a cannon. But the barren stone endures — an ironic witness to the hollowness of human vanity.

As we approach the moment when our clocks and calendars announce the year 2000, the utter truthfulness of this story becomes oppressive. "Time, like an ever flowing stream, bears all its kin away... We fly forgotten, as a dream fades at the break of day." Even the greatest, the richest and the most powerful among us are unable to break free from the namelessness that time imposes on us all.

Except One. This date points to him.

How astonishing to think it should be he. When the world provided no abode, he was cradled in the arms of his adolescent mother. He wandered through forlorn and forgotten villages in the shadows of an Empire preoccupied with greatness, wealth and power. He touched lepers, prostitutes and outcasts of every kind. Eventually he himself was raised on the crossed beams of an executioner's tree and buried in a borrowed grave.

His enemies set a great stone for him, but they intended to destroy his memory, not preserve it. They gave him a plaque too, but to ridicule, not remember. Stone and plaque vanished centuries ago, but not his name. He is called upon everywhere; his name is known in every part of the earth. He inspires great art, greater deeds and the greatest hope of all. He leads us "beside still waters" where the tyranny of our illusions is transcended. He teaches us that true greatness lies in serving, true wealth in giving, and true power in loving.

Yeshua bar Yosef. Jesus, born of our sister Maryām. Jesus of Nazareth. Jesus, the Christ. Jesus, the Prince of Peace. Emmanuel. God-With-Us. Even now He goes before us into the next millennium.

Passing the Peace

Very early in the history of the church — perhaps even in the New Testament church itself — a desire and charge came to be enacted ritually in what was called the "kiss of peace". Cyril of Alexandria was just one of a multitude who described its importance for the early Christian communities. He wrote:

> "Then the Deacon cries aloud, 'Receive ye one another; and let us kiss one another.' Think not that this kiss is of the same character with those given in public by common friends. It is not such, but this kiss blends souls one with another, and courts entire forgiveness for them. The kiss therefore is the sign that our souls are mingled together, and banishes all remembrance of wrongs. For this cause Christ said, 'If you are offering your gift at the altar, and there remember that your brother or sister has anything against you, leave your gift on the altar and go your way; first be reconciled to thy brother or sister and then come and present your gift. The kiss therefore is reconciliation, and for this reason holy: as the blessed Paul cried, saying, 'Greet one another with a holy kiss', and Peter, with a 'kiss of charity'."

These words are embarrassing for modern ecclesiastical ears. Outside of Orthodox churches, almost universally we now practice the "handshake of peace" and even this makes some of us uneasy. But it is meant to convey a very important message from our past: our forebearers experienced intimacy within the beloved community of Jesus. The implication is that we may also.

The place of the kiss (or passing) of peace in the liturgy was never fixed. Sometimes it followed an act of repentance as a symbol of reconciliation. Sometimes it followed the prayers of the people and sometimes it followed the presentation of offerings and gifts for the communal table. But whenever it occurred, it conveyed the essential message that the peace of Christ resides in the community. It is not a priestly prerogative. Each one of us imparts it to another. We are bearers of shalom for one another. The "passing of the peace" affirms in the most touching manner that all of us are both penitents and priests. In this little ritual we symbolize our most sacred calling: to be channels of the peace of Christ, a peace that passes human understanding, a peace not known in the world, nor ever given by it. This is a peace within and a peace without, a peace that "lives the questions" when the answers are not clear, a peaceful center in a conflicted world.

Yesterday's Tomorrow

A Minnesota humorist once created a motto for the Future Historians of America: "Planning Today for the Yesterday of Tomorrow." I thought of that as I visited my father. He was living in a nursing home in Clearfield, UT, about as far from our West Virginia hometown as he could imagine. He inhabited a tomorrow he never dreamed of yesterday.

My dad had been a Methodist lay preacher. After I moved north to attend Princeton Seminary, he took over a little church in Wardensville that I had served. "Like son, like father," he liked to say. One summer evening he gave a sermon in our hometown church. It happened to be taped. That particular homily was about the Good Samaritan.

"Never waste an audience," someone told him. Well, he didn't. His plain speech, earthy humor and common sense are abundantly apparent on that tape. Since dad himself was always going the extra mile for folks who needed help, the integrity in that speech must have touched the hearts of his listeners. He loved the Bible. He loved a good story. He loved charming people into faithfulness.

After a routine dental appointment he suffered a massive stroke that left him paralyzed, speechless, and with limited comprehension. We had to transport him and my mother to Utah where my sister lived. No one else could provide the quality of care and advocacy that they needed.

I felt all the conflicting emotions one would expect when I flew out from Minnesota to visit: tenderness, fear, helplessness, love, guilt, anger, appreciation. Once so energetic in his caring for others, now he lay in his bed or sat in his wheelchair for hours. Once so spontaneous and playful, now his daily life was organized by the routines of institutional care. Yet even here there was so much more to him than disability and confinement. The many disciplines of his previous life continued to serve him well: his enjoyment of simple things like colored glass, his friendly way with others, his patient disposition. And, almost certainly, his faith.

Dad listened frequently to that recorded sermon. Because of the damage the stroke inflicted to his brain, he heard it for the first time every time it was played. A kind of "beginner's mind" perhaps. The voice on the tape, his own voice, came from 20 years earlier and 2000 miles away. With nary a thought of Utah, strokes or nursing homes, that voice spoke of a life well lived, a life lived for others. It spoke with the conviction of one who knew that we cannot know what the future holds, but who believed that God is good.

Each time he heard it, my father smiled. He nodded his approval of yesterday's father's words. Never an erudite historian, nevertheless dad excelled at "planning today for the yesterday of tomorrow".

A More Interesting Church

The translator was sure it was a mistake.

It was strange enough to have a woman in the pulpit. In his hometown of Minsk, in the Republic of Belarus, this almost never happened. But there she was for all to see. She was wearing the robes of her office and standing with authority behind this modern pulpit. And, yes, she was about to deliver the sermon. He had a copy of this very sermon in his lap. He hastily read through it. But as he translated it for the headmaster, I saw confusion on his face.

Mayflower Church had organized an exchange between the children and staff of Saint Joseph's Home for Children in Minneapolis and School Number 31, a state run Orphanage in Minsk. The Byelorussian children and their teachers were sitting in the Minneapolis pews beaming happily and not understanding a word of our worship. The headmaster was seated apart, in the front, where he had been introduced and made a few remarks in Russian. Now he too was smiling benignly while the translator squirmed and sweated in discomfort.

Sandy, a young seminarian, was the preacher. More at home in the north woods than in this well-appointed sanctuary, she began with a striking question. "How could God make me both Christian and gay?" She told us that her gay friends had pretty much written off the church as hopelessly homophobic and oppressive. Most of her Christian friends could not accept homosexuals with anything other than disdain. To make matters worse, she said, not only was she Christian and gay. God also called her to ministry and to openness about her sexual orientation. What was God thinking?

This was a courageous and important sermon for Sandy to give. It was equally important for the congregation to hear. Both she and I wondered how traditional churchgoers would receive her words.

The receiving line took longer than usual that day. One by one people came through. They wanted to shake her hand, to express appreciation for her candor. They began telling her stories out of their own experience. It was clear that she had touched their hearts.

The Byelorussian children came through, with many *zdravseytvuyte's*, *privyet's*, *dobray ootra's* and *spasibo's* — traditional "good morning" and "thank-you" greetings. Then came the headmaster. He smiled broadly and pumped the young seminarian's hand. He told her — through the translator — how very good the whole service was for him and the children. He said he wished there were more pastors like her in Belarus.

We took the headmaster and his staff to lunch along with a few members of our church and the Director of Saint Joseph's Home for Children. I asked them what they thought of the sermon. Since I had been to Belarus shortly before, I knew they were reserved in discussing any matters of sexuality, and particularly homosexuality. I wanted to know their reactions to what my colleague had said about her call.

The translator listened to my question but he refused to translate it. Instead he explained that even though he had a manuscript he had been quite sure it was a mistake. He had not translated this part of the sermon at all. The headmaster never heard it!

It was my turn to be astonished, but I quickly recovered. I asked him to tell the headmaster now, along with the other staff, what he had failed to translate in the service. As he did so, I watched their reactions. They revealed an obvious surprise as the words flowed into Russian, but — good guests that they were — they seemed to be interested and supportive. Finally, the headmaster spoke. "I still wish there were more like her in our country. It would be a more interesting church!"

◊

Imagine how the traditionalists felt when Lemuel Haynes was presented to their church for ministry. No African American had ever served a white congregation before, and Lemuel Haynes didn't look like promising material to be the first. Born in 1756, he was the illegitimate child of a Black man and the daughter of a socially prominent white family in Hartford, CN. At the age of five months he had been abandoned by his parents and indentured to a white family in Massachusetts. In 1775 he had marched north with Benedict Arnold to join Ethan Allen in the attack on Fort Ticonderoga. He studied Latin, Greek and theology in his twenties. Lemuel Haynes fell in love with a young white woman in his Connecticut congregation. She proposed to him, and they were married in 1783, producing ten children.

But all who lived within the sphere of his life's energy — even the most traditional — beheld God's Spirit upon him, and God's hand above his shoulder. Upon this man, they affirmed, God's holy mantle had fallen. They licensed him for ministry in 1780; he was called to fill pulpits in Bennington, Manchester, and Granville, NY, before his death at the age of eighty. Lemuel Haynes was chosen by God to become a "fact" to transfigure the "framework" of received practices. He was the harbinger of a dream not yet fully realized in this land of his birth.

◊

Congregationalists founded Oberlin College in Ohio. It was the first coeducational school to grant college degrees to women and the first in our nation to accept students of all races. It was intended to break new ground. Even so, though women were admitted to the school, they also were expected to clean the rooms, do the laundry and serve the meals of their male counterparts. In 1847, having finished the course of literary study to which women were admitted, Antoinette Brown, a decidedly gifted young woman, wanted to read theology. She encountered strenuous objections even from this "liberal" faculty. They did not think it an appropriate field of study for a woman. However, the school charter decreed that no student could be excluded on the basis of sex, so Brown prevailed. Although she finished the theological course in 1850, the college faculty refused to award her a degree. (It was eventually awarded to her — 28 years later.)

She was active in the temperance movement and women's suffrage movements. She declared that she was called by God to be ordained into Christian ministry. She had to overcome a great deal of discrimination. Male clergy sometimes shouted her down when she spoke in public. But on September 15, 1853, Antoinette Brown was ordained a minister of the First Congregational Church in South Butler, New York. She became a "fact" that challenged the prevailing "framework" and expanded the possibilities of her era. Antoinette Brown was called to a unique and transforming ministry. The Holy Spirit came upon her. She became an author, speaker, educator, pastor and social reformer. In 1920 when she was 95, she was able to vote for the first time after the Nineteenth Amendment gave American women the right to vote. She died the next year. Today, less than five generations later, women bishops are presiding in many denominations around the world and women clergy are serving in every field of ministry.

◊

Two contradicting tendencies are present in these stories; both are essential for the church to endure. There is the tradition that carries the great content of God's story and ours. Without it the church would be nothing at all. It forms our identity and informs our capacity to believe and live out our faith. The orthodox, traditionalists and conservatives are right to be concerned that we value and conserve this core.

But it is a living tradition. At the center of this core, like the nuclear reactor at the center of the sun, there is a radical and expansive freedom. It is God's freedom. The Holy Spirit moves like wind and fire among us. It destroys and creates. It presses against our carefully drawn boundaries. It pushes us beyond our comfort zones. It makes all things new. It constantly challenges us, and keeps us from making idols of the frameworks in which we are pleased to dwell.

A few years after her sermon, Sandy knelt before the same congregation. The people who gathered pronounced upon her that great affirmation from our ordination service: "By the grace of God, she is worthy. Let us ordain her." Today Sandy is the Director of Pilgrim Point, the Minnesota Conference Camping Center. She is proving, as our Byelorussian guest foresaw, that it is becoming a more interesting church.

The Middle Way

Christian practice has drawn inspiration from two distinct and some-times competitive modes of self-understanding. One might be called the "religion about Jesus" and the other, the "religion of Jesus".

The religion about Jesus believes that Jesus Christ is the lens through which we gain a glimpse into divine reality; he is the mirror in which to see our truest selves. The God of the Universe in revealed in a displaced child who sleeps in a manger and flees imperial violence. The Prince of Peace rides on a donkey and wears a crown of thorns. The hand that shaped the universe breaks bread with friends and enemies alike, washes the feet of others and is nailed to a wooden cross.

The religion of Jesus was formed and shaped by the beliefs and practices of ancient Israel. The Shema was for him the greatest commandment, and the Leviticus principle of love for neighbor was "like unto it". His life was formed within a community of people whose backs were against the wall. Yet he demonstrated a profound ability to look beyond the stereo-types and roles of a polarized society and to address the deepest longings in the human heart. He was a realist who taught an ethic of prudent non-violence. Although he believed that human beings are first of all spiritual beings, he understood how money, power, health and relationships affect our souls' development.

Jesus taught that love is the primary spiritual energy. The self is most fully realized when it behaves unselfishly. He called for generosity to-ward others, and "repentance" from all that is false and separates us from God and each other. He counseled a turning toward that which liberates us to live with integrity in the present, and in harmony with others.

In both the religion about Jesus and the religion of Jesus, there is a profound reversal of common assumptions about wealth, power and happiness. God is to be sought and served in the "Other". Fulfillment comes through sacrifice. Generosity is more satisfying than self-aggran-dizement. Stewardship trumps acquisition. Enemies are to be engaged, forgiven and loved, not hated or destroyed.

The most important step we can take is to develop loving hearts and a cherishing attitude toward all creation. The first act of love is to see — to see beyond external qualifiers into the intrinsic loveliness and uniqueness of other persons. The second act of love is to understand — to try to fathom the depths from which the other emerges. The third act of love is to cherish — to value the person as he or she really is, and to seek the best for that person even if it is costly for oneself.

Therefore opportunities need to be multiplied where people of differing backgrounds and values come together safely to see, understand and cherish one another. These can be as local as neighborhood gatherings and Habitat housing projects, or as global as pilgrimages together. They need to be as free as possible of all distinctions based on status, wealth, power, religion or ideology.

Terms of Engagement

As the world grows more interdependent our own communities are becoming more diverse. Interaction between people with differing assumptions about God, creation, and life itself is becoming more commonplace. This can lead to grievous conflict or it can stimulate us to a deeper and broader spirituality. It is important for all of us to identify and overcome our secret fears or hidden prejudices. We wish to foster a safe and respectful society and to encourage the development of a more cosmopolitan spirituality.

Much of the prejudice in the world today simply reflects a lack of knowledge or familiarity with other traditions; it usually dissipates with increasing exposure. Other prejudices are rooted in the core assertions of our faith. Dealing with these creates genuine opportunities for spiritual growth.

In *The Love Song of J. Alfred Prufrock*, T. S. Eliot commented on the shallowness of what passes for life: We "prepare a face to meet the faces that (we) meet... We measure out our lives with coffee spoons." Jean Paul Sartre described much of life as dancing the "dance of respectability". Howard Thurman wrote that often when we come together "our shoulders touch but our hearts cry out" because they are far apart. We want more than this but prejudices inhibit us from transcending the narrowness of our lives.

Let us assume with the Psalmist that "God knows the secrets of the heart." How indeed can we eliminate unacknowledged and secret prejudices against those of differing faiths and cultures? How can we become more trustworthy and trusting of each other? One answer lies in respectful dialogue with others. There is dialogue that consists of exchanges of information, and there is dialogue that leads to mutual transformation. Both are important if we would challenge old prejudices.

What do we want? Do we desire a more complete knowledge of one another? Do we want more intimate communion with each other? Do we seek more peaceful relations with each other? If so, perhaps you will allow me to share a few principles of dialogue that I have tried to follow in recent years.

Paradoxically, we begin with ourselves. We first must swim in the river our own spiritual tradition. We must become aware of the breadth of it, explore the depths of it and learn its different currents. We need to experience the vitality and life of our faith and allow the Spirit to become a real and nurturing presence through it. Otherwise we may speak correctly but not truthfully; our shoulders will touch but our hearts will remain apart.

My second principle comes from the first word in the *Rule of Saint Benedict:* Listen. Listen to others. Cultivate "deep listening" as Thomas Merton, Howard Thurman and Thich Nhat Hanh advise — a listening that is compassionate and non judgmental. Listen to the words of others. Listen to the breath. Listen to the silences. Listen for the "still small voice" of the Holy One who is speaking in this encounter.

I learned my third principle when I was a draft counselor with the Fellowship of Reconciliation. We often had to deal with people who were, shall we say, less than receptive to conscientious objectors. I was taught a simple lesson that has stood me in good stead in many situations ever since: Never posit malice. Never assume the worse. Always assume the best possible motivation and interpretation.

The fourth I learned from my friend, Wayne Smith, who founded the Friendship Force and World Pilgrims. Pay attention to what is in my neighbor's heart more than what is in my neighbor's head. Both head and heart are vital, but I concur with Pascal that, "the heart hath reasons that reason knows not of."

Francisco Dokushô Villalba, a Spanish Soto Zen Buddhist, distinguishes between "horizontal religions" and "vertical religion". Horizontal religions are systems of beliefs, rituals, practices and sociocultural norms that strengthen individual and cultural identities. They exist in space and endure through time. They offer cohesion, consolation and coherence to the people who live within them. Sometimes they encode ethnic and cultural norms. They are often organized and energized by particular agreed upon beliefs.

Horizontal religions occasionally push against one another in fierce competition. When we speak of "communities of faith" this is often what we mean. Many interfaith dialogues and programs simply bring horizontal religions into conversations or cooperative ventures. In today's world, this is terribly important to do. Such occasions provide information and education. They teach us civility. They promote an understanding that counters many of the naive prejudices we harbor. But in such settings it also is possible to "hide" our prejudices behind the faces that we put on to meet the others.

Vertical religion, on the other hand, is experiential. It offers access to a special consciousness of what Villalba calls "la Unidad" — unity, union, *henosis* or similar mystical states. This provides the stimulation and the consolation of an experience of transcendence. People who practice vertical spirituality open their hearts to the totality of experience. This totality includes followers of other spiritual paths. Therefore he believes that all encounters with the Transcendent in vertical religion lead to unity. It cannot be otherwise. Prejudices are not so much refuted as they are simply dispelled.

Horizontal world religions gather around vertical religious experiences. These vertical and unitive experiences in all religion are encounters with the one and the same "Unidad." If I fill my glass with water from the ocean, then all of the water in my glass will be ocean water, but not all the ocean is in my glass.

My fifth principle comes from the *Guidelines for Inter-faith Dialogue of the Interfaith Network of the United Kingdom*. Keep in mind that all of us at times fall short of the ideals of our own traditions; never compare my own ideals with other people's practices. It is unfair to compare the best expressions of my tradition against the worse of yours.

Finally: Embrace paradox. Honor the tension between the particular and the universal, the horizontal and the vertical. "I cannot be at home everywhere until I am at home somewhere," said Howard Thurman. "I cannot speak without using a particular language," say the rabbis. As much as possible, do not flee from contradictions or attempt to resolve them simplistically. When differences emerge, avoid "either/or". Seek "both/and". Stay with the tension and allow it to have a voice.

There is an Asian proverb to the effect that when a finger points to the moon, a dog sees only the finger. At their best, all religions are the fingers that point to something which can never be adequately described or captured with words: "Those who know don't say," said Lao Tzu, "and those who say, don't know," At the core of many traditions is the ultimate affirmation that — after we have expressed everything we know and all that has been revealed — nevertheless, "God Is greater." God is greater than our religions, beliefs and orthodoxies. "Why do you call me good?" said Jesus, pointing. "There is none good but God."

The Way of Reverent Service

Thus the Lord showed me, and, behold, the Lord stood beside a wall made with a plumb line, with a plumb line in his hand, And the Lord said unto me, "Amos, what seest thou?' and I said, 'A plumb line.' Then the Lord said, 'Behold, I will set a plumb line in the midst of my children Israel.'"

(Amos 7:7)

Nearly everyone knows what a plumb line is. It is one of the simplest and oldest of tools, a pointed piece of heavy lead attached to a long piece of string. Masons and carpenters hold one against every wall, pillar or post they erect to see whether these are perpendicular and true.

The plumb line has not changed in form since it was used on the banks of the Euphrates and Nile thousands of years ago. Primitive builders might not recognize a rotary saw but they would have no difficulty working with the plumb line.

If we watch a carpenter as she erects a wall, we will see her step back and holds the plumb line against it. This little dangling weight at the end of the line will tell her all she needs to know. This simple instrument has remained sufficient and entirely adequate through all the centuries of human use, and through the evolution of other building instruments.

Why is this little tool so valuable? The answer is as simple as the instrument: it tells every person who uses it, whether in this culture or another, whether in this age or another, anywhere on the planet, whether his or her work is true to the one center. When the plumb line is placed against a wall it is immediately clear whether it is true to the center of the earth. This must be the case if one's work is to survive.

In these days of competing ideologies, Republicans argue with Democrats and Marxists with both. Gurus from India, Korea, Japan — and California — are tripping across the continents. Pamphleteers of every persuasion are proclaiming their own latest brands of certain salvation and hucksters of every sort are pushing pills, travel or merchandise as the long sought panacea. I think we need a plumb line.

We need a simple principle by which we can test our own and others' work, by which we can measure our lives in relation to the one true center. Without such a guide, our efforts will be haphazard and our work without lasting significance. We may meditate. We may exercise. We may volunteer, study and perform and yet find ourselves with a haunting sense of pointlessness. But with such a guide, we can carry on the work of our lives knowing that it is consistent with the requirements of the one true center.

There is such a principle for us. It is as ancient and simple as the plumb line of our analogy. When misinterpreted it produces the most repulsive forms of spineless and cowardly obsequiousness. When proclaimed but not practiced, it is the occasion for ridicule and cynicism. But when understood and implemented, the human spirit takes flight. The life in which it becomes incarnate is the flower of creation, nature's loveliest work of art.

I call this principle "the way of reverent service." I realize that in the market place of ideas this is simply one more competing against the rest. So be it. Yet it stands at the heart of the Christian affirmation; it has been a motivating dynamic in American church life for generations, and I hope it will become increasingly a part of my own life as well.

When Jesus described the last judgment in Matthew 25 he was articulating this principle for us. How were the sheep separated from the goats?

Was it prestige? No. He did not say, "The Kingdom has been prepared for you because you were a queen, you a prince and you the greatest artist in the land."

Was it accomplishment? No. He did not say, "The Kingdom has been prepared for you because your silk, your medical skills or your plays are known throughout the world."

Was it education? No. He did not say, "The Kingdom has been prepared for you because you studied with Aristotle, you with Plato and you with Gamaliel".

Was it doctrine? No. He did not say, "The Kingdom has been prepared for you because you believed in the Trinity, you in the virgin birth, and you in the miraculous resurrection."

The basis for the separation of the sheep from the goats, the principle, the plumb line, was "service" — service freely given out of the generous impulses of our own nature.

"For I was hungry and you gave me food. 1 was thirsty and you gave me drink. I was naked and you clothed me, a stranger and you welcomed me.

305

I was sick and you visited me, in prison and you came unto me... Truly I say to you, as you did it unto the least of these, you have done it unto me." Jesus is articulating a very basic principle for life and its fulfillment: the way of reverent service.

In the New Testament Jesus is the personification of this principle. He is a friend of outcasts and sinners. On the very night of his death he comforted his disciples and not the other way around. He — their master and teacher — washed their feet in a gesture of one's proper attitude toward status and position. "Greater love has no one than this," he said, phrasing once and for all the ultimate ramifications of this simple principle, "that he lay down his life for his friend." Far from being an extreme demand, this statement announces the greatest joy and personal liberation. Jesus is saying that love has so permeated and filled his being that he can relinquish his life, confident that it rests upright on the one true center of the world. To actualize our potential, we must serve others.

Twelve centuries later, Saint Francis of Assisi phrased the same point most eloquently: "It is in giving that we receive; it is in pardoning that we are pardoned; it is in dying that we are born to eternal life."

This way of reverent service has more than an individual dimension. Whole families can be involved. When I was a child our family decided to give up sending Christmas cards and used the money to purchase food for others. I remember sawing wood, washing windows and painting fences for shut-ins. These are among my most cherished memories, perhaps because they measure well against the plumb line of reverent service.

When translated into social terms, the plumb line leads us to seek a society where, in the words of the Psalmist, "love and truth meet; justice and peace kiss." (Psalm 85:10-11.) When translated into ecclesiastical terms or church structures, this principle becomes known as missionary activity, benevolence, social concern or social action.

At its best, social action is an expression of reverent service. It does not result from political correctness or a guilty conscience. It does not result from noblesse oblige, an austere sense of duty or any form of enlightened self-interest. Rather it springs from an overwhelming gratitude for the gifts of life and a desire to extend this joy to others.

306

The Courtyard

I made my way to my church, the one in Georgia, the one where I was a pastor. As I walked down the sidewalk, under the arbor, past the pond with its fountain and flowers, nothing looked out of place yet nothing was quite the same. But when I opened the door an unimaginable din overwhelmed me. As far as I could see, to the left, the right or straight ahead there were masses of people. People of every hue dressed in every imaginable costume and speaking every conceivable tongue were mixing together in what appeared to be an infinitely vast hall. There were cellists and baseball players, Ghanaian dancers and Ojibwa elders, Korean executives and Mexican mariachi players. Children were running, gymnasts were vaulting and nurses were changing IV's. The scent of incense mingled with the smells of cooking meats, open landfills, fragrant spices and burning diesel fuel.

Preachers were expounding doctrines and soldiers were practicing with their weapons. Couples were courting. Mechanics were fixing airplane engines and criminals were doing drug deals. Midwives were delivering babies. Students sitting in hard chairs at library tables were fixating on their books. Teenagers were tapping to the unheard music of their iPods. Groups were gathering in deep grief beside lifeless bodies. Old women in ragged clothes were pawing through dumpsters. Nuns in modest dress were kneeling in prayer. Children were jumping around their birthday cakes. Young women were strapping on explosive vests. All of humanity was gathered in this narthex doing everything that human beings do. But each person was so intensely involved in her or his own project that they did not see the living cornucopia of which they themselves were part.

I pressed into the crowd. Some I knew, but most I did not. As I moved to my left, I discovered that this hall curved ever so slightly like the deck that surrounds a baseball stadium. The more I walked, the more I realized that it was circular, a huge ring in which the masses of humanity were dwelling. I continued toward the center.

It was long and exhausting but I spotted an opening in the wall ahead. I walked through it and the noise behind me subsided. The space I entered was hushed and dimly lit. The air was pleasantly cool. As my eyes adjusted I could see a display case in front of me, and a few people were looking in. I heard soft sounds of distant chant. In the glass case I saw Bibles, vestments and holy implements. An infinite array of these stretched before me.

I saw a time line spiraling around the black walls of the dark room. On it were pictures and words from thousands of years of history. Abraham, Sarah, Hagar, Moses, Maryām, David and Isaiah were on it. So were Mary, Joseph, Jesus, the Disciples and the Myrrh Bearers. The Popes, the Saints, the Queens and Kings, the Presidents, the Tycoons all had their places. Benedict, Felicitas, Augustine, Pelagius, Theresa were there. I saw Heloise and Abelard, Dave Brubeck, Billy Graham, and Sojourner Truth.

I saw the cathedrals of the world — all in miniature but real nonetheless. I saw storefront churches and people gathering on beaches, in restaurants and living rooms for prayer. I saw women and men organizing campaigns for and against many issues, appealing to God and sacred scripture.

I saw hungry people and skeletal figures in refugee camps, and women and men distributing food, building and repairing homes, digging wells, and carrying medical supplies and clothing. I saw a young pregnant woman facing savage beasts before roaring crowds. I saw farmers and shop keepers shielding Jews from the clutches of the Gestapo, and proper New Englanders caring for black slaves who had mutinied at sea and killed their vessel's crew.

As I continued my exploration, I came upon Inquisitors extracting confessions from tortured Jews in Spain, and Klansmen hanging tortured Black bodies from trees in Georgia. I saw cross marked Christian knights on horseback rampaging through bloody streets in Jerusalem. I saw armed Christian militia from North Carolina on maneuvers in rural Idaho. I saw hymn-singing churchgoers buying and selling slaves like cattle. I saw missionaries cutting off the hair of indigenous children, silencing their languages, and shaming their culture and inheritance. I saw Christians fighting Christians from Cochin to Belfast to the Maginot Line, and Spanish Conquistadores pillaging Aztec villages.

I heard great congregations singing, and small choirs in country churches, and tambourines and saxophones. I heard the erudite accents of learned sermons in Scottish accents, and the staccato cadences of spirit-filled Indiana preaching. Strains of Bach echoed through the hall, and Russian chant sung by Japanese voices, and Audio Adrenaline's amplified praise.

After spending an infinite time in what appeared to be a museum of Christian reality, I saw huge arched doorways leading into more rooms on either side. On the left was a similar hall overflowing with Buddhist artifacts. On the right another hall was crammed with the diversity and devotion of Islam. Gradually I came to realize that each great hall was linked to others in a vast inner circle; all of the religions of the world were here in their totality, their shame and glory revealed. It was possible to move laterally from one religion to another and to immerse myself in the fullness of each one.

At first I was fascinated. I was greedy to see and learn everything. Gradually, however, this endless circle of religiosity overwhelmed and oppressed me. As vast and various as these rooms seemed to be, they also were dark, enclosed and self-contained. I couldn't breathe.

I made my way through the various displays. Eventually I saw a small wooden door with glass panes in the wall directly in front of me. It suggested an exit more than anything else. Light streamed through; there were glimpses of green boughs softly swaying beyond. I came to understand that there were similar doors in all of the great halls of the great religions.

I approached and pushed down the handle. The door opened. Fresh air wafted in. A gentle breeze brushed lightly against my cheek. I was blinded by the brightness of the light.

I passed through the door into an outdoor courtyard bathed in this light. As my eyes adjusted I saw small branches swaying imperceptibly and a few small birds circling far overhead. Nearby a stream trickled over rocks. Other than these, everything was still. The courtyard itself was devoid of familiar furnishings. There were not even shapes or angles that I recognized. But in its austerity it was absolutely complete.

Time itself disappeared into the formlessness of this space. I sat down. I became as empty as this place, and as filled with light. All of the weight and weariness of my life drained from me. I became one with the sky, the dancing branches, the gurgling brook and the encircling birds. I experienced wonder and joy beyond comprehension.

I could go back. But should I? The door through which I had come opened in both directions. I remembered the faces of all the people in the narthex, their happiness and suffering intermingling. I remembered the great encouragement of the religions I had traversed, but also their decay into self-righteousness. I saw them anew with the eyes of cherishing. My heart was breaking with compassion. As deeply as I rested in this place, my work was not finished. I rose from my place and started slowly for the door.

My Faith

I consider myself a Christ-centered universalist. I am a universalist because I believe there are intimations of God's presence everywhere to be found. I constantly seek insight from many disciplines and sources, and am hungry for knowledge of other authentic religious traditions. Yet in Jesus Christ I find a life of astonishing beauty, integrity, and power that commands my devotion. I have learned from Albert Schweitzer that people may come to know Jesus through three interrelated and equally essential ways: the head" (rational investigation), the "heart" (empathic intuition) and the "hand (ethical action). It is our task and our privilege to know, embody and present the wholeness of the Christ event in ways which respect modern sensibilities yet challenge modern complacency.

At the center of my theological vision are three texts: Psalm 139:1-18, Matthew 25:31-46, and Luke 4:16-21. The Psalmist suggests a divine presence in all creation, and God's searching love for us before we were "intricately wrought in the depths of the earth" or formed in our mothers' wombs. Such a faith is "too wonderful" and it forms the bedrock on which we can build a meaningful life. Matthew's vignette gives us the criteria for a righteous life: to feed the hungry, clothe the naked, visit the sick and imprisoned and welcome the stranger. In Luke, all who would be Jesus' disciples receive the charter for a purposeful life: to proclaim good news to the poor, sight for the blind and release for those who are oppressed.

There are many contemporary issues that beg for the church's attention. These center around nurturing hospitable and inclusive communities in which people are known, understood, appreciated, challenged, encouraged, empowered, cared for, and may experience transformation. Our task is to provide people with the means and opportunities to discern and respond to God's movement in their lives.

Our religious communities are embedded in a profoundly unstable social order. Consequently, even the local church must find a new niche in the emerging global society. The church at every level must address creatively and forthrightly problems caused by exclusion, the lack of understanding across cultures, the erosion of values that dignify individual effort and sustain community, and the volatile despair arising among growing numbers of poor and alienated people. America's metropolitan areas require that we forge new communities across urban and suburban divides as well as across ethnic, racial, class and religious boundaries. I believe the Christian message calls us to this ministry. It is big enough to affirm both the oneness of the human family — and, indeed, of the whole created order — and the God-given diversities that enrich our world.

The Community of Faith

Neither the one who plants nor the one who waters is anything, but only God who gives the growth.

(I Corinthians 3: 7)

I was the organizing pastor for a new congregation in Reston, VA when I was summoned to California for a family emergency. My mother and father were visiting my sister when my mother fell. My mother had brittle bone disease and was rushed to the hospital; she was undergoing an emergency hip replacement. While she was there my sister began to hemorrhage badly and was taken by ambulance to the same hospital but to a different floor. They determined that she was suffering from Crohn's disease. The doctors needed to perform emergency surgery that same night to remove a large portion of her intestine. They told us it was a life or death situation with no guarantees.

My father and I waited nervously in the dimly lit waiting room as the hours went slowly by. We paced and prayed. We talked occasionally, but mostly we were silent. Then my father spoke words I will never forget. He is the shining example of faithfulness. He was my sister's Sunday School teacher and my scoutmaster. He was always there to reassure us and never wavered in his trust in God's Providence. But that night he did. Around 2:00 am I heard him say these words, "Oh God, if there is a God… This is your daughter, and this is child abuse!"

I am happy to report that both my sister and mother got better, though their recoveries were long and painful. My father's faith returned and soon he accepted a lay ministry position in a small Methodist Church.

I flew back to Reston on Saturday night, and returned to my new congregation the next day. We were creating a multiracial congregation within a multi-denominational parish. We were meeting in an elementary school cafeteria; I had the (mistaken) belief that the success or failure of this venture rested entirely on my shoulders. But as I stood in the pulpit on the first Sunday morning after my sister's surgery, I looked at the eager and caring faces of my loyal congregation. I felt empty. I had no words of encouragement for these waiting people. I apologized to them. I gave them an update. I told them the experience had been traumatic for our whole family, that our faith was challenged, and that I had nothing else to say. I was sure that the fledgling congregation would collapse and everyone there would lose their faith.

One of the lay leaders of the church arose.

> "Budd," she said, "faith is God's gift to the whole community, and not to any one individual. Not even the minister. All of us have times like this when we doubt whether God is even there. It shows us you're human. Even Jesus had crises like this. But you need to know that we're here with you and for you. The faith of the church is lodged in all of us and not in you alone. It is lodged in the community. You can lay your burden down for a while and we will carry it. You can question God, and God won't go away. We won't go away either. Faith won't disappear. This is how faith is transmitted — by the community."

She was right. Our texts, songs, liturgies and fellowship all exist to strengthen this faith. Because of it, even in the midst of the bubonic plague in Europe, Julian of Norwich could avow, "All shall be well, all shall be well, and all manner of things shall be well." Even though violated, chained and beaten, American slaves could turn Jeremiah's question into an affirmation: "There is a balm in Gilead!" Even though looking deeply into the horrors of the Holocaust, Fr. Gregory Baum could see that, "There is no situation, however destructive, in which an inner strength is not offered to us, allowing us to assume greater possession of our humanity." No matter what befalls us, the community of faith helps us to know that, "We'll understand it better bye and bye."

The survival of a church does not depend solely on its leadership, but on the quality of faithfulness transmitted from one generation to the next. My lay leader's words that morning were a beautiful gift and profound lesson. Pastors come and go but congregations endure. Thank God for the good sense of lay people that often prevails over ego-driven fancies of their clergy.

About the Author

An ordained minister in the United Church of Christ, Gilbert (Budd) Friend-Jones has devoted his life to parish ministry. He has served congregations in Maine, Minnesota, Virginia, Georgia and Illinois.

Friend-Jones graduated from the Divinity School of Howard University (D. Min.), Princeton Theological Seminary (M. Div.) and Frostburg State University (B.S.). He is an Oblate of the Order of St. Benedict at St. John's Abbey in Collegeville, MN, and the author of *When Easter Interrupts: Reflections on Lent and Easter.*

CPSIA information can be obtained
at www.ICGtesting.com
Printed in the USA
FSOW02n1110181216
28730FS